# Acknowledgments

*The White Bear Center for the Arts wishes to thank the many people who so graciously shared their memories, their photos, their history and their hearts with the readers of this book.*

*It is with sincere gratitude that we wish to thank Liz Kasper of Northern Design Group for donating her time and talent in directing the production of this book. We also wish to thank Frank Zeller for donating his beautiful art print, "Manitou Montage", for use on the cover. Our thanks would not be complete if we did not include the staff from the Ramsey County Library, White Bear Branch, for their enthusiasm and time invested in research on this project. In addition, we would also like to thank Gene Johnson and the White Bear Press for their encouragement and for allowing us to reproduce articles and artwork from archival editions of the newspaper.*

*We are also very grateful for the many people who assisted with this book by transcribing, editing, proofing, scanning and formatting text, photos and artwork: John Henricksson, Deb Barnes, Market Communication Arts, Inc., Marcia Dornfeld, Sue Rutford, Helen Peterson, Susan Maki, Virginia Merrill, Jean Cook, Eileen Berger, Joe Steinworth, Tom Hagen and Susan Seltz. We would also like to thank Mark Sather, our city manager, for his efforts in bringing this project to completion and for recognizing the value of the arts in our community. Our thanks would not be complete if we didn't acknowledge the Mayor and City Council of White Bear Lake for their support.*

*The White Bear Center for the Arts wishes to express their deepest heartfelt thanks to the following businesses, organizations and individuals who showed their support for this project by financially contributing to the production of this book. It is due to their love of this community and recognition of the importance of this unique historical collection, that we would like to acknowledge their support.*

The Rotary Club of WBL

James and Rebecca Matson

Virginia and Kenneth Merrill

White Bear Lake Lions Club

Bang Printing

Joanne Larson of
The Country Goose

Kowalski's Market

Magnepan, Inc.

Coldwell Banker Burnet

Kara Anderson at
KAD Design, Inc.

HealthEast Care Center—WBL

North Country Auto

Edwin and Susan McCarthy

Bob and Eileen Whitaker

Dr. C. M. Ingham

Peter and Linda Seed

Hamilton and Ann Luther

Sherry and Paul Chapin

Gerald and Audreanna Oestreich

Bill Patterson

Hope Healy Koontz

Elsie Bahnemann

Karen LeVasseur Merth

Lyndon and Jane Long

Carol Adams

Mr. and Mrs. Clayton Jorgensen

Anonymous

Paul and Valerie Ackerman

Gail Ruther

Tom and Paula Dosland

William and Theresa Huot

Rich and Ginny Power

Anonymous

Beverly Bosse

Antoinette M. Nolles

Jeannie Ramsey

Louis Hauser

Polly Shank

John Henricksson

Carol Sawyer

Patricia Terry

Tom and Lynne Hagen

Sarah E. Weddell

Jan Chamberlin

Eileen Berger

James and Harriet Blilie

Clayton Jorgensen

Edward Holtz

Ethel Woestehoff

Cary Cardozo

Thomas and Ann Patterson Gibson

Jim and Liz Kasper

Pat and Lisa Jarvis

Paul and Charity Huberty

Jerry and Mavis Wheeler

*Please accept our apologies if we inadvertently left your name off of this list.*
*It was our intention to include everyone.*

# Prologue

By Pat Terry

Just as Krumkake is nourishment for the body, *Krumkake, Tales of Wit, Wisdom and Wanderings* is intended to be nourishment for the spirit. *Krumkake* endeavors to be a salute to our unique White Bear Lake area history and heritage.

Long ago, our ancestors journeyed from all corners of the Old World, seeking a new life. Many settlers came to this area and made their homes on the shores of White Bear Lake. A hundred and more years later, those original settlers are gone, but many of their descendants have remained here. Why? What is it about a community that makes one want to call it home?

The generations of people who lived in the nineteenth and twentieth centuries may have been witness to more changes than any previous generation. It is from some of these people, and their personal observances, that we might find the history of ourselves.

What was the recipe that brought us all together here in this quaint Minnesota village? What stirred the hearts of the original citizens of White Bear Lake? Are there stories that may tell us how the area was shaped and molded? What have our parents and grandparents passed along to us and how do we tell the next generation our stories? Just what are the ingredients that bind us as residents of the same area?

Today, as we begin a new century, we have many distinctive tales which have been mixed, stirred, and folded together to preserve a heritage we can savor as ours alone.

*Krumkake* is an artful culinary blending of some of the stories that flavor this area. These writings are combined with a pinch of this and a dash of that to make an interesting legacy. It is this legacy we strive to share with present and future generations. Krumkake is not only a dessert to tempt your palate but a treat to appeal to all your senses.

*So grab your spoon, sample our batter, and get
ready to consume a most delightful concoction:*

# Krumkake

**Tales of Wit, Wisdom and Wanderings
from the White Bear Lake Area**

# Krumkake

## Tales of Wit, Wisdom and Wanderings
## from the White Bear Lake Area

*Compiled by:*
Patricia A. Terry
and
Lynne Davenport Hagen

*Published by:*
White Bear Center for the Arts
2228 Fourth Street
White Bear Lake, MN 55110
Phone: 651.407.0597

WHITE BEAR
CENTER
FOR THE
ARTS

First Printing April 2000
Bang Printing
1473 Highway 18 East
Brainerd, MN 56401

Layout and Design by:
Patricia A. Terry
and
Lynne Davenport Hagen

Production by:
Cap Systems
Patrick Jarvis Design
Mavis Wheeler Design
Northern Design Group

Published by:
White Bear Center for the Arts
2228 Fourth Street
White Bear Lake, MN 55110-5747
Phone: 651.407.0597

ISBN:  0-9674711-0-9 (pbk)
0-9674711-0-7

# Krumkake

## Tales of Wit, Wisdom and Wanderings
## from the White Bear Lake Area

*Cover Art by Frank Zeller*

**Manitou Montage**
*White Bear: Wind, Water and Whisperings*

In this print, artist Frank Zeller captures both the Manitou legend and several major White Bear Lake landmarks, including a typical lake cottage (The Fillebrown House), Manitou Island Bridge, the Geist Gazebo in Matoska Park and the lake itself, winter and summer.

Frank Zeller's paintings have won many regional and state awards. He exhibits regularly in juried art shows and his work is represented in several galleries and corporations throughout the Midwest.

Limited edition art prints of cover are available
500 numbered and signed by artist
17" x 19 1/2"
$55 unframed—includes shipping

Inquiries to:  Frank Zeller
2610 Valley View Drive
White Bear Lake, MN 55110
651-429-4264

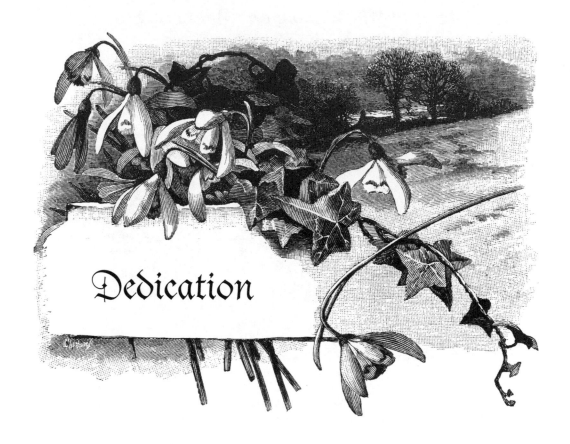

# Dedication

*This book was compiled for*
*all the people...*
*past, present and future,*
*who sometime in their lives*
*let the waters of White Bear Lake*
*touch their souls.*

# Introduction

## A Tribute to White Bear by the
## St. Paul Pioneer Press in 1890

### Submitted by Lawrence R. (Bob) and Eileen Whitaker

"White Bear Lake lies like a sapphire set round about with emeralds, a dazzling brooch which rises and falls upon sweet Nature's bosom, overlooked by her blue eyes, brightened by her sunny smiles, and swept by her fragrant sighs. Nowhere can be found a lovelier place. Such is the unanimous opinion of scores of Nature's lovers who go there to court her as soon as her young sister Spring pays her annual visit, and leaves only when Autumn shakes out her bright dresses and folds them for Winter. White Bear is to be the lake of this region and the suburban glory of St. Paul."

Manitou (or Spirit) Island (1890) is one of the most enchanting and lovely places, consisting as it does of about 60 acres with high and nicely wooded banks, graced throughout with imposing and picturesque cottages, where dwell, during the summer months, many of St. Paul's most estimable and wealthy people. An arched bridge from the mainland reaches the island. Throughout its entire length is a labyrinth of shady, well-kept walks and driveways. An additional interest is lent to this lovely spot by the fact of its previous occupancy many years ago by Indian tribes, and many are the weird legends told of it. The name of Manitou, which it bears, is from an old Chippewa legend, to the effect that the island was created in a single night by the Manitou or Great Spirit, who appeared in the form of a white bear. Here now, where once the Indian warrior wooed his mate, and skimmed over the surface of the lake in his primitive canoe, abounds all the elements of modern civilization and culture. Not the least important feature here is the system of water works put in by a stock company.

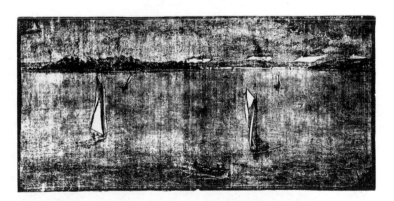

## "Moonlight on the Lake"

### Scene on White Bear Lake as Published in Vol. 1 of White Bear Life in 1896.

### White Bear Lake

No pleasure can equal that of boating on a beautiful stream or lake. White Bear Lake has an enviable reputation over the country as being one of the most beautiful spots in the Lake Park region, and the village of White Bear, located on the west shore of this wonderful lake, is one of the best towns in the northwest, and is growing with remarkable rapidity and stability.

The facilities for reaching the village of White Bear are almost unlimited—six steam trains per day and a trolley car every hour give excellent transportation, and we are promised a still better service as the season advances.

Valuable improvements will begin soon—a Carnegie library, a new bank and two new school buildings are among the talked-of projects of the near future—and the contracts have been let for a portion of this list. With the loyalty of our people in patronizing our home station there is good prospect for a new depot.

### Summer Resort

White Bear Village is excellently located for a summer resort. Situated as it is between Bald Eagle Lake and Birch Lake and on the shore of White Bear Lake, and within easy reach of several smaller lakes our Village has few equals as to points of natural interest which appeal to the summer visitor.

Elsewhere in this issue will appear reproductions of summer scenes along the lake, also a winter scene, ice boating on White Bear Lake.

That the public at large, within a radius of many miles, appreciate the pleasures afforded by frequent visits to our village is manifested by the mammoth crowds of pleasure seekers that throng our locality during the excursion season.

### BOOST!!
#### For White Bear, First, Last and all Time

*Courtesy of White Bear Press.*

# Kissemepa and Kagoka
## A Legend of White Bear Lake

Written by Francais J. Whitaker
Submitted by Lawrence R. (Bob) and Eileen Whitaker

Every spring, for perhaps a century, or as long as there has been a nation, an island in the middle of White Bear Lake had been visited by a band of Indians for the purpose of making maple sugar. Tradition says that many springs ago, while upon this island, a young warrior loved and wooed the daughter of his chief, and it is said, also, that the maiden loved the warrior. He had again and again been refused her hand by her parents, the old chief alleging that he was not brave and his old consort calling him a woman!

The sun had again set upon the "sugar bush" and the bright moon rode high in the blue heavens when the young warrior took down his flute and went out alone, once more to sing the story of his love. The mild breeze gently moved the two gay feathers in his headdress, and as he mounted upon the trunk of a leaning tree, the damp snow fell from his feet heavily. As he raised his flute to his lips his blanket slipped away from his well-formed shoulders and lay partly on the snow beneath. He began his weird, wild love song, but soon felt that he was cold, and as he reached for his blanket some unseen hand laid it gently on his shoulders. It was the hand of his love, his guardian angel. She took her place beside him and for the present they were happy, for the Indian has a heart to love, and in his pride he is as noble as in his own freedom, which makes him the child of the forest.

As the legend runs, a large white bear, thinking perhaps that the polar snows and dismal weather extended everywhere, took up his journey southward. He at length approached the northern shore of the lake which now bears his name, walked down the bank and made his way noiselessly through the deep heavy snow toward the island. It was the same spring that the lovers met. They had left their first retreat and were now seated among the branches of a large elm, which hung far out over

*The legendary Manitou Island Drive. Photo courtesy of Lawrence R. (Bob) and Eileen Whitaker.*

the lake. (The same tree stood and excited universal curiosity and interest until it was removed as a safety precaution. It stood just opposite the entrance to Shady Lane.) For fear of being detected they had talked almost in a whisper, and now, that they might get back to the camp in good time and thereby avoid suspicion, they were just rising to return. Suddenly the maiden uttered a shriek, which was heard at the camp. Bounding toward the young brave, she caught his blanket but missed the direction of her foot, and fell, bearing the blanket with her, into the great arms of the ferocious monster. Instantly every man, woman, and child of the band were upon the bank, but all unarmed. Cries and wailings went up from every mouth. What was to be done?

In the meantime this white and savage beast held the breathless maiden in his huge grasp and fondled his precious prey. All at once, a deafening yell from the warrior was heard above the cry of a hundred of his tribe. Dashing away to his wigwam, he grasped his faithful knife, returned almost in a single bound to the scene of fear and fright, rushed out along the leaning tree to the spot where his treasure fell, and springing with the fury of a mad panther, pounced upon his prey. The animal turned, and with one stroke from his huge paw brought the lovers heart to heart, but the next moment the warrior, with one plunge of the blade of his knife, opened the crimson sluices of death and the dying bear relaxed his grasp.

That night there was no sleep for the band or the lovers. As the young and the old danced about the carcass of the dead monster, the gallant warrior was presented with another plume, and ere another moon had set, he had a living treasure added to his heart. Their children for many years played upon the tanned skin of the White Bear from which the lake derives its name. The maiden and the brave remembered long, the fearful scene and rescue that made them one. Kissemepa and Kargoka could never forget their fearful encounter with the huge monster that came so near sending them to the happy hunting ground.

*Editor's Note: In keeping with tradition, our city fathers have instituted an annual event, "Manitou Days," a local celebration commencing with an evening parade and culminating with many varied festivities.*

*Lake Avenue of White Bear Lake. Photo courtesy of Lawrence R. (Bob) and Eileen Whitaker.*

# Krumkake Recipe

1/3 cup Whipping Cream
3 eggs
1 cup Sugar
1/3 cup Melted Butter
1 1/3 cup Flour
1 teaspoon Ground Cinnamon
or
1 teaspoon Almond Extract

Whip the cream. Beat eggs lightly and add to the cream. Add the remaining ingredients. Bake on a Krumkake iron on top of the stove. Turn the iron once while baking each cookie. Remove Krumkake from the iron with a spatula. Roll at once around a wooden Krumkake roller; cool and remove.

Yield: six dozen 5" cookies

*Try filling with sweetened whipped cream and fresh fruit or strawberry preserves.*

# Contents

# Butter

# Flour

# Spice

# Hot Off the Iron

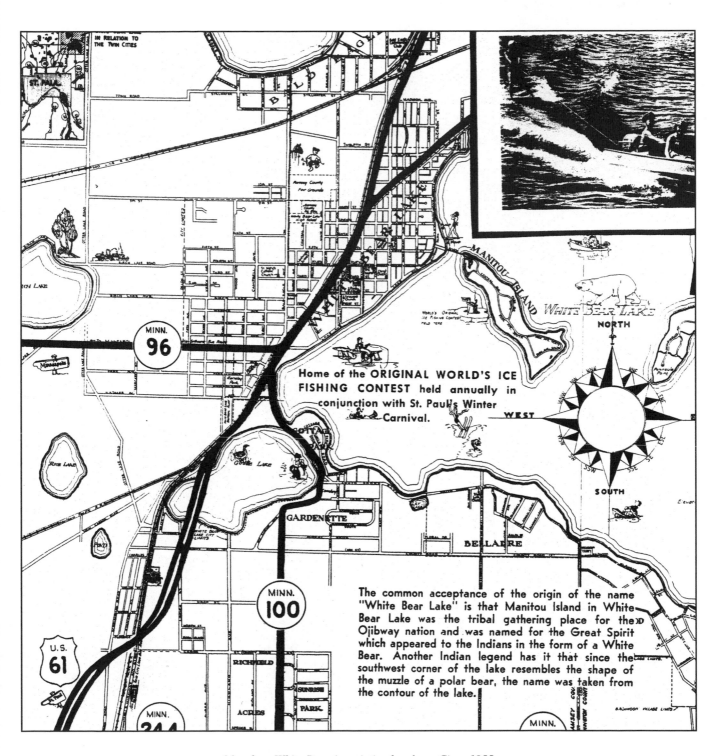

*Map from White Bear Association brochure. Circa 1955*
*Courtesy of Paul Chapin*

Whipping Cream

# Airplane Accident

*As Remembered by*
*Lyndon A. Long*

I, Lyndon A. Long, was riding my bicycle at the intersection of Clark and Lake Avenues. It was summertime in about 1927. An amphibian biplane appeared and seemed to be trying to land on the lake. So, being interested, I watched as it approached the lake; a lake that was like a mirror, as the wind was nil.

The pilot apparently couldn't make out the mirror-like surface, so he landed either above or below the water surface. The plane nosed into the water bringing the tail up over the bow, turning the plane upside down. The plane didn't sink because, being amphibious, the undamaged hull kept it afloat.

I rode as fast as I could to Johnson's Boat Works to find Buster Johnson working down on the dock. He hadn't seen the plane come in, but we immediately got into a motorboat and sped out to it.

When we got there, the pilot was in the water wearing a bowler hat, and an unlit cigar dangled from his mouth. He was completely surrounded by fuel floating on the surface. We threw him a large rope, which he attached to the plane. We then took him aboard and proceeded to tow the plane to Johnson's boat dock. He turned out to be Dr. Young who owned a string of optometry shops in the Twin Cities.

I remember being so proud because Buster Johnson asked me if I could tie the rope to the boat using a knot, that no matter how tightly wrapped, could still be untied. Well I had just learned about the bowline knot in the Boy Scouts so I was able to do the job superbly!

## 300-MILE AN HOUR 'MYSTERY SHIP' AT STATE FAIR

*Courtesy of White Bear Press.*

# History Repeats Itself

*As Remembered by*
*Elsie Bahnemann*

"Mama, tell me about when you were a child in White Bear Lake!" As a youngster growing up in the West Side area of St. Paul, I was fascinated by the stories my mother, Anna Paar Eue, would often relate to me about her early White Bear Lake years.

Anna was the youngest of nine children born to Adolph and Elise Paar. Adolph emigrated from Germany in 1853, coming to St. Paul before Minnesota was a state. Elise emigrated from Germany a few years later, and in 1858 they were married. They were destined to become the grandparents whom I would never know.

In 1884 Adolph was stricken with cancer of the liver. His father, Christian Daniel Paar, who was still living in Kassel, Germany, urged him to come to his country for medical help. So Adolph, his wife Elise and three of their children (including my six-year-old mother Anna) made the trip back to Germany, and lived in Kassel for about a year. Unfortunately, there was no cure for Adolph's illness; he died in Kassel on February 13, 1885.

*The home of Anna Paar located on Clark Avenue. Photo courtesy of Elsie Bahnemann.*

So now, the newly widowed Elise and the three children who were with her returned to St. Paul. With the rest of the family joining them, they all continued to live in their large family home on Wabasha Street in St. Paul. It was not long, however, before Elise put their mansion up for sale. On Clark Avenue in the town of White Bear Lake there was a sizeable tract of land on which three houses were already standing. In 1887 Elise purchased this piece of property and the family subsequently moved in. Some of the older children were already married; the three houses on the land were put to good use almost immediately.

"I was about nine or ten years old when we moved to White Bear Lake," my mother would tell me. "I loved playing in the lovely big garden that surrounded the houses. And the trees, they were great for climbing!"

*Clark Avenue (before paving) with view of E. B. Gibbs Civil War monument erected May 30th, 1913. Photo courtesy of Lawrence R. (Bob) and Eileen Whitaker.*

"You mean you really climbed trees?" This seemed unbelievable to me.

"Of course—I really was quite a tomboy! And we had a wonderful big dog; a St. Bernard called Bismark, who would follow me all over. People spoke of me as the "little girl with the big dog."

"Tell me about your school," I would plead as I held up an old photograph.

"Well, yes, this is a picture of my fourth grade class, and the child way over to the right is me, your mama."

*Miss Gundlach's fourth grade class — Washington School 1888 Photo courtesy of Elsie Bahnemann.*

I looked closely at the photograph and spotted my mother. I put a mark above her picture, so that I would not forget. "'Who was your teacher, mama?"

"She was a lovely lady by the name of Miss Gundlach, really a good teacher. I learned a lot from her. Elsie," she said, "if you had lived at that time, you would have loved her."

Years went by, and little Anna grew up. At fifteen years, she was confirmed in a German Evangelical Church in White Bear Lake. In 1904 she married my father, Friedrich Wilhelm Eue of St. Paul. The wedding ceremony was held in White Bear Lake with H.C. Westphal, the Evangelical Lutheran pastor, officiating. After living in one of the houses on the family property for a short time, the young couple moved to St. Paul's West Side, where they built their home.

I was born in 1910. In 1923 I attended the first half of the eighth grade at the old Crowley School on the west side of St. Paul, a temporary measure, as a new junior high school was being built and was not quite ready for students. In the meantime I found that the old Crowley School had its charms for me. One teacher in particular fascinated me, an attractive older lady with beautiful white hair. History was the subject she taught. Her name, however, fascinated me even more. She was known as "Miss Gundlach." The name "rang a bell" for me. "Mama," I said to her one day, "I think you would like my history teacher—her name is Miss Gundlach."

"MISS GUNDLACH! REALLY? ARE YOU SURE?"

"Yes, that's her name!"

We both wondered if she could be the same Miss Gundlach that had taught my mother in the White Bear Lake school so long ago. So, one day I asked her. "Miss Gundlach, did you ever teach in the White Bear Lake school and have my mother, Anna Paar, as one of your pupils?"

"Yes! Yes!" She responded excitedly. "Could it be that you are REALLY Anna's daughter?"

Of course I assured her that I was indeed Anna's daughter. And so we learned that history had repeated itself. For Miss Gundlach, mother and me, it was the beginning of a beautiful and loving friendship, as we frequently visited each other that year.

Although Miss Gundlach died a long time ago, her image has stayed with me all these years. She was my teacher in St. Paul and my mother's teacher in White Bear Lake.

# Life at the Hotel Leip in the 1880s

*As Remembered by*
*Frederick E. Whitaker*
*Submitted by Lawrence R. (Bob) and Eileen Whitaker*

Young men growing up in White Bear Lake in the latter half of the nineteenth century did not approach the character of Mark Twain's Tom Sawyer or Huckleberry Finn. Life of the youth, Frederick E. Whitaker, Senior, was a much more serious business. Insight into this was recently revealed to the author in a notebook owned by Mr. Robert Whitaker of White Bear Lake. This fascinating notebook of Frederick E. Whitaker, Senior, recalls his adventures as a bellboy at the Hotel Leip in 1881–1885.

Frederick E. Whitaker, Senior, was born on August 6, 1873, at Hotel Leip. His father, Robert Whitaker, was then the clerk and manager of the hotel. When Fred was between the ages of eight and twelve years old, he was hired as a bellboy.

Here are some of his personal reminiscences:

*Dear Snooper:*

*Our Dad was clerk and manager at Leip's Hotel and Cottages. He met lots of fine people from around St. Paul, but most of them were Southerners who came up on the steamboats in big family parties and stayed all summer. You see, White Bear Lake and Lake Minnetonka were in the frontier in those days. St. Paul being at the head of navigation, received them all, and from this point, spread them around. White Bear was a real resort in those days. It had Greenman's Hotel in Cottage Park (burned down), Leip's Hotel and Cottages (the main building held 125 rooms, then they had seven cottages), Williams House with three cottages, Chateaugay, The Lakeside of Mrs. Drake and Bloomer Hotel at Mahtomedi. Those hotels could accommodate quite a big bunch.*

*The summer I was 8 years old, Col. Leip asked Dad if I wanted a job as a bellhop. Dad said yes. I went down to Lake Shore on the 7:15 A.M. train every morning and walked back home some time between 7:30 to 11:00 P.M. I was 9 years old on August 8. For three more years I worked there every summer.*

*Sometimes on Sundays and holidays, big crowds would come and I would have to turn the freezer. This was a pretty big job for such a little skinny boy, but I always managed to get a dish of ice cream or a coke. Sometimes they had big picnics. Although they had grounds and lots of tables we had to hustle because some of them ate in the hotel. Others rented a room for the day if they had a big family and needed a loafing place for a little one. The St. Paul-Duluth Railroad sometimes would bring 12 to 16 coaches full. Almost every year The French Society of St. John de Baptiste came to the hotel and all the prominent people of St. Paul would be there. Old Man Leip was a German, but he spoke French like a native.*

*Capt. Leaman's Launch, one of many White Bear Lake excursion boats. Courtesy of White Bear Press.*

*Of course, the hotel had a big and very fine saloon at the end of the big pavilion. The pavilion was a part of the big rowboat and sailboat dock. There wasn't a good bathing beach there. A rickety bus and two plugs always met the trains at Lake Shore Station. The Station had a summer agent, Miss Maud Johnston, who kept it going almost until the automobile killed the business of local train passengers, and the depot was removed.*

*I put in four years at the magnificent salary of five dollars per month and two meals a day. The third year I nailed the Old Man for more, and he gave me a raise to eight dollars. Of course, there were tips quite often, and I saved all I could. The Southerners were generous on tips.*

Like Tom Sawyer, Fred Whitaker still thought like a boy and he recalled one incident only a boy would remember. " *While working there in the middle of a hot summer night, we had a warm rain. In the morning when I went to work there were small black and yellow lizards all over the place. The Old Man told me to get rid of them, for they had crawled into the office, which didn't have a screen door. When they were stepped on and killed, there was blood all over the floors, and the heat caused them to smell badly. Some the ladies were scared stiff!"*

At seventy-eight years of age, Frederick E. Whitaker, Sr. still remembered these incidents of his youth in White Bear Lake. They reveal to us the candid views of his youth growing up in a popular resort town in Minnesota in the nineteenth century.

*The Alden Hotel was typical of the resort hotels located along Lake Avenue. Photo courtesy of Lawrence R. (Bob) and Eileen Whitaker.*

*Ramaley's Pavilion (1910), located near the present day VFW, accommodated over 2000 persons. The building included a dance hall, concert stage, restaurant and room rentals. Photo courtesy of Lawrence R. (Bob) and Eileen Whitaker.*

# Ceiling Falls in at Ciresi's Liquor Store

*As Remembered by*
*Eugene D. Johnson (Gene)*

Prior to 1956 the White Bear Press was located on the second floor in the Getty Building in downtown White Bear Lake. In 1944 the Huber-Hodgmann four-page newspaper press was installed. Over the years the weekly vibrations were bound to cause some wear and tear on the building.

One day when I was the shop foreman, I was running the cylinder press with heavy lead pages. The plaster let loose from the ceiling in Ciresi's Liquor Store, located under the press on the first floor, and came crashing down amid dust and noise. Within seconds, Sam Ciresi, who was then the owner, came charging up the two flights of stairs and confronted the publisher, Aaron Litman, about the terrible damage his press had caused.

## White Bear Press

*Formerly White Bear Life*

HERBERT J. KEELER

WHITE BEAR, - - MINNESOTA.

Published Weekly at 214 Clark Avenue.

Tri-State Phone 17.    N. W. Phone 268.

Subscription, $1.00 per Year in Advance.

**Advertising Rates:**

DISPLAY, rates on application.

PURE READING and LOCALS 7 cents a line. Liberal discount for contracts.

CARD of THANKS, 25 cents.

CLASSIFIED ADS, 5 cents a line first insertion; additional insertions 3 cents a line. Count six words to the line.

Liberal discount from legal rates on Probate Notices, Foreclosures, Incorporations, etc.

Entered at White Bear Lake Post Office as Second Class Matter.

THURSDAY, OCT. 1, 1914.

*Advertising Rates for the White Bear Press during early 1900s.*

*The Getty Building, shown here with its original facade, still stands at the corner of Third Street and Clark Avenue. Photo courtesy of Lawrence R. (Bob) and Eileen Whitaker.*

I don't know all about the conversations that ensued but it wasn't very many years later that Aaron Litman purchased land and began building at 4779 Bloom Avenue, where he relocated the White Bear Press and where it operates today.

Ciresi's Liquor Store ceiling was restored, bottles replaced and business went on as usual.

Aaron Litman purchased the White Bear Press from Vernon S. Tegland in 1948. The Litmans owned the paper until 1970 when it was sold to me.

# Bonin Leaves Free Press Notes

*As Remembered by*
*Eugene D. Johnson (Gene)*

Each publisher in the history of The White Bear Press has played a significant role in the newspaper's development, including myself. I purchased the newspaper 29 years ago. I was a hometown boy coming back after cutting my teeth in the publishing business on two rural Minnesota newspapers. I bought the Press from Mrs. Aaron Litman in 1970.

Actually, I had worked for the Press beginning at age 15, feeding the newspaper press and making up handset type ads.

At 34, I was able to turn the fledgling 1,800 paid-circulation tabloid into six different newspapers reaching over 60,000 homes weekly.

Looking back to the early days, I recall the 70's market as very competitive. A Forest Lake publisher had moved in with a shopper to meet merchant needs. Suburban Sun Publications had an office in White Bear Lake and the Lillie Newspapers of North St. Paul were stretching outward.

We had a lot of encouragement from people such as Dick Long, First State Bank president, Fred Brass of the Village Shop, Bob Brass of the Ben Franklin store and Dick Parenteau of Parenteau's Clothing and Shoes. Some said it would be difficult to succeed.

I tried everything to "grow" the circulation, and it eventually reached 5,000 homes. But that wasn't enough to attract the advertisers that were needed to make a suburban newspaper successful.

One night in 1973 when I got home I found notes in my refrigerator, under my pillow, in my closet, all over the house that said "Free Press, Free Press, Free Press."

It was the work of Phil Bonin who had joined the Press advertising team in 1973. His idea was to launch a free-distribution shopper with some news and call it the "Free Press."

We did it, it was successful, and we gained market share!

During the recession of 1982, I decided to merge the "Free Press" with the White Bear Press and make it a total market coverage voluntary pay newspaper. The "Free Press" name was dropped, but many people still use the moniker today.

Progressively, Press Publications began its expansion campaign with adjoining newspapers, first in Vadnais Heights, then Little Canada, then on to Stillwater, Lino Lakes and, most recently, Forest Lake.

# X Marks the Spot

*As Remembered by*
*Eugene D. Johnson (Gene)*

t was in 1974–75 when a full page White Bear Press ad for Summit Liquor Store came back from the printers with advertised liquor prices showing through what was supposed to be large X's.

At that time, the Minnesota Legislature had provided a liquor control commissioner who prohibited price advertising.

This particular ad was designed by Press advertising representative, Phil Bonin, along with the Summit Liquor owner, Tom Hanson. They thought they had a clever idea of printing the price, then putting the X's over it. Little did they realize, the X's would not block out the prices adequately!

So one night in the back room of the Press, volunteers were invited to help cross out the prices on the full page ad for the entire Press run, which at that time was over 10,000 copies.

It took a carton of felt-tip pens and the determination that the paper would come out in a legal manner.

When people who worked for the Press in those days reminisce, they still laugh about it. Phil Bonin continues in his 26th year at Press Publications. That's just one of those stories that goes on in the life of a community newspaper.

*Ad courtesy of White Bear Press, circa 1978.*

# A Class With Class

*As Remembered by*
*Virginia Zollner Terry Merrill*

The most remarkable thing about my White Bear memories is the high school class with whom I graduated. This wasn't any run-of-the-mill type class; it was the White Bear High School Class of 1951 with 120 plus graduates.

At the time we attended classes, I don't think anyone realized that we were different from any other class. It was after we left school that we began to distinguish ourselves.

Can you think of another class that has:

- *A reunion every five years without fail—and has about a 60 to 70% attendance?*

- *Another event between the five years, usually a cruise, with 10 to 15 classmates and their spouses?*

- *A breakfast meeting each month with anyone who is in town attending frequently?*

- *A group of the classmates living near each other in the south in the winter?*

- *An informal gathering, (or two) each summer up north?*

- *The best Sven and Lena jokes in the upper Midwest?*

- *A real concern for each other? Perhaps that comes from reaching maturity and gaining wisdom, and leaving behind the teenage worries and competitions.*

Whatever the reason, the result is a lot of laughs and fond memories to carry us through till the next time this crazy group meets again! Thanks everyone!!

*The Division Street side of White Bear High School (now the Central Middle School) after its 1924 and 1935 additions.*
*Photo courtesy of Lawrence R. (Bob) and Eileen Whitaker.*

# White Bear Lake's Tornado of 1941

*As Remembered by*
*David Gehrenbeck*

he cyclone that transported Dorothy Gale from Kansas to the Land of Oz may be better known, but White Bear Lake's devastating tornado of September 4, 1941 was for real.

It happened over the lunch hour during the first week of the new school year—barely three months before Pearl Harbor. I was ten years old and in Miss Lola Benson's fifth grade.

Living directly caddy-corner from the old (1888) Webster School at Fifth Street and Stewart Avenue, my brother, Richard, and I had walked home for our noon meal. Suddenly the sky darkened, the wind picked up, the rain and hail followed. Nothing to be particularly alarmed about, we thought, until dishes near the kitchen windows crashed to the floor. By this time Mother realized this was no ordinary storm, and called on her two boys to get to the basement. We, however, were so entranced by the fury of the elements that we didn't get beyond the dining room.

Minutes earlier Barbara Choate had come by on her way back to school. Mother urged her to stay with us, but Barbara ran on and made it safely home. Another classmate, Janice Daggy, had quite a joyride. She had started out from her home at Fifth and Johnson, and later reported having been scooped up by the wind and carried along Fifth Street for several yards. Miraculously, she landed gently.

In another five, maybe ten, minutes, it was all over. The power was off, of course. Mother, though obviously relieved, scolded us for having disobeyed her. We tried to look out the windows, but the screens were saturated with water and plastered with leaves. For several minutes we could hardly see daylight at all. Once the fury was past, we cautiously opened the front and back doors. No, we were not in the Land of Oz.

Even more cautiously, we ventured outdoors. Every tree in our yard was down—except a white birch which later we reasoned had bent almost to the ground before springing back up (cracks in the earth at least suggested that). In our yard were five apple trees, wonderful for eating but even better for climbing. They, and most all of the elms, maples, and oaks in the neighborhood were uprooted, leaving huge craters, now filled with muddy water. Power and phone lines—and poles—lay in tangled webs all over. Directly across Fifth Street, the sidewalk in front of the Presbyterian parsonage was cracked to smithereens. But worst of all for us was the destruction of the little playhouse Grandpa had built for us in 1938. Until that day it had stood next to the sandbox in the backyard. Now, having been hurled into an apple tree on the other side of the house, it lay in ruins. Yet its little wood-burning stove remained intact—and functional.

By now the sun was shining. As it turned out, we were lucky: not a pane of glass in our house was broken, no doubt because we weren't fast enough to close all the windows so the air pressure differential outside versus inside was minimal. But the roof was a mess. Shingles were scattered, and branches and chimney brick were lying all over.

A block south, at Fourth Street and Stewart Avenue, the devastation was worse: trees had crashed into walls and roofs, and on Mrs. Chisholm's home the roof had disappeared. A cache of love letters, at one time consigned to the attic, was now strewn all over the area.

How widespread the storm was, we had no idea. By nightfall, once Father had finally gotten home from 3M, we learned that our neighborhood was among the hardest hit. Downtown White Bear Lake, only three blocks west, survived relatively unscathed, although the Armory at Fourth and Cook took quite a beating. South of town, along Goose Lake, some of the units at Jantzen's Cabin Camp were turned upside down.

*Webster School 1889*
*The original Webster School was a four-room building on the corner of*
*Fifth Street and Banning Avenue. Photo courtesy of Lawrence R. (Bob) and Eileen Whitaker.*

It would be years before it was all cleaned up, tree stumps lingering along some properties throughout World War II. The Webster School withstood major damage, although, its soaring steeple soon had to be removed. Returning to my classroom in mid-afternoon, I found many of my classmates huddled together in the middle of the room. No lessons were being taught, nor was anyone counted tardy who didn't make it back by the one o'clock bell.

But there was a lesson, after all: never underestimate the potential of a thunderstorm. Tornadoes like this aren't apt to repeat themselves in the same spot, we hear. Once in a lifetime is quite enough.

# Constables

*As Remembered by*
*C. M. Ingham*

Constables were the first kind of police protection in most small towns and villages. There was no money for a police department in these communities. The criminals who were caught funded most crime control.

The constables were elected to their position along with the mayor and village councils. It was the least sought-after position and in many cases the elected refused to serve or were elected as a joke on some poor soul. Some men, however, took the position seriously and prospered, as well as kept order.

The normal procedure for the constable was for him to be available to apprehend miscreants, speeders, drunken drivers, thieves and any other criminals.

In the village of Birchwood there was a very serious, honest man who took to his elected position conscientiously. He had a black 1930 Model A Ford coupe that he converted to the police car by painting the letters on each side and replacing the parking lights with red lenses. He put a siren on the front bumper wired to an electric battery on the dashboard.

Three corners of the County Road E and East County Line crossroads had speakeasy saloons. The fourth corner, overgrown with trees and brush, served as the cover for our brave constable. The low life fringe of the criminal element would hang out in the area because of the slot machines and gambling. They all seemed to drive big, fast cars; they drove them through stop signs and dared anyone to complain.

Our constable tried to stop them with his little black four-cylinder coupe, but they just laughed at his meager efforts and his little putt-putt.

So, not to be outdone, our constable talked to a friend in White Bear who was an ace mechanic. They concocted a great scheme. Bert Lindbeck put a V-8 engine with super-charger twin pipes under the hood of the little black coupe.

The next night as the fast crowd poured out of the saloons, they saw the little coupe sitting behind the bushes, waiting as usual.

As cars roared through the stop sign, the constable took out after them. In a big Buick, the first law offender headed for North St. Paul, four miles away. As they hit 60, the constable with his little coupe, pulled alongside the speeder, flashed his little red lights, tapped his siren and had his man.

He repeated the process frequently enough to make a good living for himself and the Justice of the Peace, who was very tough. Between the two of them they cleaned up the east side of Washington County of the fast cars and some of the St. Paul hoods.

"I KNOW ALL THAT BUT—

*Courtesy of White Bear Press.*

One night our constable found a body lying in a ditch near his ambush spot. He called the Justice of the Peace to ask him what to do. The justice told him to "Check the body. If he's dead, shove him into Ramsey County. If he's drunk, take him to Stillwater and put him in jail. We'll fine him tomorrow!"

Another of our elected minions of the law was a sometime contractor, who loved his new position. He was so eager he went out and bought his own Police Uniform with belt, badges, leather puttees, and striped jodhpur pants. He equipped his car with flashing lights, siren, shotgun and a souped-up transmission.

He loved to chase speeders or people who looked like they could afford to be arrested, whether they were speeding or not. He frequently caught people, found them guilty and fined them on the spot by telling them he would pay the judge.

There was one constable who loved to arrest speeders and drunk drivers. He arrested my brother for going 32 mph in a 30 zone and took him before the Justice of the Peace. When the judge saw the constable, who was staggering drunk at the time, he threw the case out and arrested the constable for drunk driving!

*Ads courtesy of White Bear Press, circa 1914.*

# A Girl and a Float

*As Remembered by*
*Edward Holtz*

In 1958, Superintendent I.V. Johnson requested that the White Bear Teachers' Association build a float for the school district for the city-sponsored parade which was in honor of the 100th anniversary of Minnesota's becoming a state.

We decided to have two girls from the class of 1958 ride on the float and to find the oldest graduate and have him/her also ride the float. I found Emogene Cummings, who was living in the White Bear Beach Area. She said that she was a graduate from the second class of 1897. Miss Cummings was about 79 years old at the time of the parade in 1958. She indicated that the first high school classes were held upstairs in the building on the corner of Banning and Third Street which is on the southeast corner of that intersection. It is now Edward Jones Investment on 2208 Third Street. I believe that at one time it was occupied by the Hardy Grocery Store.

Emogene attended her freshman and sophomore years, 1894 and 1895 at the Third and Banning location and at Washington School thereafter, which was built in 1896. Washington School was the only original building still standing that was used for high school education in White Bear Lake, until it too was replaced by a new building.

*The 1958 White Bear Lake homecoming float with three special graduates.*
*Photo courtesy of Edward Holtz.*

# Tuba Time

*As Remembered by*
*C. M. Ingham*

In our high school-middle school (grades 5–12) we had the opportunity to join the band when we were in the 7th grade. Several of us signed up to learn to play instruments. This was a new program for our school, so we all started out as beginners. No one knew anything about anything! Our band director, Mr. Nelson, told us that we needed 3 trumpeters, 3 trombones, a baritone, a bass, 3 clarinets, a piccolo, a snare drum and a bass drum.

Mr. Nelson came from a large family of band directors who owned many instruments. He rented them out to several schools, and was hired to teach students to play them. Our band practiced in the lunchroom once per week.

*Some very serious brass players—photo taken in front*
*of Washington School. Photo courtesy of Janet Griemann.*

We all signed up for the various instruments. I thought I would like the trumpet, so I was issued a nearly new silver one with a book of instructions. Each of us was told to read our books and start practicing.

When I got home I announced the new career I had signed up for. I couldn't understand what my parents were looking at on the ceiling. I had a sit-down talk with my mother, whom I had to convince I was serious. She was skeptical after my failure to accept piano lessons from her because I hated practice. I told her this was different because I would be doing it with other kids who were eager to play music, too. Dad said, "Just don't practice when I'm home!" I tried practicing and learning the instrument, but had trouble with the notes, which were too close together.

After six months, Mr. Nelson suggested that maybe the trombone would be easier. Shoving that long arm in and out was monotonous and a classmate of mine, June Phillips, who was A-One on the trombone, had the number one chair. There had been several early aspirants who had dropped out so Mr. Nelson pleaded with the remnants to hang in there and work harder. I was switched to a baritone horn with valves. I should have taken the piccolo, but Merlee Reynolds was fumbling with that one. The next year I switched to bass drum.

The music was simple and I was big enough to carry it. When we went to a concert we had to go by streetcar. I couldn't sit in a seat with the drum so I had to stand on the back platform and keep people from kicking it in, while trying to stay warm in the winter.

The following year I was asked to try the tuba. It was a C# Sousaphone, which I climbed into. The music was easy to read and I really didn't need to practice 20 hours per week, but I did need to practice some. My favorite place to practice was two blocks away in a wooded pasture that was home for several horses and cows. When I practiced, the horses left to the far end of the pasture, but the cows gathered around and mooed to my oompas.

My sophomore and junior years of high school were a lot of fun because of all the activities I was doing. Besides my paper route, I was in football, classes in chemistry, plane geometry, French, algebra, English, biology, Glee Club, drama, and sang in a sextet. I was also tootling the tuba with relish.

In football I played blocking guard on offense and tackle on defense, but I had to play the tuba in homecoming parades and during halftime. I'd give Merlee my tuba mouthpiece to wear in an inside pocket so it didn't freeze while I was playing football. She also put a mitten over the valves.

During the summer between sophomore and junior year we gave a combined concert in Phalen Park in St. Paul. I carried my tuba on the platform of the streetcar with the bass drummer.

When we arrived at the park I noticed a group of smart alecks lining up in the front row with lemons in their hands. It was always a pain to have these guys around because they would noisily suck on those lemons when we played. That sight can cause your salivary glands to dry up and you need a lot of spit to play a wind instrument. The tuba, like all other wind instruments, does collect saliva and needs to be drained periodically. Since it is a large instrument, it collects a lot. I maneuvered myself to the front of the stage directly in front of the lemon suckers. When they pulled out their lemons I emptied my drain all over them. They disappeared, much to the glee of the rest of the band.

Later that year I was talked into joining a group of other guys from an Old Time Band with a job at Treager's Dance Hall in Hugo, Minnesota. We would play Saturday nights from 8–12 P.M. for $2 each. There were five of us and I was the rhythm section, since we had no drummer. We had a lot of fun but all were underage so had to forgo the beer tips. We were asked and agreed to play an extra hour for $1 each. What a deal!

I sat in a couple of other bands as a sub where we also played waltzes (3/4 time with emphasis on the 1 beat), mazurkas (3/4 or 3/8 time), polkas (double-time) schottisches (2/4 time, slower than a polka). I carried my tuba in the rumble seat of my first car, a 1924 Ford Model T. When I left high school I left the tuba because I could not afford to buy it. It was fun, but the piccolo would have been easier to carry around. I was invited to play the tuba in a pickup Dixieland band in Mahtomedi but declined: still too expensive. But it spurred my interest in Dixieland music, which I dearly love to this day.

# An Entertaining Village

*As Remembered by*
*Janet (Michaud) Griemann*

In first grade we were excited to meet Santa Claus as he arrived by sleigh at the White Bear Lake Armory. But, it was a bitterly cold day and Santa arrived very late, as we all had waited outside. Most of us froze our faces.

As a child I remember people gathered at homes for fun and dancing. The kitchens were usually large and could be cleared for dancing. My dad, L. Desire Michaud played the violin or 'fiddle' as some called it. There was usually a piano or organ accompaniment. My mom said she never danced much because Dad was always playing.

Dad sang in a quartet with Bill Leudke, Bob Collison, and Ed Belser and later with Cleo Smith. Various organizations would put on shows by local talent. Mabel Thompson was usually the accompanist. Sometimes, traveling shows would hit town and put on a show featuring local talent and would share the proceeds with a local sponsoring group. I have a playbill from such a show, years ago. It is not dated—but it does mention 'Masters' Rex Campbell and Sterling Price. If living now, they would be about eighty-eight years old. In the late thirties and early forties, dances were held at the Armory. Events such as "March of Dimes" honoring president F. D. Roosevelt on his birthday, January 31, were frequented.

As children, on Halloween, we waxed the windows on the stores and shops in downtown. The wax was extremely hard to remove. Everyone had paraffin as it was used for canning by most families. Later, Bon Ami was substituted and was much easier to remove.

Weekly band concerts were looked forward to each Friday night during the summer. We were usually treated to an ice cream cone at the Park Sweet Shop afterwards.

*A view of Railroad Park and bandstand circa early 1900s.*
*Photo courtesy of Lawrence R. (Bob) and Eileen Whitaker.*

Before the Avalon Theater was built we had movies in the auditorium. On Saturday afternoon, if an adult accompanied children, each child could get in for ten cents. We had one lady in our neighborhood that would go each week and take a group of us. The auditorium was next door to the Armory. It later became a furniture factory. It eventually burned down. My aunt, Marvel Michaud Auger, played for the silent films. Even after the Avalon was open some of the films were silent movies.

*The Armory building at the corner of Fourth Street and Cook Avenue now houses the White Bear Center for the Arts (WBCA) on the Fourth Floor. Photo courtesy of Lawrence R. (Bob) and Eileen Whitaker.*

## AVALON THEATRE

White Bear Lake, Minn.

**FRI. AND SAT., MAY 22-23**
George Arliss, in
**THE MILLIONAIRE**
with a cast of stars, Evelyn Knapp, James Cagney, Noah Beery, Ivan Simpson. This is a different picture from the usual Arliss pictures. One with action and that every one will enjoy. A great attraction.

**SUN. AND MON., MAY 24-25**
Joan Bennett and Warner Baxter, in
**DOCTORS' WIVES**
Unforgetable as Doctor and wife, Warner Baxter and Joan Bennett, with Victor Varconi and Helene Millard in supporting cast. Also a Laurel and Hardy comedy, Laughing Grady.
Sunday Matinee at 2:45 o'clock, 10 and 35 cents

**TUES. AND WED., MAY 26-27**
Victor McLaglen, in
**THE DEVIL WITH WOMEN**
also a long feature comedy
Joe E. Brown, in **GOING WILD**

**THURS., FRI. AND SAT., MAY 28-29-30**
**SHIPMATES**
with Robert Montgomery, Ernest Torrence, Dorothy Jordan and Cliff Edwards.

**—SOON—**
Secret Six, White Shoulders, Day Break, Seed

*Ad courtesy of White Bear Press.*

*Looking west on Fourth Street near the Cook Avenue intersection—circa 1940. Photo courtesy of Lawrence R. (Bob) and Eileen Whitaker.*

*Washington School Christmas Program—1924. Photo courtesy of Reinholdt Roessler. This photo was also submitted by Bernice C. Selden.*

*The Lion's Club annual show included the "Happy Whistlers"—circa 1960's. L to R: Ralph Colaizy, Richard Isaaks, John O'Connor, Robbie Shield, Michael O'Connor, William Welch.*
*Photo courtesy of White Bear Lake Lion's Club.*

Easter was a pretty big deal. We always got new outfits to wear and that was the first day I could wear halfsocks replacing long stockings and winter underwear. As a student at St. Mary's School, some classmates and I would try to get by with the half-socks exposing our bare knees. The nuns would bring their long black stockings to class and we had to put them on over our socks.

High school was the center of our activity. We had many clubs and various activities, and our social life centered on these during the school year.

Our main entertainment in summer was swimming. We had a public beach by the Clark Avenue and Lake Avenue intersection. We were delighted to be the audience for the cast from the Plantation nightclub as they practiced for their shows. They'd do calisthenics and exercise on the beach. Ballroom dancers, Yolanda and Velez, were watched closely as they practiced their routine on the beach. Yolanda was the only person I'd seen that had more than one swimsuit. She was very petite with long black hair. Her suits were a black, a white, and an orange one.

We used the trains for our clocks—as the trains became more frequent we knew it was time to skedaddle for home and dinner.

We skated in winter. Usually the lake would freeze by Thanksgiving. Later we'd skate at the Hippodrome on Wednesday and Saturday nights, as well as Sunday afternoons. We would slide and ski on the hills of White Bear Yacht Club golf course.

**EIGHT DARLINGS FROM DANCELAND**

This is the combination of merry makers who appear twice nightly at The Plantation, under the direction of Glyde Snyder, and who make the tired businessman forget his troubles, while the envious swains wonder "where they get them." From left to right they are: Amelia Rogers, Dorothy McGuire, Helen Dax, Irene Gelden, June McNaulty Helen Marvin, Irene Vosburgh, Dorothy Kay.

*Photo courtesy of White Bear Press.*

# Working at Hoffman's Store

*As Remembered by*
*Lorraine Corrigan Berger*

Not too long ago, the road which runs past White Bear Floral and Sweet Cravings Coffee Shop was part of Highway 61. When the state decided to remove the curve and make Highway 61 a straight line at County Road E, a bit of history eventually disappeared. For at the end of the 1920's and during the 1930's, a vital commercial center thrived there. There was the big Hoffman Store, Scheuneman's Market, which was across the street, seven beer joints, two gas stations, a big garage, a dancing establishment, and an octagonal white building selling a revolutionary new idea: the hamburger!

From 1931 until 1938 Henry L. Hoffman hired me to help in his ever-growing establishment. I was about thirteen years old when I started. Our house, located where Tousley Ford is now, was very close, so it was convenient to walk there. I wore a white uniform and on summer weekends much of my day was spent scooping ice cream cones for 5 cents each. Eight flavors gave the customers a big selection to choose from. Back then the home icebox could not be kept cold enough for ice cream, so ice cream cones were very much in demand. Many Saturdays and Sundays I would sell over 500 cones! On the Fourth of July and on Labor Day, the number went up to 700! For ten cents, the customer could get a triple dip. That was hard work for a high school age girl!

My duties included more than dishing up the cones. The customers would come in with their slip of paper listing all their needed items. In those days customers did not go back in the main store, but waited at the counter for service. The clerks would read the list and bring the completed order up front. I'd take the long hook to pull down canned goods stored high on the shelves. Once a can of tuna tumbled down and hit my front tooth. That really hurt!! To this day there is a slight chip still showing.

People would bring in empty glass containers for vinegar. I'd go to the back of the store where big kegs of vinegar stood with a spigot to fill the gallon jugs. The price was 45 cents a gallon. The vinegar would spill on my fingers and I'd smell it for hours. Washing hands was not a big priority in those days.

Mr. Hoffman, a progressive businessman, installed a cooler within the store where he kept beer, meat, butter and the eight huge buckets of ice cream. In the back storage shed he stored blocks of ice, cases of strawberries set on the ice, empty baskets, wheelbarrows, and sacks of potatoes as high as the ceiling. It was quiet back there, cool and dark, and smelled of gunny sacks and potatoes. I would have to transfer the potatoes from the sacks to pecks and bushels, which were displayed out in front of the store. As I'd reach in the bulging sacks, sometimes one finger would hit a soft mushy spot. Ick! I'd wipe off the rotted potato from my fingers with a nearby rag, fill the baskets with potatoes and carry them out front. Then I'd return to scoop up more ice cream cones!

Sometimes when Mr. Hoffman got busy behind the meat counter, he'd want me to help scoop out hamburger and package it. Then too, back I'd go to the ice cream cones!!

Outside the store, attractive displays of fruit and vegetables beckoned to the customers. Cherries, raspberries and strawberries were much in demand. One customer from Manitou Island always sampled the cherries. Dangling it by a long stem in front of his mouth he'd sing out 'Life is just a bowl of cherries' and plop it into his mouth. Cucumbers and sweet corn in great numbers were purchased for canning. The smell of fresh dill filled the air. Many women canned 60 to 80 quarts of each item each summer.

Local farmers brought cases of eggs to the store. The eggs were white and brown. They would have to be transferred to boxes or carefully placed in a brown bag. Often we had a big container of eggs displayed on the counter.

Bananas hung by huge clusters from the ceiling. I was nervous cutting off the fruit as tarantulas sometimes lurked among the thick fruit. Mr. Hoffman caught them and displayed them in a tightly shut jar on the counter to shock the customers.

*A typical grocery of the early 1900s, Joseph Hardy's grocery store was located at the corner of Third Street and Banning Avenue. This store was one of the first mercantile shops in White Bear Lake. Mr. Hardy is pictured at right. Mr. P. J. LeVasseur (center) later opened his own grocery on Bald Eagle Avenue. Photo courtesy of Lawrence R. (Bob) and Eileen Whitaker.*

Many times, customers would want a hunk of ice to take home for their icebox. I'd have to estimate a 25 or 50 pound hunk, cut it with a saw, grab it with tongs and carry it out to their car. For all this labor I was paid fifty cents a day. I did get a promotion where I earned the grand total of one dollar a day! And I felt wealthy! My hours were early in the morning to late at night, and on the Fourth of July until midnight.

But it was not all hard work. Girl's softball games took place weekly in the summer. Mr. Hoffman would excuse me for two hours when someone came to pick me up

*The exterior of the Hardy Store. Photo courtesy of Lawrence R. (Bob) and Eileen Whitaker.*

and take me to the ball field. I was the pitcher. I had no time to change so at times I'd pitch in my white uniform. We won most of the games. Often, someone would drive me back to finish my work at the store.

Often people in the area would come to use the telephone, as hardly anyone owned a phone in those days. Mr. Hoffman rarely charged anything. They would call relatives in St. Paul or place an order. Mail order was one of the best ways to purchase unusual items. Next door to the store, Bob Hoffman opened one of the first hamburger stands in Minnesota. He had just come back from a trip in California where he saw how popular this meat patty between a soft bun could be. He called it a California hamburger. It had slices of tomato, onion and lettuce, just like the ones he had tasted out west. Business boomed in his white, octagonal building next to the store. St. Paul residents coming to the lake for the day stopped in for a hamburger and a five-cent bottle of beer.

On the east side of the railroad bridge stood the Red Barn Beer Parlor and Dance Hall owned by the Burlingame family. Many weekend dances were held here. On summer nights we could hear the polka, music and the sound of voices.

Dances were also held at Scheuneman's Store. Scheuneman's Market was not nearly as big as Hoffman's but they had a room inside the store with benches along the wall. Augie and Annie Scheuneman, another old family in the area, owned the place. The couple was short and rotund and very friendly. I'd guess Mrs. Scheuneman was about 72 inches around the waist. Their building provided a popular place for bridal showers and wedding receptions. On Friday nights the card game 500 proved very popular.

Eventually, I graduated from high school and went to Glacier Park to work for the summers. So ended my years at Hoffman's Store. After some years, the corner of Highway 61 and County Road E was zoned commercial and the Corrigan home was moved three blocks north, where it still stands today amid a thick grove of trees.

Note: *The author of this story lived in White Bear Lake until she married Dr. Emil Berger in 1942. Presently she is a resident at Lyngblomsten Nursing Home in St. Paul.*

*Cereal ad of that time period.*
*Photo courtesy of White Bear Press.*

# The Three R's

*As Remembered by*
*Bill Patterson*

It is now said that "I learned all I needed to know in Kindergarten" but mostly I remember trying to color pictures and sing songs. I do remember that we brought two cents to school every day and got a small bottle of milk. I wanted chocolate, but my mother said "NO."

First grade, in 1927, brought Miss Miske as my teacher and some new friends. Among them was Eileen Helfman, whose father operated the Standard Oil station on Lake Avenue. They lived next door to the station where later the Podvins lived. Across the street where the Hanscomes later lived was Betty Jane Smith. Among others was Mary Ann Buchan, the only classmate that was with me all thirteen years in school. Merrill Bernier started with me, switched to St. Mary's and graduated from high school a year ahead of me.

In first grade it seemed I spent most of my time trying to catch up with the girls – academically speaking. It seems to prove that girls learn faster than boys do in the early years. It's a limited sample, but experience with our children and theirs seem to be the same.

*Washington School (shown here after expansions) housed grades K–8.*
*Photo courtesy of Lawrence R. (Bob) and Eileen Whitaker.*

Washington School was old when I went there. It was built in 1887, which seemed very long ago at that time. Time takes on different proportions, as we grow older, because our frame of reference changes. One day in the life of a five-year old is a larger proportion of our frame of reference than when we are older. At any rate, the school was old and the floors were creaky. The windows were big and it was quite light in there when the sun was shining. The ceilings as I remember them as a five-year old were as high as a cathedral—probably about 12 feet or so. The front entry was up several steps and opened onto a center hall. There was one room on either side as you entered, back of which were stairways on either side. The back center housed rest rooms and nurse's office. Hallways on the East and West led to two more classrooms. The Kindergarten was on the West and second and third grades were on the East. The upstairs was similar with a gymnasium and one classroom and offices. By the time I reached seventh grade the enrollment had increased and the gym was converted into a large classroom for seventh and eighth grade.

The basement was used for some Phy Ed classes in winter and for special events such as listening to educational radio programs. The "American School of the Air" was the source of the programs, which were generally scientific and historical in content. The school had one Atwater Kent radio to serve all eight grades. Also, in the basement was a machine to clean erasers. It was a large wheel turned by a hand crank. Holding the eraser against the spinning wheel caused chalk dust to blow into the air. (I wonder if that was good for our lungs). But the erasers got clean and the cleaners got full of dust!

For some reason second grade is not too clear in my memory. The teacher, I believe was Mrs. Magnuson, Dorothy Haas' mother. It was located on the most easterly room on the first floor. One notable event of that year was the presidential election between Herbert Hoover and Al Smith. Even at that young age I had a great interest in presidential politics. Smith was the first Catholic to run as a major candidate for President and there was some bigotry in the campaign. While I can never remember any words of hate or bigotry coming from my parents, it was obvious that they preferred Hoover. There was a concern that the Roman Catholic hierarchy would influence Smith and threaten the Protestants somehow. In retrospect, if Smith had won, the Democratic Party would be seen as responsible for the Great Depression and it could have changed the future somewhat—for good or bad.

*Ad courtesy of White Bear Press.*

In my remaining years in grade school I became a reasonably good student. My third grade teacher was Clara Steen. I recall her as nice and a good teacher. There are no specific recollections of that year. It was the year of the great stock market crash and the start of the "Great Depression" which lasted until the start of World War II. The depression had a lasting effect on all our generation. One living and growing up today cannot imagine the effect of 40% unemployment on the life of the country.

1932 was the year of the election of Franklin Roosevelt to his first term as president. I have a strong memory of March 4, 1932 (inauguration day then). Mother and I were home and listening to the inauguration on the radio. She was very upset that 'that awful person had defeated Herbert Hoover, who was such a gentleman'. Hoover was the victim of the worldwide financial collapse and was later recognized for his great humanitarian work during and after WWI and for contributing much to the country after his defeat in 1932. He did lack the personality attribute, which we now seem to overvalue.

High school started for me in 1935—Washington School—built in 1895–97 and finally torn down to make way for a senior citizen development in 1978—had been my school home for almost nine years. White Bear High School in 1935 consisted of one building—now part of Central Junior High—and housed four classes—freshman through senior.

I'd be hard put to name the members who entered with the class of '39. Most of us had grades 6–8 together in Washington School and a few had been together since kindergarten. We also joined with those from St. Mary's Catholic School and from Hugo/Centerville—probably about 100 all together.

The school was beginning to get overcrowded and lacked satisfactory athletics, home economics, shop and stage facilities. During our freshman year the South wing was added and included a new combination gymnasium-auditorium along with new classrooms and locker rooms—a great advancement from the old.

The basketball court was of most interest to me, as the "old gym"—still in use—was a small, acoustically horrible and inadequate facility. It was used for Phy. Ed. classes during inclement weather (which we had much of in Minnesota, then as now), for interscholastic basketball and for school dances. During games, the benches for the participating teams barely fit between the wall and the court boundaries. Sitting on the bench could be as exciting as playing! With the caliber of basketball at White Bear then, it was probably more exciting! It was bad!

One of the first big events of the year for us freshmen was the All-Hi Dance. It took place fairly early in the year, like October—and my friend convinced me we should double date. My sisters gave me some fast dancing lessons. I got a date, and away we went. The dance was held in the old gym with the High School orchestra playing. Can't remember what all the songs were, but Tiger Rag was one of their favorites. Aided by the sensational acoustics of the old gym, they were (if nothing else) loud!

This was in 1935–36, and the Depression was still in full swing. Having a dollar to spend on a date was pretty good. My money for such things came mostly from my caddying in the summer at White Bear Yacht Club.

My education in White Bear Lake was a lot more inclusive than just the three "R's", and I'm happy to say that it contributed to the wholeness of my life.

Eggs

# The Lake is Home

*As Remembered by*
*Debora L. Houdek*

I grew up in Birchwood in the 50's. There were a lot of things that impressed me, were significant, memorable, or fun, but when you get right down to it, there's one thing that stands out. I mean the Lake itself, of course. There was summertime and the smell of water drifting between the leaves. There was the constant sound of boats and birds and kids yelling as they plunged in. Always there was the Lake.

Oh, there were times when we ignored it; riding bikes to the village hall for arts & crafts, picking raspberries off the bushes along Hall Avenue, or making dents in the hot blacktop at the road's shoulder (it was too hot to get near the middle, barefoot). We ignored it while running the three-legged races in the little park across from Butlers' after the 4th of July parade. But the Lake was always there. It was in the smell and feel of the air and in the brown tanned bodies running around in the sunlight. It was in the multitude of small conversations about docks, boats, and even "the itch," which showed up with the algae in August. It was in the assumptions about how we'd spend our days. It was essential to the very nature of the community formed on its edge, and a part of the nature and perspective of each one of us.

*Unknown girls at the lake. Photo courtesy of Bernice C. Selden.*

Our neighborhood gang would run around in swimsuits all summer long. We went swimming three times a day. Every spring the men would get together to put the dock in, and every fall they'd take it out. Often they'd climb the hill afterwards to one house or another and the families would sit laughing and lounging around a table full of chips, lemonade and beer. They'd have been different kind of neighbors but for the Lake.

Groups of moms would get together mornings in someone's kitchen, or around the picnic table on the patio out back, to drink coffee and compare notes on life, kids, husbands, or paper towels, while their kids were at swimming lessons. Sometimes they'd head for the beach, too. They'd set up a card table in the shallows to play bridge and watch us swim. Boats were always a part of the mix, whether for fishing, water skiing, or just sunning and everyone knew something about racing sailboats, whether they sailed or not.

The whole vocabulary of lake people is specific to the water they live with: rafts, jumps, boat racks, docks, drop-offs, C-boats, "itch," the races, ice houses, clearing a rink, put in, take out, weedy spots, rocky sides, the shallows, and the deep end. The connotations of each word was known and understood in relation to the Lake.

The Lake became a friend of mine, and still is. Years after I left (with much kicking and screaming), I come back to sit on the end of the dock and breathe the lake air. I return to commune with the Lake. I've stood there in the moonlight in my Halloween costume, or mid-winter in dress clothes after an evening out, telling the frozen water what had gone on in my life since last time. I sit with my feet in the warm July water, and talk with the shimmers that stretch out to meet me from the spot where the sunlight hits, at the tree's shadow line. The glistens on the water feel like family, cousins and siblings of my waterborne childhood. The Lake is home.

As I sit watching the Lake from a friend's dock, she comes down the hill bearing a plate full of quarter cut peanut butter and jelly sandwiches. I just grin. No words needed. We'd grown up together on the Lake.

# Spring Park Villa Resort on Bald Eagle Lake

*(1905–1978)*
*As Remembered by*
*Ruth Mattlin*

The Spring Park Villa Resort was built in 1905 for the wealthy vacationer. It was situated on the southeastern corner of Bald Eagle Lake in White Bear Township, consisting of a stately hotel and 20 cottages.

The Victorian summer hotel was three stories high with a large lobby, elegant fireplace, and refined stairway leading to 6 bedrooms and 2 baths on the second floor. Also in the lobby was a square grand piano (an 1882 Matheuchek), and gas lights. Other amenities included an exquisite dining room, an enclosed porch to serve meals to guests, and a huge wrap around porch where people could sit and enjoy the lake.

For others who were interested in fun and excitement, the Spring Park Villa offered tennis, horseback riding, croquet, and a rousing game of horseshoes. For those seeking the lake, there was canoeing, swimming, sailing, fishing and boating. On the beach they had a gazebo for sing-a-longs, programs, and just plain relaxing. There also was a natural spring, which was made into a well. Many early residents used to come there to get their water, hence, the name "Spring Park Villa."

*Spring Park Villa was built in 1905 and survived until 1978 when it was demolished.*
*Photo courtesy of Ruth Mattlin.*

The resort was owned and operated by the Mahlon D. Miller family. They had six children, Grace, Cora, Beatrice, Faith, Mahlon Jr., and Harold. The father, Mahlon Miller died on May 26, 1907. His wife and children continued to operate the resort, with the daughter Grace taking over after her mother's death. During the Depression years and the drought of the 1930's, the cottages were turned into housekeeping, and the hotel then stopped serving meals.

In the spring of 1956, Carroll and Ruth Mattlin, and Harold and Mary Mattlin purchased the Spring Park Villa property, which by then had dwindled to 15 cottages and a hotel. Carroll and Ruth Mattlin continued to operate the resort for the next 22 years. The cottages were rented furnished by the season. The hotel was winterized and rented as a one family residence. As the lake property increased in value the decision was made to take down the cottages and hotel in 1978. An era had ended.

*Porch sitting room of Spring Park Villa, located on the southeast shore of Bald Eagle Lake, in the year 1908. Photo courtesy of Ruth Mattlin.*

### *Epilogue*

Charles Davies built the Spring Park Villa as a summer resort, open from May 15th through September 15th. Many vacationers from all over the Midwest came to stay. Among the most famous was Cass Gilbert, the architect of our own state capitol. Guests arrived by train at the Bald Eagle Depot, which was located at the intersection of Soo Line and Northern Pacific Railroad tracks, one mile north of White Bear Lake.

Horse and carriage then drove them to the hotel, located in the area of East Bald Eagle Boulevard, Park Avenue and Division Avenue. The Spring Park Villa property and lake had been used as an Indian camp in the nineteenth century for fishing, hunting and wild ricing. Bald Eagle Lake and its natural springs were considered a healthy area in which to vacation.

# From Coal Collector to Winter Carnival Queen

*As Remembered by*
*Antoinette Marie (Carpentier) Nolles*

I am the only daughter, and middle child, of five children born to Mary Ann and Philip Carpentier, residents of White Bear Lake, Minnesota. My parents were married and maintained permanent residence in White Bear from 1908. My mother was part of the large Auger Family, farmers in the White Bear area since the early 1800's. My mother grew up on a large farm that is now subdivisions along County Road B, from Highway 61 to Bellaire Avenue.

My four brothers and I were born a year apart; beginning with Clifford in 1910, Telesphore in 1911, me in 1912, Edward in 1913 and Willis in 1914. We all were born, and raised, in our home on the corner of Lincoln and Bald Eagle Avenues. We played (and collected fallen coal) on the nearby railroad tracks that ran behind our home, the tracks being our "communication" with the city, St. Paul, Minnesota. My brothers and I attended St. Mary's parochial elementary school, and White Bear High. Some good friends I went to school with, and who still live in White Bear are: Sterling Theroux, Lyndon Long, Joe Kieffer, Bob Whitaker, Leon Ratte and Fran McHugh Vadnais.

In the early years of the 20th Century, White Bear was a popular, if not famous, summer resort town. Wealthy people from all over (and as close as St. Paul) had summer homes along White Bear Lake and Manitou Island. The train and streetcar provided convenient transportation for others to swim and fish on the lake. Popular weekend dancing and entertainment at the pavilion and other clubs were also very well attended.

My four brothers caddied, and played golf at Dellwood Hills Golf Club. My brother Clifford was the manager of the Avalon Theater for 40 years, and tended bar at the "617", a popular cocktail lounge in White Bear. Both the Theater and the "617" were owned by a gentleman by the name of Paul Albright, one of the city's "movers and shakers". It was said that if anything was going to happen in White Bear Lake, it started at the "617". My brother Willis worked at Johnson Boat Works, on White Bear Lake, for 50 years as one of the noted craftsman who built the popular yachts from White Bear.

My father, as his primary job, worked for the City of White Bear for 20 years, and eventually became the Street Commissioner. However, during the heyday of the "resort" atmosphere, he made a good living moving the furniture and belongings of "summerhouse" people, who moved their possessions from St. Paul to White Bear and back, throughout the season. Quite often, he traded furniture for the moving fee.

One of my favorite memories was being crowned Queen of the White Bear Winter Carnival in 1935. The White Bear Fire Department sponsored the pageant, giving the winner a beautiful Russian diamond ring. We were always curious as to where the Fire Department got those diamond rings.

In 1936 I married Ray J. Nolles, son of James and Lillian Nolles, new residents to White Bear in 1933. My future in-laws owned Ma's Inn, a small Cafe and Gas Station on Highway 61, just as you entered White Bear. We served the best hamburgers and homemade pie in town. Having a beer license as soon as Prohibition was partially lifted, made for a very busy inn. Bootleg whiskey was a popular item also, though not on the menu. The Nolles also owned a cabin on Bald

*Antoinette (Carpentier) Nolles, White Bear Lake*
*1935 Winter Carnival Queen.*
*Photo courtesy A. Nolles*

Eagle Lake, where we spent most of our free time. It was a place so quiet and serene we had no idea that the cabin just two lots away was often occupied by the likes of Al Capone and Bugsy Siegel (they liked it quiet, too). In 1940 we purchased a resort in northern Minnesota, splitting the year between White Bear and Boy River, Minnesota.

Things changed dramatically when the war started in 1942. My husband and four brothers joined the service almost immediately, with me joining my husband, Ray, in Hondo, Texas a short time later. After the war, we returned to Minnesota and the resort business, but never returned to White Bear Lake. We missed it very much, but our families still lived there, so we visited often.

Presently, I live in Phoenix and Payson, Arizona with my children, grand- and great-grandchildren. My memories of White Bear Lake are wonderful. It is fitting that I am now reading Tom Brokaw's book "The Greatest Generation." I know I was part of it in White Bear Lake.

# WOMAN'S CLUB WILL FAVOR FOUR GIRLS; ALL GET DIAMONDS

### Royal Russian Jewels Now on Exhibition; To Boost Truck Fund of Firemen's Carnival

Arrangements for the fire carnival to be held in White Bear July 16-17-18, are taking shape. One big feature will be the contest in sale of tickets.

Four young ladies will be chosen by a committee of the White Bear Woman's Club to receive beautiful rings each set with diamonds.

These diamonds are of the royal Russian jewels acquired by the Firemen's Association and offered in the fire carnival contest. These rings are to be won through the efforts of these young ladies and their friends. These beautiful jewels are now on exhibition in the Peterson jewelry store window.

The lady, responsible for the sales of the largest number of tickets will receive the ring containing the largest diamond—ring No 1. The next successful in sales will receive ring No. 2, and so forth.

The total amount of sales made by the firemen will be distributed equally between the four contestants.

A bulletin reporting the progress of each lady's sales will be posted frequently in a prominent place in the business district and published in The Press.

The tickets are available at the Luedke residence 131 Clark avenue.

The names of the chosen ladies will be announced later. Give these girls your support and the firemen your co-operation.

*Story courtesy of White Bear Press.*

# Legion Park Flagpole

*As Remembered by*
*C. M. Ingham*

One of the wealthiest residents of Mahtomedi was Walter Reidell, President of Sanitary Farms Dairy. They owned and ran a very successful dairy in St. Paul and around White Bear Lake. Mrs. Reidell was our local philanthropist. She paid for the entire school population to have vision tests through the school system. I was fourteen at the time, and found I was half-blind. I thought everyone saw everything blurry. I thought that when people spoke of stars in the sky it was like the Easter Bunny, and was a nice fantasy. I could make out a blurry blob in the sky that I assumed was the moon, but that was all. I always asked the teachers to let me sit in a front seat so I could see what was written on the blackboard, but was relegated to a back seat because I was so big.

After I received my glasses, the whole world changed for me, and I was so thankful to Mrs. Reidell. The fact that I chose frameless glasses and broke them ten times the first year because of fistfights at being called "Four-Eyes" did not diminish my desire to see. Dad finally said, "Why don't you take off the glasses when you get into a fight?"

"I can't see the guy I wanta hit!" was my answer. After the tenth repair I was assigned silver solid octagons, and never broke them again.

Years and years later Mr. Reidell died and Mrs. Reidell bought the "Triangle" where Mahtomedi's main highway and the Stillwater Road met at the edge of Willernie. The Triangle was a slice of land a block long on two sides attached at the end by a piece of land 60 feet long. It was a wasteland of ditch, culverts and trash collections. She had it cleaned up, filled the ditch after laying new culverts and had a small grove of pine trees planted across the narrow end. She had erected a flagpole and dedicated the whole area to the American Legion as a park in honor of her husband, Walter. As the area grew, the empty space at the two long sides of the Triangle became a parking lot for the stores, taverns and cafes across the street. It also became the place where the American Legion held their annual Memorial Day services.

The members of the Legion sodded the area between the pine trees and flagpole and erected wooden crosses and Star of David emblazoned with the name of our deceased veterans from our area.

The year I was the Commander of the Legion we had purchased a new flag for the ceremony and were going to replace the old one. My brother, Bob Ingham, the Postmaster of the Willernie Post Office, monitored the flag, which was about 100 feet away. It was a community symbol that signified when there was a death in the village, state or nation: at those times it was flown at half-staff. People would pass it daily, know someone had died, and call the Willernie Post Office to see who it was. It was a small town telegraph system.

Two weeks before Memorial Day the Northern States Power Company drove their huge truck into the Legion Park and erected a power pole five feet from our flagpole. Within three days our six-foot flag was in shreds from whipping against the power pole.

Bob Ingham called me and I called NSP in White Bear Lake to ask them to move the pole. Their answer was that they have the right of eminent domain and they refused to budge. I asked to speak to the supervisor whose office was in Stillwater. He also gave me the same answer and refused to buy us a new flag. He told me to move our flagpole with all the flagstone around it.

I explained to him that the property belonged to the American Legion, who had members who had been members of the C.B.s (Construction Battalion) in service, plus several who were lumberjacks familiar with the workings of power saws. The supervisor said, "You wouldn't dare."

I replied, "You have one week to move that pole."

NSP: "Do you realize you could cut all the electricity to the stores, bars, stations and cafes there?"

I: "Yes, and they are behind me! There is a spot between two filling stations behind their driveway fences that is open and available!"

NSP: "We would have to dig up the pole and disconnect all that power. We refuse."

I: "Okay by me, but it would be easier to do it now, rather than clean up the mess later. We'll even cut the pole into fireplace lengths for you, free of charge."

A week went by and no action, so I called the NSP super and reminded him. He said to me, "You're just as hard-nosed as your dad. He made us move our poles from the middle of the Village Hall parking lot when he was mayor!" I thanked him for the compliment and suggested that their planning department in the future think before they act. He did not thank me for the suggestion.

Three days before the Memorial Day ceremony I reminded him again, and invited him to watch. The next day NSP removed the pole, moved it to the spot between the filling stations, filled in the hole and re-sodded. I called the super to thank him, told him he could drop off the new six-foot flag at the Post Office, and invited him to the Memorial Service, where I promised to buy him a cup of coffee.

He didn't show.

# Bald Eagle Water Ski Club

*As Remembered by*
*C. Allen Lindholm*

In 1951, my good friend, Tom Chapin returned home from the east coast to get married. He and his cousin came down to my dock that morning to get in a few ski rides before his big event. It was after 12 o'clock when Tom said, "one more ride, Al." Tom and Anzel got married at 2 o'clock and he has been skiing ever since. Tom was a competitive skier on either snow or water, and took it to a different level. Tom and Anzel returned to good old Bald Eagle two years later, in 1953, just in time to join the Bald Eagle Water Club as a charter member. Ralph Samuelson started water skiing on Lake Pepin, Lake City, Minnesota, in the 1920s. We used to watch Movietone News, short subjects at the Avalon Theater in White Bear, to learn and get new ideas about water skiing. Every time Dick Pope, Jr. came up with a new trick his dad would call the media in New York and they would send their photographers down to Cypress Gardens. It would be in the theaters in short order.

Bud Jameson was in the service and was stationed at Wold Chamberlain. He took a 30 day leave and spent the entire time on the end of my dock. I would pull my brother and Bud every day and they got to be pretty good skiers. I can still hear Rinee, standing at the top of the stairs hollering, "Damn you Bud, get home, it's suppertime."

*Bald Eagle Water Ski Club. L–R: Bud Jameson, Tom Chapin, John Lindholm. Photo from White Bear Association brochure circa 1955. Submitted by Paul Chapin.*

Bud would say, "One more time around the bay."

Buds first boat was, "Hellsapoppen," and he had that before he went in the service. It had a 22-hp Johnson motor. Bud, Bill Scanlon and John Benson used to try to ski behind it but the boat was not quite adequate. It was fun taking our boats to different lakes and rivers. We would line up in front my house and go in a caravan and most often it was to Stillwater. Most of my friends were single, and as the caravans got longer, we sure didn't have a shortage of pretty girls vying for rides.

Boating and skiing on the river was different than on the lake. We did not have life preservers and we always had to look out for deadheads. This was more of a problem in the spring and early summer when the river was high. Later, when the river was low, there was less debris but we still had to know where the sandbars were. The channels were marked, but not always accurately. I'm referring to the river north of Stillwater up by O'Brien State Park and Osceola. If you ran wide open you could go in much shallower water because the boat ran higher on the water.

We were invited to cruise with the 10,000 Lakes Family Boating Club many times. They enjoyed our water skiing exhibitions. However, we were all young and had faster boats so we did not like to go at their speed. When I was pulling my brother John and he got tired, he would jerk on the rope and I would whip him to one side and turn back. John would ski to the boat and land on the deck. He would not even get wet. They were really impressed. The Commodore from 10,000 Lakes encouraged me to start a boating club on Bald Eagle to promote our sport in safe boating and enjoyment, which I later did in 1953. His boat was a beautiful mahogany strip runabout made especially for the Chicago Boat Show.

I remember when Al Letourneau and Stan Earhardt broke a shirr pin on their motor. They climbed the riverbank and pulled a nail from a fence. It worked so there was no need to tow the "Barracuda" back to the landing. Good old American ingenuity!

One time I was leading a group of us up in the white water under the bridge at Taylor's Falls. The water was swift and boiling and it was very exciting. The noise of our motors was bouncing off the rock walls and very loud. People were running out on the bridge to see what was going on down there. We went down river to gather with the rest of our group in calmer water and I did not anticipate the current when I stopped in front of Pete's boat. He punched a hole about 4 inches wide and 10 inches long in my boat. It was right at the water line so I could not turn left without taking on water. It was a very interesting ride back to Stillwater especially for my passenger with no life preserver. My brother Jim was working at Amundson's Boat Works so he knew how to patch the hole. He fixed it so you could not even tell where the hole had been.

Although water skiing had been done for many years, it really exploded in 1949 when Johnson Evinrude came out with their 25-hp Big Twin motor with a neutral shift. At that time we were experimenting with different kinds of skis, surfboards, water toboggans, freeboards and saucers. We actually had more fun with surfboards to start with, because of the planing surface. Later we had slalom, turnabouts and jumpers. We broke a lot of jumpers until they made them strong enough to withstand the shock of the landing. Jimmy Henkle got two pair of skis from his sister, which were 8 and 10 feet long. Dude Lowell broke both of them when he went off the ramp.

*White Bear Press ad for local boat builder, 1914.*

We were always looking for new ways to ski. One of John Benson's pilot friends gave him a tow with an airplane on snow skis over the ice and I thought we should try it on water. Benny used to say, "I was too scared to hang on and too scared to let go."

In 1952 John Benson brought his floatplane, a J3 CUB, down to my dock to give us a tow. I went out first around the island. Then Bud Jameson tried it and then brother John. When John returned, he dropped a ski and kept going. Bud's knees were still knocking when John finally got back to the dock. We had never skied so fast! I had to warn them to be ready when the second pontoon came out of the water because the plane gained speed so fast it could pull you over. We never did use the airplane to jump the island, but we sure talked about it a lot.

One time I was pulling Brother John and Bud through the channel in the weeds, across the bay from my dock. Bud attempted to go through the second channel. The rope was not long enough so I pulled him right into the cattails. There were two fishermen fishing nearby and they nearly fell out of their boat laughing. Bud was always good for a laugh, which is why he was such a good clown in our ski shows.

Bald Eagle Lake had more activity than any lake its size. We had canoes, rowboats, and sailboats. There was swimming, fishing, skin diving, motor boats, floatplanes, and water skiers. Dwight Long, who belonged to the St. Paul Yachting Club, used to bring his rowers out. Later, pontoon boats, water ski shows and tournaments, fishing tournaments, and barge parties were common. One might also see Tom Wienhagen running around on his motorized water skis, or an Army Duck or Elias' aqua copter.

The Minnesota Power Boat Association brought high-powered boats out to test their performance but they made too much noise for the residents. We had water ski jumps and slalom courses. Bald Eagle was alive and well!!

The lake level has always been a concern for many residents and still is. When dams were installed on the west side and the north end to raise the lake level, a lot of residents lost land. Somebody was always knocking out the top planks of the dam. The St. Paul Waterworks eventually won the battle. The Bald Eagle Water Club used to have a representative from the Minnesota Department of Waters give talks on the subject.

In 1954, the Bald Eagle Water Club started to put on ski shows to raise money. The airplane act was the top act; however, the conditions had to be right to pull it off. The area needed to fly the plane and the wind had to be just right. If the waves were too high, the ski tips might snap off at high speed due to intense vibration. I was the first one to do it in a show on Bald Eagle. Ski jump acts were the crowd favorites. Triple over and under jumps, distance jumps and helicopter spins were performed by our talented skiers. The pyramid and pole acts were well received. We had pretty girls, clowns, kids and even dogs in our shows. Later on there were kites and parasails, 360-degree boat spins, barefoot skiers and many specialty acts.

I was really into our boating and skiing activities. I designed the club logo for the patches to be used on our boats and jackets. I also wanted our club members to stay amateur. There were boat liveries on Bald Eagle Lake in 1956: Joe Rogowski's, Joe Kieffer's, Gil Sensifer's, Herman Benson's Pastime Inn, Pat Ryan's Plaza and Collet's Boat house. The boating boom drove them all out of business. Bobber's Boats is presently in business on the north end of the lake.

In 1953, Mark Hamden got some railroad flares that we taped to 4 foot poles. Each water skier was to carry the flares in a boat parade just before the 4th of July fireworks were displayed from the island. The Bald Eagle Sportsman Club was in charge of the fireworks. All the flares were lit and the boats started out with their skiers from docks adjacent to mine, lined up in single file, and went around the lake.

In 1953 a man came to our house and wanted my folks to sign a petition to put a speed limit on boats on Bald Eagle. He did not know their sons had a speed boat on the lake. Needless to say, my folks did not sign it but it got me thinking about organizing a club to stop that effort. One Sunday morning Bill Neilson and I were parked out in the middle outer bay and I told him we should start a club. We knew most of the boaters and skiers on the lake and thought it would be possible. I talked it up to all of my friends and everyone liked the idea. Don Harding offered his shanty for our first meeting. We invited John Temple, who was an officer with the St. Paul Yacht Club, to come and help us get organized. Our first meeting was July 17, 1953 and we elected Terry Rooney as our first president. Bud Jamesen got Tom Lyons to draft a constitution. We all signed an autograph book, and decided there was work to do to promote our sport. That day the Bald Eagle Boat And Water Ski Club was born. The original mission of our club was to promote all recreational activities on the lake, including boating, skiing and sailing.

Some of us wanted to get a better launching ramp because we were pulling our boats in and out of the lake so often. We had a lot of opposition, so Bill Ball eventually built one himself. Harry Robins wanted to get scuba diving going but found there was not enough interest. We were definitely leaning toward being strictly a water skiing club with tournaments and shows.

In 1954 Tom Chapin sent for some plans for building a water ski jump that we could use in our ski shows. When Swede Brandl was tack welding some barrels together, the top blew off one of them. That sure got our attention! The completed jump was 8 feet wide and adjustable to 5 feet or 6 feet. When we put it in the water, I wanted to be the first one off, so I ran up to the house to put on my swimsuit. By the time I got back down to the lake, Stan Earhardt had already gone over it. He soon learned how a waxed surface can grab your rear end pretty fast if you are not balanced on your skis. We anchored the jump right in front of my dock. I really liked it there, however, because of all the activity, some neighbors wanted it moved. Over the next few years, the jump was moved all over the lake, until it was finally located on the west side by Dick Fenstermakers' property.

On Saturday, February 6, 1954, the last weekend of the St. Paul Winter Carnival, Bud Jamesen called me and told me he could get a rubber wetsuit from the Navy Seabee Attachment in Minneapolis. If we could get a boat, we could go water skiing! It was unseasonably warm, which made many of us think about water skiing. I told Bud I would call Vern Rippon of Midway Marine to see if he had a boat available. We were going to go for it! The newspapers were called. Bubs Goette got his sister, Dorene Selig, and Gerry Hanson to put on their swim suits for pictures. Bud did his thing and it made great publicity for our Bald Eagle Water Club. A few years later Don Kosek, from the Bald Eagle Water Club, skied on New Year's Day. He and others did it for many years. Don was a terrific clown in the ski shows for many years.

I was a member of the Sunset fast pitch softball team and sometimes after games we would cool off down at my dock. One time I taught Pete Arcand how to get up on skis. After his third try he got up and I pulled him near the jump. To my astonishment he went off the 6-foot ramp. He bounced off the end. When I picked him up he said, "I didn't expect it to be so damn slippery." I know of no other person to go off a ski jump the first time up on skis.

My brother John was the first one to do a 360-degree turn off the ramp, and the only one to go off backwards, land backwards and make it. He had scars on his forehead from hitting the lip of the ramp but he finally did it. Eventually he learned to do the jump on one ski, which was very difficult.

Terry Rooney always had his swimsuit in the cab of his truck, so when he drove by and I happened to be down on the dock, it wouldn't take him long to change and come down for a spin around the bay. Terry made some stilt skis for the shows, and a pair with a shower attachment so he could take a shower while skiing. Terry, Brother John and Bud Jameson were the first clowns in the shows.

On moonlit nights some of us would grab a 6-pack and a pretty girl and head out to the south side of the moonlit island for a game of "hide and seek". We would gather on the south side of the island and someone would be chosen to be "It". Usually it was the last person out there. "It" would turn on his running lights and give everyone three minutes to scatter and hide, usually behind someone's sailboat, raft or dock. When "It" found someone, they also had to turn on their running lights and help find the others until everyone was caught. You were caught when you were spotted in "It's" spotlight.

Some of us liked to be on the move in the dark, but running into someone was always a big concern. I didn't like the possibility of meeting up with Bub's Chris-Craft so I hung a battery powered taillight on the back of his boat, unknown to him. He always wondered why he was the first one caught. Tom Weinhagen got a super bright spotlight that enabled him to see for a half a mile. I never could get away from him. One time Jack Ostberg put his boat in Roger David's boatlift and pulled a tarp over it. Everyone thought that was breaking the rules.

When all the boats returned to my dock, we always had our running lights back on. One time though, as we were returning, Jerry Fournell, the local police officer, met us and said our spotlights were bothering some of the lakeshore residents and others didn't like the noise. He was nice and just warned us to be careful. My mother and her friends used to like to watch us from the top deck of my barge. Mother liked to see the lights on our boats and was unaware of any danger.

*Ad courtesy of White Bear Press.*

# Lutefisk

*As Remembered by*
*C. M. Ingham*

As a child living in the North central area of the country, which is inhabited by thousands of Scandinavians, I often heard of lutefisk—but we never had it at our house.

We had some close dear friends, John and Minnie Larson, who were direct from Sweden, and had kids our age. We spent many hours eating Mrs. Larson's delicious cooking such as sandbakkelse, head cheese, blood sausage, great coffee cakes and tea rings and cookies, but never had lutefisk.

When I asked one of the twins, Bob or Dick Larson, why, he told me it was a secret dish only for Swedish people. When I asked my Dad, he told me it was like Scotch haggis, but we didn't have that either. When I asked Mother she told me we were lucky we had neither since both were not good to eat!

Many years passed and I finally looked up the meaning and contents of haggis. It is described as a traditionally Scottish dish that consists of the heart, liver, and lungs of a sheep or calf, minced with suet, onions, oatmeal and seasoning, baked in the stomach of the animal.

I have talked to many people who have traveled to Scotland and they all have been served this dish with great pomp and ceremony, but few have asked for seconds. Of all the world travelers who have been in the Scandinavian countries none has ever been served lutefisk. It must be a very special ethnic custom!

I have eaten hearts, liver, sweetbreads and kidneys and enjoyed them. My Dad bought brains, lungs and tripe for us, but he was the only one who tried them, so he said.

When we had our paper route, one of our customers was Alex Krapner, a square-set butcher, complete with straw hat and sawdust on the floor of his shop. During the winter I noticed he had some barrels behind the store, which had long, thin somethings stacked upright in them. As the winter progressed they changed color from white to yellow.

I asked my brother Bob what it was and he told me it was lutefisk and the reason it was yellow was because of the dogs! (As he explained to me: "If a dog couldn't eat it or make love to it, he peed on it!")

That did it for me and lutefisk.

I understand the preparation, when not peed on, is unique also, but still a secret. The result is a gelatinous translucent fish covered with a strong odor and white cream sauce. I know no one who has seconds on this dish either.

---

Norwegian

## Baked Lutefisk

2 lb. lutefisk
2 c. water
1 tsp. salt
melted butter

Rinse lutefisk well in cold water and soak overnight; drain. Place fish in glass or enamel pan (not aluminum). Add water and salt. Bake covered with foil at 400 degrees for 20 minutes or until done. Served with melted butter poured over the top. Accompany with boiled potatoes and lefse.

4-6 servings

# Childhood Magic

*As Remembered by*
*Kerm Molkenbur*

rowing up in White Bear Lake 60 years ago, and living across from the current city hall was like—maybe heaven. A population of approximately 2,000 to 4,000 people provided for just about knowing everyone.

World War II had just ended and the area from the train depot south to where the bank is now located was piled with German tanks and shells and many things recovered from the war. It was then shipped down to the old St. Paul Auditorium for people to view.

Our family grew a garden and placed a white wooden "V" in the garden to show we were growing vegetables for our family during the war.

Summers were spent (age 8) lying in the surplus wheat, barefoot, in bib-overalls, watching the clouds go by. On our farm at the time were four huge bins that contained the wheat.

*Looking North—the White Bear railroad depot showing the 1893 passenger awning. Photo courtesy of Lawrence R. (Bob) and Eileen Whitaker.*

Opening weekend of deer season was spent sitting at the train depot watching all the cars go by with deer mounted on them. At the end of the war, bums would get off the train and knock on your door, asking for something to eat. In return they did small jobs around the house.

The Ramsey County fairgrounds were located by the old Hippodrome and high school. Mondays were spent looking for loose change in the wood shavings after the fair was over.

The Old Plantation Inn was located east of where the White Bear Shopping Center is now, and the building was right on the bay of the lake. Friday and Saturday nights were spent watching the bootmen open the car doors on big black Cadillacs to let the paying customers in. I just stared at them while hiding in the bulrushes.

At that time we had two movie theaters in town. One was the Avalon and the other was the White Bear Theatre. Sicklers Peerless popcorn was 5¢ a box. The price of the movies was 12¢ with an empty toothpaste tinfoil or 14¢ if you did not have an empty toothpaste tinfoil. The foil was saved to help out with the war. Saturday mornings were a double feature with Roy Rogers, Hopalong Cassidy, and the Lone Ranger. After the movie, it was over to Kohler's Ice Cream Romance Parlor for a cherry cola at 5¢ a glass.

The coaster wagon was taken twice a week over to Miller's Pure Oil for ice for the icebox in 50 or 75 pound blocks. On the second trip back, my brother and I would each get half-Popsicles.

*The private entrance to Manitou Island.*
*Photo courtesy of Lawrence R. (Bob) and Eileen Whitaker.*

At 10 years of age, I had a paper route and a red cart with balloon tires. The cart was loaded down with papers. I walked from downtown White Bear Lake out to the end of Manitou Island every day. It was the best route in town because you never had to collect. The people living on the island sent their money in to the Dispatch. I received many Christmas presents on Labor Day, when half of the residents would leave to go south for the winter.

My years of 12, 13, and 14 were spent out at the Yacht Club caddying from sunup to sundown. I hitchhiked or rode my bike out to the Yacht Club.

At age 18, you could buy a lot on the lake for $500 to $800. Today, it's more like $3,500 for a running foot of shoreline!

*Streetside view of the White Bear Yacht Club circa 1900. Photo courtesy of Lawrence R. (Bob) and Eileen Whitaker.*

# The Midwife

*As Remembered by*
*Josephine Morrow*

In the 1920's when a baby was expected, one could either travel to a hospital in St. Paul for delivery or make arrangements to go to Mrs. Kirkby's (I believe that's how the name was spelled—as kids we called her Mrs. "Kirpy"). Mrs. Kirkby was not only a midwife who assisted with births, but she also opened her home on west Fourth Street for "rooming-in." A cheery closed-in porch on the west side of her house held beds where the new mothers could spend a week. If one could not afford to go to Mrs. Kirkby's, then one of the Drs. J.H. or T.S. (Scott) McClanahan would go to the home for delivery. Mrs. Houle, another mid-wife, would assist him. Mrs. Houle, who lived near the northwest corner of Third Street and Miller Avenue, was always on call.

On July 4th, 1928, everyone was enjoying the out-of-doors picnicking and swimming and Dr. T.S. McClanahan was no exception. He had to be summoned out of the water at the 12th Street bathing beach, and by the time he arrived at my home, Mrs. Houle was already there to assist with my birth.

*White Bear Press ads circa 1900—a cure for what ails thee.*

*The White Bear Sanitarium became part of the healthful healing attributes associated with the White Bear Lake area resorts. Photo courtesy of Lawrence R. (Bob) and Eileen Whitaker.*

# The White Bear Telephone Company

*As Remembered by*
*Helen Lindbeck Peterson*

In 1947 I received a call from the chief operator at Northwestern Bell Telephone Company in White Bear Lake. She wanted to know if I would come to work as a telephone operator on a part-time basis after school. Some of my friends had regular jobs and some of us baby-sat or had other chores we did on a more sporadic basis. This sounded so good to me, I could hardly wait to start in March of 1947.

I worked from 4:00 to 8:00 PM on school days and sometimes a few hours on weekends. When school was over for the summer, I could work full-time. That included Sundays and holidays. In the White Bear office, reigned over by Frances Keep who had hired me, we worked every other Sunday and four hours on holidays.

There were eighteen boards in the office, three for incoming long distance and local, and the rest for local calls or outgoing long distance. One block of numbers had only rural eight-party lines, but the other nine or ten had either private lines, two- or four-party lines. The switchboard was painted frequently with dots to designate type of service, firemen, changed numbers, etc. A call to Hugo or to St. Paul or beyond was charged a long distance rate, and the operators wrote the tickets and kept track of the time. All the operators, service assistants, and the chief operator were women.

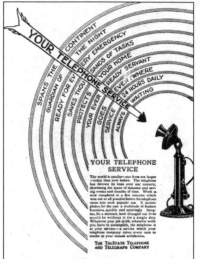

*White Bear Press ad 1914*

There was a volunteer fire department in town, so when a fire was reported to the chief operator (she was the only one with the authority to take a fire call), the siren was activated and the firemen would call in to learn the location. Then off they would go to the fire or the station, whichever was closest to them.

The office was located on the second floor of the Getty Building on Third Street. The White Bear Press was at the west end of the second floor and the telephone company occupied nearly all the rest of the floor. Outside the southern windows of the operator's room was the tarred roof of the floor below. When the breeze cooled by the lake blew in our direction, that tarred roof again heated it, and the room became stifling hot. In an effort to cool it, two galvanized washtubs were brought in and a large block of ice was put in each. Two fans circulated the now humid, hot air.

*The original telephone company was housed
in the second floor of the Getty building.
Photo courtesy of Lawrence R. (Bob) and Eileen Whitaker.*

In the early 1950's all numbers in White Bear were changed to Garden 9 numbers and Mahtomedi became Garden 6 and the system was converted to dial. Many of the White Bear employees transferred to St. Paul, but some took their severance pay and went to other jobs rather than commute.

# A Skating Rink

*As Remembered by*
*Helen Lindbeck Peterson*

In 1938, my family moved to a house on the northwest corner of Fifth Street and what is now Bloom Avenue, where the First Presbyterian Church now stands. The house seemed huge to me. We had three bedrooms upstairs and a kitchen, dining, and living room downstairs. There was a 'summer kitchen' on the back of the house with a pantry and a back entry, as well as a glazed-in front porch. An outside entrance led to a cellar. There was a pump in the back yard and a double garage with a shed that housed the outhouse. After the first winter in that drafty house, the landlady, Mrs. Bunghard, had city water piped into the kitchen. Daddy arranged to tap into the water pipe in the cellar and to add a spigot.

In the Summer we had a large vegetable garden. In the Fall Daddy would hire Joe Vadnais to come with his team to plow and disc the garden. After the ground had been thoroughly churned and turned, they would hitch a two-by-twelve plank to the team and, with Joe on one end of the plank and Daddy on the other, level the area. Sometime between Thanksgiving and the end of the year the weather would be cold enough to flood the prepared ground and the beginnings of a skating rink could be detected. Each freezing night Daddy would haul the hose from the cellar and sprinkle a mist of water over the entire area, layer after layer, slowly building a sheet of ice. He erected two poles and hung a light over the center. The two by twelve plank that had been used to level the earth in warmer days became a bench where skates were donned. On one of the poles he posted regulations. They included his rules such as "No climbing on snow banks," "No stuffing snow in overshoes," and "No stealing caps or mittens"—all common sense directives. On school nights the lights were "blinked" at 8:00 P.M. That was bedtime for school children, but on Friday and Saturday nights I could skate until 10:00 P.M. In the first year or two, he posted hours for hockey players, but that proved to be so little used, it was soon abandoned for pleasure skating only. The light was turned on at sundown and off at 10:00 P.M. Then the shovel or shovels came out and the rink was cleaned and a new sheet of ice sprinkled over the top. Many times he did this alone, but sometimes a volunteer or two or three would stay to clean the surface before flooding. He flooded a path of ice from our back door to the rink, and often I crawled across the kitchen floor to the table for supper so I didn't have to take the time to change from skates to shoes to skates again.

There was a large cardboard carton in the summer kitchen that contained an assortment of used skates, darned and mismatched mittens and heavy stockings. If a youngster came without skating gear, Daddy would take him or her in the house and outfit little feet with the best he had to offer. When someone came with new skates from Santa, Daddy would offer the kid a quarter for the old ones and, after they had been sharpened by my uncle, put them in the box for another to use who had none.

One Saturday night two or three cars we didn't recognize drove into the yard. I went to see who they were and to ask what they wanted. They were looking for the hippodrome a couple of blocks north of us. Then they asked whose rink this was and could they see the owner or manager. I skated out onto the ice and told Daddy they wanted to talk to him, then followed him back to the cars. They asked what the charge was to skate. I remember Daddy pointing to his posted rules and telling them if they could abide by them, they were welcome. They were a part of the troupe from Shipsted and Johnson's Ice Follies on their way to Forest Lake. We all stood in awe while they donned white figure skates and then put on a performance for us all. My mother and a couple of aunts who didn't skate stood piled up in the kitchen window to see the show. Those of us on the rink stood around the perimeter fascinated for about an hour while they dazzled us with graceful arms outspread executing jumps and pirouettes and spins.

When Spring, and then Summer returned, I was reacquainted with weeds and potato bugs in the garden.

*Skating photo, circa 1932, courtesy of White Bear Press.*

# White Bear Delivery Service

*As Remembered by*
*Michael Randolf*
*Told to Him by*
*James Enright: Father-in-Law*

In 1915, the gray horse barn formally located behind Mike Enright, Sr.'s residence at 2117 Fifth Street, White Bear Lake, Minnesota, housed three large mares and a delivery wagon. These were the "tools" Mike used for his employment. Mike was contracted by the Emporium (a large department store in the city of St. Paul) to deliver packages throughout the White Bear Lake community.

Being the first large department store of its kind, the Emporium occupied an entire city block, was four stories tall and sold everything from clothes to household wares. Mike's employment was good for those days. As a promotion Mike was transferred to the White Bear Lake area. The company paid for his phone and electricity service, his rent and fuel, and in addition, paid him a salary of $12 a month.

Just a few blocks from his house was the Northern Pacific Railroad station. During all hours of the night and day, large black coal-fired steam engines, billowing smoke and soot, wailed their lone whistle, stopping at the station. Mike would patiently wait with his horse-drawn wagon to collect packages from the Emporium to be delivered to customers residing around the lake. It took Mike an entire day to travel the route around White Bear Lake.

When Mike's son, James, (who is now 85 years old and still resides in White Bear Lake) was in kindergarten, he was allowed to help his dad drive the horses. That was the way of the delivery service until 1924, when a model T truck replaced the horse and wagon. It still took an entire day for Mike to traverse the town on his route.

*A horse and cart delivery wagon in front of the Reif and Clewett Meat Market located on Washington Avenue. Photo courtesy of Lawrence R. (Bob) and Eileen Whitaker.*

# Teenage Letter

*Submitted by*
*Phyllis DeLonais*

*Written March 22, 1891 by my Mother Dott Lucy Ball to her sister, Harriet Ball , whom she nicknamed Queen, who lived in Rushford, Minnesota*

Dear Queen,

I am sorry you felt so bad because Birdie and I did not write a longer letter. But it was not our fault that it did not get there as soon as the others, it was mailed the same time Monday morning. I do not control mail matters so I could not see to it after it was in the Post Office. I know it was awful mean not to write more to you. As I had more to write, too, than she did.

We started out with the agreement that she was to write to you. When I got through with the others and saw what she had written, I was ashamed and thought I must write a few words more. I was more sick than tired I guess, but I was really tired too. Birdie and I had worked like slaves before that. As soon as we got here we had to unpack some dishes and duds. Then we had to wait for some groceries Pa had ordered, before we could have supper. We had to keep working all the time to keep awake. As soon as supper was over I set up the beds, and we popped into them.

Of course we had to be up quite early the next morning because Pa had to go down to the office. We had to clean the pantry out first thing before we could put the dishes into it. I tell you it was dirty! Saturday the white-washers came and I put paper on the dining room wall. It was nine o'clock before we got the mopping done.

Friday after we got here we had a unique caller in the shape of a little French girl. Ma had to send her home, she was into everything. She has not been here since and I hope she won't be back either. One of our neighbor's little girls, Nannie O'Neil, came in to see Edith, but she had gone down to the office and there was only Ma and I at home. She is five years old but small for her age, and so comical. I couldn't keep my face straight to save my neck. She had such a pretty voice, blue eyes and brown hair. The first thing to set me laughing was when she looked around awhile and then said to Ma, "Not a soul to home but you and your girl." When she saw Edith's doll, she clapped her hands together and said, "Oh, how sweet, but that little apron takes the cake." She said your doll was "just as big as Aunt Sarah's baby." At supper she behaved like a little lady. She wasn't prying into anything.

Mrs. Bacon has 6 boys John and Jim (twins) Earnest, Charley, Elmer and Bill, the biggest. They are nice boys, too. They help their mother about the housework, do the chores, and stay at home nights. Besides that they have helped their mother work rugs. I tell you they are worth something. Bill is just sprouting a mustache. Haven't seen Jim yet, but Earnest and John were over Friday evening. Earnest has a violin. They have an organ there, too, but I do not know whether they can play or not.

Last Sunday Mrs. Bacon asked us to go to church with her. Bird and I went and enjoyed it very much. The singing was so nice. Everybody joined in, young men in the bargain. It seemed queer to see so many young men and boys in church behaving themselves. After church Mrs. Bacon introduced us to several ladies, but she did not introduce them to us, so we are not any wiser.

We went to church again today, but we were alone. As soon as it was over we left. But we had not got to the door when someone behind us said, "Wait a moment ladies please," and turning we saw the minister. When we got into the hall I saw someone staring from the other door. I knew who she was but had not had an introduction. She asked if we were the "editor's" daughters, and I told her yes. She invited us to stay to Sunday School. Bird consented to stay but Ma is sick so I had an excuse not to, but I'm in for it next Sunday, as she said I must come and I told her I would. She either didn't know our name or had forgotten it for she said if I would tell her she would introduce me to some of the others.

One of them was the Supt. of the Sunday School, one a Miss Farrar and I didn't hear the names of the others. Bird and I are going with her to the Young People's Christian Endeavor Society tonight. Yesterday her mother, Mrs. Long, was in to call on us. I took a liking to her the first thing. She said her daughter had wanted to call on us as soon as she heard there were young ladies here. I told her today to come down some evening.

She is learning the dressmaker's trade, so she doesn't have much time. Her father had her brother keep the store. They have a nice house, but they are not a bit stuck-up. I think we shall be friends. I like Mr. and Mrs. Bacon's family, too, "especially the boys." I just wish you could see my "For Dandy" or "Embroidery", as I call him. His clothes first attracted my attention. They are about the color of that stuff Ma thought of making Edith a cloak out of. Embroidered with wine colored yarn. Maybe you can imagine how funny they look. He is such a crisp little chap, too. He makes me think of August but he is not near so large.

Edith goes to school, and one night a little girl came home with her. "Embroidery" was passing by and Ma asked her if she knew who he was and she said, "Why that's my brother, Albert." She is French and her name is Ellen Taylor. The neighbor on the west side of us has a baby but I haven't seen it yet. Her husband is a carpenter and is not home. A week ago yesterday he came home to spend Sunday. They were awfully soft.

Dear me! I can't think of much to write. Oh, one day little Charley Bacon was in here and he told Ma that the next time she went to St. Paul she was going to buy a baby. He said that one night the folks that lived here before us were sleeping with Ned and Willie, (I guess they were), when Punch and Judy threw a baby through the window right onto the floor. He says also that Punch and Judy gave Mrs. Thompson her baby. Ma told him that down where we used

*Courtesy of White Bear Press.*

to live the stork used to bring the babies under their wings. He wanted to know which wing they carried them under then.

What kind of weather are you having down there? It has been warm and pleasant last week but it seems to be trying to make up its mind which to do this afternoon; snow or rain and succeeds in both.

There are lots of Catholics up here, French and Irish. I don't think the Episcopal Church is pretty at all. It is a homely shape and painted the color of barns. But the Presbyterian is very nice. That is the one Bird and I went to. Birdie and I saw some of the lake today for the first time. We were early for church so we took a walk to the lake.

Tell Mr. Crompton he ought to be up here fishing. Bill and Jim Bacon went fishing Friday and caught between thirty-five and forty fish. We haven't heard a word from Minnie since we got here. I have not seen much of the town yet, but there are pretty houses. There are some nice brick buildings up here. In one of them are Pa's office, a drug store and the post office. I will try and draw an outline of the two floors of our house. We have not got settled down yet. It has been so cold we could not do anything away from the fire.

Goodness gracious, I almost forgot to ask about Olaf and the twins! Do you ever see the "valley boys"? How are you all down there anyway? Ma is not doing well. She says it is the water. It always makes her sick to change the drinking water. Jingo ! It is getting cold up here. I mean upstairs. Have you had high water down there yet? Have you seen Mrs. H. and the children lately? How is Winnie? I'm just aching to get hold of a baby.

I wish we lived nearer the track so we could see the trains. We have to cross 10 tracks to get to the office, and, there are trains here nearly all the time. There are lots of dogs here but the most of them are large. It seems funny to walk down street without having a dozen little dogs barking at your heels. It was an uncommon sight at Rushford to see a dog "hitched" up to a sled, but here it is all the rage. About every other dog is hitched up to a sled, drawing a big boy, so you may know the dogs are big. I guess I can't think of any more to say at present so good-bye.


Your Biggish Sister,
Dot


P.S. Pa says for you to go to the printing office and ask if they will exchange papers. Birdie and I went downtown and picked out a dress for you. I hope you will like it. Ma will make it as soon as she can. There is not much chance to pick anything here, for only a small amount of goods is kept. Ma says she is aching to see you all and sends her love.

# Early Mahtomedi on White Bear Lake

*Submitted by*
*Hope Healy Koonz*

*Excerpts from the book to be published in January 2000: Healy Families from County Mayo, Ireland and Minnesota*

Long before we came to live in Mahtomedi, Sioux Indians lived in the area. The Sioux (Dakota) name for white bear was 'mato' and lake was 'mde.' According to their legend the spirit of a bear haunted the lake. The bear was slain by an Indian brave as the bear was about to attack his sweetheart on Manitou (Spirit) Island. Manitou Island is part of White Bear Lake.

When we moved to our home on the lake in Mahtomedi in 1923, there were few winter homes. Many summer cottages dotted the landscape. Mahtomedi was just a township named Lincoln Township. It existed for three miles to Willernie and had a width of two miles. The town, Mahtomedi, was incorporated in 1931.

The "main road," a dirt road, ran through the township. Petunia Lane curved off the main street to our home on the lakefront. When the road was paved with tar in 1925 it was fun to stand aside and watch the men lay the surface. It was more fun to pick off and chew a piece of soft dripping tar from the machine!

Our home was just one block from the railroad depot and the end of the streetcar line. The local grocery store and post office, both run by the Spink family, was located in between them. Spink's not only held groceries, but also had that wonderful penny candy. A nickel or a penny would buy a jawbreaker, a tiny bottle of colored syrup in a wax bottle, or an all-day sucker. We had such a choice of pieces that it was most difficult for us little children to make a decision on just what to spend our nickel on, on a Saturday afternoon.

Chandler's grocery store, just up the road from Spink's, had hand-packed ice cream. As we finished eating our Sunday dinner, one of us would run down to Chandler's for the ice cream. We could not keep it in our icebox because there was no refrigeration except a block of ice. Mame Chandler could pack the ice cream in so tightly that we thought it would come out of the carton. They had great candy also. We could charge anything we bought at either store.

The St. Paul & Duluth Railroad ran trains out to Wildwood, Mahtomedi, Dellwood, and White Bear Beach, for a round trip fare of $.50. Besides passengers, the trains hauled logs, coal, mail and ice to and from Stillwater on the St. Croix River, just nine miles away.

The Northern Pacific Railroad took over the St. Paul & Duluth line. A turntable, to turn the train around, was located near the depot. Two train employees pushed the engine around this great big circle. That was a delight to watch; such an extraordinary sight. We stood and watched in wonder when the old coal engine puffed out its huge bursts of steam.

Sometime after 1892, the Twin City Rail Transit extended its streetcar line from North St. Paul to Mahtomedi. Train travel was seventy-five minutes compared to the streetcar trip of sixty minutes and the streetcar fare was only eighteen cents a ride.

To build up the number of passengers to and from St. Paul to Mahtomedi, the Twin City Rail Transit developed Wildwood Park on the south end of White Bear

Lake in 1898. It was a marvelous amusement center and picnic ground. On Sundays and summer holidays extra streetcars from St. Paul and Minneapolis, via Como Park, came out at ten minute intervals bringing tourists from miles around.

The transit company furnished ice, good water and convenient facilities. No intoxicating liquor, no gambling and everything in perfect safety, were very attractive features. Swimming, fishing, boating, sailing, and launches traveling around the lake made it ideal for everyone.

The amusements were a "must" for all of us. There were "funny" mirrors that made one look huge, skinny, fat or grotesque. A "Fun House" with water flowing up rather than down, which just amazed us, was a grand attraction. Guns in booths to shoot for prizes were always a come-on. A penny arcade drew us there for a raucous laugh. For a penny, one could see hilarious or risqué movies. They were not exactly movies. One had to crank a machine to make the pictures revolve and the faster it turned, the better the picture. We could ride the bumper cars, the Tilt-A-Whirl and the merry-go-round until we got sick. Time after time we rode the merry-go-round trying to snatch the brass ring for a free ride.

The roller coaster was one of the largest in the United States and a terrific thrill and horrible scare to ride. One could hear the screams of those on that terrifying roller coaster as it wound up, around and down to its depths. Many, many times we also screamed as we rode it.

*Wildwood Park, White Bear Lake—1905.*

A two-level high diving board on a fifty-foot tower enticed a few braves. My brother, Chuck, was the only one in my family who dared to dive from the high board. The rides and amusements, mixed with the heavenly fragrance of popcorn, hot dogs, candy and candyfloss, attracted everyone.

A large pavilion for dining and dancing captivated the adults. Famous and popular orchestras such as Paul Whiteman's and singer Rudy Vallee, delighted the crowds. My sister, Dorothy, was fortunate in being able to dance there with her boyfriends. If Dorothy and her partner danced cheek to cheek they would be asked to leave! It was a no-no!

When the lake was calm late at night we could lie in our beds on the sleeping porch and listen to the music from Wildwood. We could even hear the screams from the roller coaster.

With the coming of the automobile and better roads, it was not possible to keep out unruly passengers as the transit company did on the streetcars. Gangsters such as "Machine Gun Kelly" and "Babyface Nelson" occasionally visited the park as well as other underworld characters. One night in the early 1930's some gangsters had a gunfight, leaving three dead. As the morning commuters to St. Paul stared out the windows of the streetcar, they saw the bodies.

People began to venture further out in the country in their automobiles. This eventually sounded a death knell in 1938, for one of the most picturesque enterprises of the time.

*Sources: Minnesota Historical Society, Althea Rohlfing – friend of Hope Healy and Mahtomedi historian, and Healy Families of County Mayo, Ireland. To be published in 2000.*

# Water and Ice

*As Remembered by*
*Cynthia E. Vadnais*

Activities and events are what I remember about White Bear Lake. White Bear was a very exciting place for a child growing up in the late fifties and early sixties. For me, summer and wintertime stand out the most.

As kids, my sister Shari, other friends, and I would spend our days down at Memorial Beach. The journey would start from our house, located at what is now 1924–6th Street. We would ride our bicycles over to 5th Street, down to Division Avenue, then up 9th Street, stopping at the old Cheese Shop for a snack. Of course there were always the unusual items that we would consider such as chocolate-covered ants or bees, and fried grasshoppers. The large cheese-making operation was also able to temporarily hold our attention until the heat got the better of us and we once again were off to the beach. After crossing Highway 61, we would follow the bike path along the railroad track, that is, the dirt path created by the kids, taking us close into the lake. We would go to Memorial Beach because we were not allowed to go to Ramsey Beach.

Memorial Beach was then a private beach that you needed to wear a tag to get into. The tag consisted of, if memory serves me right, a small circle of colored plastic with the name Memorial Beach, a number, and the current year. We would bring along a bag lunch and spend all day in the water, then ride our bikes home in late afternoon.

In the evenings, during the summer, after doing the dinner dishes and sweeping the kitchen floor, we would go outside to meet with all the neighborhood kids, of which there were many. We would play games such as hide-and-seek or red rover until it was time to go to bed.

An event that all of us kids, as a neighborhood would organize, was a Muscular Dystrophy (MD) carnival. We would take our wagons uptown to the local merchants and solicit them for prizes. Any we asked were always willing to donate something. It seems to me we generally raised around sixty to seventy-five dollars each year and gave away many great prizes. Our carnival culminated in a parade that all who had helped with the carnival would participate in. Our various skills, still to be honed, were mostly acquired at the Larkin Dance Studio. We would parade in our finest costumes, perched on wagon floats, on decorated bikes and on foot, right down the middle of the street, for as far away as five or six blocks.

My weekly allowance, until I became a teenager, was twenty-five cents a week. I was to wash or dry dishes nightly, sweep the kitchen floor daily, and help clean house on Saturdays. Twenty-five cents went a long way. Many of the candies at Johnstone's grocery store were two for one cent. The Avalon Theatre had special Saturday matinees that were only five or ten cents. A special treat was to have a cone at Dean's Ice Cream, where the murals of monthly sundaes were painted on the walls. One could easily get lost in the magic of those paintings with, for example, sundaes sliding down a mountain of snow on a sled.

A favorite summertime activity was going over to Lincoln School for the Summer Recreational Program. We would take a bus once a week and go to North St. Paul to roller skate. There was a morning, every week, that we would do crafts. Every Friday morning we would gather and, as a group, walk up to the Junior High Auditorium to watch a movie. Horseback riding was also a favorite. There were special events throughout the summer such as going to Como Zoo, Excelsior Park, the annual walk to the Dairy Queen on Highway 61 and the big carnival at the end of the program.

A lot of enjoyment was had going up to the old Carnegie library for an afternoon and checking out a stack of books. Throughout the summer, the returned books were always traded for a new stack of books.

*The Andrew Carnegie Foundation donated the public library, which was opened in 1920 at the present-day library location. Photo courtesy of Lawrence R. (Bob) and Eileen Whitaker.*

During my early to mid-teens, I was a member of the girls' drill team, the Trojanettes. We spent our summers practicing on the football field at the Junior High School, marching, and competing against other drill teams. We were always quite proud on Memorial Day when we marched in the White Bear Lake parade and had a chance to show our neighbors just how good we were.

It is easy to see why as a kid, summertime seemed to last forever.

How can one live in Minnesota and not love the winters? My mother, Bev Vadnais, always thoroughly prepared us for the worst cold. She would take a big, wide, wool scarf and wrap it around our torso, pinning it securely. Of course, boots were not all that waterproof so we would wear plastic bags on our feet to try to keep them dry.

Dad was a great hockey player and long blade skater and hence, we spent a lot of time on skates. I remember well the first two pairs of skates that I had. The first was the training pair with a pair of runners on each skate. My second pair, at about age five, were my bunny-hugs. They laced, buckled, and then finally laced again. Needless to say, my ankles didn't even have an opportunity to bend. Maybe I should just say that I didn't walk on my ankles.

When the ice was good, early after freezing, my dad, Jack Vadnais, would put on his long-blades and take us skating along the shoreline of White Bear Lake. We would chase along behind him listening to the ice crack way out into the lake as we moved across it. As we got a little older, we would go to the Hippodrome on the weekends. The warming room was the only heated area and was quite popular when the thermometer dipped low. There were also many winters that part of our backyard was flooded and lit so the whole neighborhood had its own place to skate.

There were the occasional trips onto the lake in the winter where Mom and Dad would tie our saucers to the bumper of the Travel-all and take us for spins out on the ice. It was so much fun to go flying across the lake at speeds probably approaching five to ten miles per hour.

*"Ice boat" canoe located near Stewart and Lake Avenues. Photo courtesy of Lawrence R. (Bob) and Eileen Whitaker.*

*"Dat vas a big un, eh?" Winter Carnival ice fishing contest. Photo from White Bear Association brochure, circa 1955. Submitted by Paul Chapin.*

White Bear Lake played an important part in the St. Paul Winter Carnival. The White Bear Rod and Gun Club annually sponsored what was billed as the largest fishing contest in the world. Each year, a different design was plowed on the lake. This was quite the family event for us. My Aunt June and Uncle Ralph would join us. My mother would put on a big parka and pin on all of her previous year's carnival buttons. Dad would wear a big jacket that looked like polar bear fur. We all fished and hoped to catch the big one. Dad, being one of the organizers of the event, always made sure that each of us kids had an ice-fishing button with the year of our birth on it. The carnival royalty would come to the event as well as the Vulcans. Small planes could be seen flying over the contest taking pictures. It was an enormous event that everyone seemed to be participating in.

I went to grade school at St. Mary's Catholic School. We lived about four blocks from school and would walk to school in the morning, home for lunch, back to school and then home again after school. In the winter, for the whole distance to school no matter which way we went, the sides of the roads were lined with huge snow banks that we would walk across the tops of on the paths that had been beaten into them. On the walk home after school we would often stop on the largest of the snow banks and play King of the Hill or have a spirited snow fight.

Christmas time was magical. Railroad Park was all lit up and stocked with Christmas trees leaning against makeshift fences. It was a family event to go up and select a tree to bring home and decorate. The Post Office had a wonderful, large manger scene displayed out under the flagpole. All the street poles were also decorated for the holidays.

A favorite holiday activity was to go Christmas caroling. My brothers and sisters, friends, and I would go out several times during the season. It didn't matter how cold it was, the smiling faces that would answer the door always warmed us when we started singing. Upon finishing three or four carols, many people would invite us in and offer us a cookie or a hot drink. White Bear was a small town then and no matter where you went, everyone seemed to know who you were.

My childhood was a wonderful time. I think that, in part, it was because it was spent in such a wonderful town. Even though I don't live in White Bear anymore, I am still drawn "home" on a regular basis and continue to create memories with family and friends.

# A Little Bit of This and That

*As Remembered by*
*Lorraine Billingsley (Hogan)*

uring the hot summer days, one of the favorite things to do was to follow the ice truck and get a sliver of ice to suck on whenever the ice truck stopped on its rounds of selling ice.

The fire whistle (not siren) would blow at noon (time to go home for lunch), at 10:00 P.M. (curfew) and for fires. When the fire whistle blew, I would rush outside and watch Fred Lenhart burst out of Lenhart's Bar running as fast as he could down to the old fire station that was on Clark Avenue. You could see others running to the station, too. It was very exciting.

In the winter, we would "belly flop" with our sleds down the middle of 4th St., just west of Highway 61. The road was hard and snow packed all winter and there were very few cars. The boys used to grab the back bumpers of cars for a free ride.

One winter my two brothers, Ronald and Clarence, were walking back across White Bear Lake after a day of skiing at the Yacht Club, when the wind came up. It blew the snow and it became very cold. After an afternoon of skiing and being tired and the wind coming up, my brother Ronald wanted to stop and just sit and rest for awhile. My brother Clarence wouldn't let him lie down. They walked to a house on the island where the people were wonderful and let them come in and get warmed up.

The "hill" we used for sliding was the platform, as we called it. It was located west of the railroad depot by a railway siding. The platform was used to unload cars from railroad cars. It was a sturdy platform as high as a railroad car door and had a ramp leading down to the ground. It made an excellent hill for sliding and all the neighborhood children enjoyed it.

I remember when Memorial Beach first opened. You had to wear an elastic band with a metal tag around your ankle to show you belonged and had paid to be a member and could swim there.

When Highway 61 was being built across Goose Lake, no one believed that enough fill could be brought in so the highway could go across it because there was a peat bog there. I guess we were wrong, weren't we?

*White Bear Lake Fire Hall.*
*Photo courtesy of White Bear Press.*

# Hometown Advantages/Disadvantages

*As Remembered by*
*Harriet Bissen*

rowing up in a small town had many advantages. Growing up during WWII in a small town such as White Bear Lake had some disadvantages. I didn't realize that.

There was never a time when I couldn't remember the street lights, paved streets, curbs and sidewalks, movie theater, grocery stores, butcher shops, ice cream parlor, Carnegie library, doctors, bank, piano teachers, parks, fire and police departments, county fair and indoor ice rink. There were about 3,000 people living in this beautiful little town with maple trees, green lawns, and lakes. Winter and summer, White Bear, Bald Eagle, Goose and Birch Lakes were a wonderful advantage for all of us.

By necessity, whenever and wherever I went, it was on foot or by bicycle. I didn't realize that might be considered a disadvantage. Getting the family car was not even an option. There was gasoline rationing as well as a shortage of tires. There were many rationed and scarce items that created difficulty for my parents. They coped and I was not aware of any disadvantages that WWII created.

School functions, such as football, basketball, and hockey, were a big part of the week for most of us. On rare occasions, the school district provided bus transportation for an out-of-town game. School districts, too, had to guard their gasoline and tire allotments. If the game was really important, such as a conference championship, a reluctant father would allow his car to be piled with friends, for that one time only.

In spite of restrictions of this sort, times were exciting during the first half of the 1940s—the war years. There just wouldn't have been time for television or computer games, even if they had been available.

White Bear Lake, like other small towns in the area, had a 9:30 curfew. It was a war-related effort but the biggest benefit was getting the teens home where they belonged every night. The siren would send us running during winter and summer. The siren was loud enough to be heard all over town, as well as the surrounding area. What would happen if one was in violation? I never asked. I just made sure to be home.

Between church youth groups, scout meetings, school functions and homework, only on Saturday night were we left to our own devices.

Most of us had little money and no wheels. We went by foot (shank's mare as it was called), which didn't allow us to roam very far. There were some high school boys already serving in the armed forces. We didn't realize their absence was a disadvantage. There was appreciation and pride to know someone serving Uncle Sam.

Looking back on those years, I have fond memories of the Teen Canteen. That is where I, along with my girlfriends, perfected the dance called the Lindy Hop. It was all the rage then. In the years immediately following the war, we saw Donald O'Connor and others of movie fame doing the Lindy. By then the dance included all sorts of gymnastics. The Canteen was in an old building on Third Street, just east of Banning. Memory tells me it was the American Legion Club rooms. The floor was of hardwood and slightly wavy. No disadvantage in our minds. It was great fun to dance to the phonograph. Over and over we practiced. Our burning ambition was to get the steps just right. The open space, the hardwood floor and the rhythmic beat of the Big Bands set our nimble feet into action.

We dressed for dancing in pleated skirts with matching sweaters. Just as today, there was security in conformity. The evenings ended with a mad dash to be home before the curfew siren sounded.

My memory doesn't tell me how long the Canteen operated. Details fade with the years. Sometime during that period, I started babysitting, which ended my trips to the Canteen. However, I do remember what fun it was. The Lindy became a life-long skill for me. It was the Big Band era. We were called the dancing generation. Swing was king. I still enjoy a whirl around the dance floor.

If the American Legion was the civic group behind this effort, they should be commended. We had so much energy. The Legion provided a safe, wholesome place to be. As a teen, I probably did not realize someone deserved a thank you for this free evening of fun. Late as it is—50 some years late—thank you Legionnaires from a happy dancer.

Growing up in beautiful White Bear Lake had many advantages. Yes, indeed.

*The Hardey's Store in 1910 was rented to Bernier Grocery. The Teen Canteen was located on the second floor, and at present is still home to the American Legion. Photo courtesy of Lawrence R. (Bob) and Eileen Whitaker.*

Sugar

# The Ragman

*As Remembered by*
*Anita Almleaf*

My parents made their home in White Bear about 1920 after having been married in Canada. Being a Purple Heart veteran in the First World War, Dad needed to be near the Veteran's Hospital in Minneapolis.

After settling in Bald Eagle, he rented a barn on the adjacent lot. He hoped to be a hobby farmer but got a little carried away with cows, chickens, geese and ducks. The barn had extra stalls, so he rented one to a man from St. Paul who had a horse and buggy. The man came on the bus every day; hooked up his horse and buggy and headed for downtown White Bear to collect used rags. Rumors were that he was a wealthy man from Summit Avenue in St. Paul. He became known as "Dudley the Rag Man," driving his buggy through the streets of White Bear, calling, "Rags, rags."

Being a 10-year-old on summer vacation, my days were boring. I would beg my mom to let me go with Dudley just one time. She finally gave in, packed a bag lunch for me, and away we went, heading for downtown White Bear. I felt like a queen sitting alongside him in the buggy!

Before the day was over the ragman had to stop at the Blacksmith Shop to have new shoes put on his horse. This was an unexpected bonus for me! What a deal! It was one of the most memorable days in my young life.

---

## THE GOOD OLD DAYS

☞ Folks must be joking when they refer to the good old days. Without going back to pioneer times many can recall something about them.

We used kerosene lamps which were dirty and required refilling. Now we touch a button. We kept a team of horses in a smelly stable and fed them three times a day besides acting as groom. Now we spring the self-starter and away we go on a tireless steed. We split kindling and split wood and carried coal, an endless job. Now in many cases the heating plant is automatic. And the cooking arrangements are well-nigh perfect.

Women spent much time making dresses and hats and then they often looked dowdy. Now the stores provide both much more cheaply and much better in every way. Same way with women's clothing of all kinds. Foods, tinned, bottled and packed, are better and more sanitary than in the old days of home preparing.

Because of great progress our physical well-being has been improved. Our mental appetites can more easily be appeased. There is something wrong in the outlook of any person who seems to hunger for the good old days. As the boy on the corner said: "That's the balony."— Toledo Blade.

*Story, circa 1931, courtesy of White Bear Press.*

---

*Editor's note: The ragman would ride through town collecting old rags. At the end of the day he would go back to the barn and sort the rags. By feeling the fabric content he would sort them into piles. It was unknown to the author of this story as to what he did with them after he sorted them.*

*L.D.B.*

# Depot Dreams Come True

*As Remembered by*
*Ruth Mattlin*

*The Preservation and Restoration of the White Bear Railroad Depot (1988-1992)*

The Northern Pacific Railroad depot of 1935 had been closed and boarded up. The last passenger train through White Bear Lake was in about the year 1967. What would happen to the depot now that it belonged to the Burlington Northern Railroad and was no longer used?

This depot was built with 40,000 bricks salvaged from the old roundhouse, (just south of the depot) which was torn down to make room for Highway 61.

Carroll R. Mattlin dreamed of preserving and restoring the Northern Pacific depot as an important piece of history for the city of White Bear Lake. That was in the year of 1988.

Mattlin, a retired general contractor, had his business on leased railroad property for 55 years. He also owned two private railroad cars, which he parked by his business on a railroad siding. The first car, a red wooden Northern Pacific Caboose No. 1285, was built about 1910. (It is now parked at the south end of the depot.) The second car was an all steel Pullman Observation Lounge Car, "The Rainier", from the North Coast Limited train of the Northern Pacific Railroad. It was built in 1946 and is now in the Duluth Lake Superior Railroad Museum.

*A view of White Bear Lake's Depot pre-dating the awning additions of the late 1800s. Photo courtesy of Lawrence R. (Bob) and Eileen Whitaker.*

The Mattlin buildings and property were purchased by the city of White Bear Lake and taken down in 1997. The Manitou Crossing development now covers the property.

Carroll R. Mattlin was born on Christmas Day, 1913 in the second floor apartment of the Bald Eagle Lake Depot, which was a mile north of White Bear Lake. His father worked there as the night tower man for the Northern Pacific Railroad. He was responsible for controlling train traffic at the junction of the Northern Pacific and Soo Line Railroads.

Mattlin had a life-long interest in making the community a better place. His dream encompassed building support from the White Bear Lake citizens. He developed a petition to "Save the Depot," and during events like the grand opening of the new City Hall, he procured 4,000 signatures. The dream started to come true when the City of White Bear Lake finally purchased, from the Burlington Northern Railroad, the depot and the 2.8 acres of land it occupies.

The city manager, Mark Sather, said that it was the intent of the city council to have the depot restored and eventually promote redevelopment of the remaining property. Mattlin, a long time railroad enthusiast, was appointed by Mayor Jerry Briggs to be chairman of an advisory committee to the city council for the depot restoration.

A committee of about 15 citizens volunteered their time and talent for the next few years. Ray Smith, Mike Parenteau, Eldon Morrison, Sandy LeMire, Sandy Briggs, Art Pew, Bill Rust, Julie Heimerl, Patti Butcher, Dick Carlson, Bernice Peterson, Don McCormack, Harry Mares, Leo Rafferty and Ken George were the committee members.

The committee, asking for their support with donations of money, time and talent sent out a letter to all residents of White Bear Lake.

Stan Hill volunteered his expertise with the fund-raising. The city needed about $75,000.00 to proceed with the project. All donations would be recognized. Those who donated $500.00 or more received a print of the depot by artist, John Cartwright. Donations of $50.00 and over would be listed on a permanent record board in the depot. They received tremendous support from individuals, businesses, and organizations young and old.

By August, 1991, the White Bear Lake Area Chamber of Commerce moved its new office space into the restored depot and has since tripled its membership.

Mattlin, along with the expert help of Ray Smith of the White Bear Lake Historical Society, transformed the baggage room into a museum. The emphasis of the museum is on railroad artifacts and history of White Bear Lake, and is the property of The White Bear Lake Historical Society.

Finally, the depot museum's "Open House" was held June 27 & 28, 1992. This was coordinated with the 28th Manitou Days celebration, the "City of Lakes & Legends," which was presented by the Chamber of Commerce.

In October 1993, Mattlin organized the moving and placing of the red Northern Pacific Caboose Car No. 1285 to its current resting place next to the depot.

Completion of the project was a wonderful, cooperative, community effort. It allowed everyone to be a proud and happy part of history. It is everyone's museum, depot and caboose!

Congratulations to the City of White Bear Lake, and to the depot committee. Congratulations as well to the chairman, Carroll R. Mattlin, who received the President's Choice Award of 1993 from the White Bear Lake Area Chamber of Commerce; for his interest and work in the restoration of the depot and for creating a new office space for our Chamber of Commerce.

# The Gazebo of White Bear Lake

*As remembered by*
*Eileen Berger*

In 1883, during White Bear Lake's golden era as a fashionable summer retreat, Bavarian-born Thomas Erd built an elaborate Victorian gazebo as a special gift to his daughter, Annie, and her new husband, Emil Geist. The white ornamental structure, as decorative as a wedding cake, stood on a bluff next to the lake and adjacent to the Geist summer home on South Shore Boulevard (about midpoint between present day Schneider's Bay and Bellaire Beach).

Sometimes called a honeymoon cottage, the building measured 15 feet in diameter and 18 feet in height. Screens and glass windows covered the top floor and a door in the lower section enabled family members to sleep there at night. An outside stairway and a bright red roof topped off the original structure. Mr. Erd added a weather vane as a finishing touch. In an interview in 1920, Ed Geist told the story of how Annie's father, a well known contractor and stone mason, built the gazebo as a surprise for them. The young couple was not allowed to visit the family for many weeks before the gazebo's completion. It became a father's final kind gesture to his daughter, as Mr. Erd died less than two years after he built it.

After the father's death, the Geist family moved into the house and enjoyed the airy, cozy pavilion for many years. In the late 1960's the home was sold to Robert and Joanne Edel. By this time the structure was in a state of major disrepair. Parts of the structure were rotted or missing, the screens were almost completely torn out and most of the glass was broken. The new owners were not interested in preserving it. Some members of the White Bear Lake Women's Club heard it might even be torn down. They felt that the little gazebo should be preserved; it was part of White Bear history and it would be a loss to the community if it were demolished. After contacting the owners, the Edels agreed to donate the structure as is. Lois Gillen, President of the Women's Club in 1970, spearheaded the project. Much enthusiastic discussion followed and Margaret Mingo headed the Beautification Committee. The organization voted that no more than $650 could be spent for the project and all estimates had to be in writing. But by August of 1971 the house had again been sold to the

*The Emil Geist Gazebo, now located in Matoska Park, was originally built in 1883.*
*Photo courtesy of Eileen Berger.*

Goodman family and the new owners said they would like to keep the gazebo in their possession. The situation became difficult and by September 13, 1971, the whole idea had to be dropped, much to the disappointment of the Club.

Time passed and by August, 1973 there was again a new owner of the property, a Mr. Harris. This time, Mr. Harris approached the Women's Club to donate the two-story structure. At this time, Margery Schneeman was President. Many opinions and debates followed as to whether or not the pavilion could be restored, how they would be able to pay for such a major reconstruction, and where they would put it if indeed it could be moved. But the Women's Club again took up the cause with gusto and perseverance. The new Gazebo Project Committee was composed of Morina Hohman, Lois Gillen and Margery Schneeman. Club member Rita Binger made a motion that if the Club accepted the gazebo, a public fund would be started, as the costs would be far higher than they first suspected. Everyone agreed, and a new Citizen Advisory Committee was invited to join the project. This group consisted of Thomas Newcome, Arthur Gillen, Nancy and Allan Woolworth, and Jean and Dr. George Geist. Lois Keetch recommended to the Park Board that the gazebo be located in Matoska Park. The budget for repair, preparation of the new site, moving the building, construction costs, repainting and re-roofing, plus insurance, came to $4,050. Many residents rallied around the cause and donations began coming in.

Many a meeting took place between 1972 and 1974. The city, in the meantime, agreed that the building could be placed in Matoska Park, located on the other side of the lake. Because of public usage, the committee felt that glass windows could be a liability and the contractor remodeled the two floors with open verandas. The plan for moving the gazebo included transporting it across the frozen lake during the winter. But when the time came to move it, there was fear that the ice that year was not thick enough. Rather than chance an accident, it was decided the structure should be moved by truck down South Shore, Highway 61 and Lake Avenue. To prevent further damage to the building the moving contractor decided to separate the top floor from the bottom. Hundreds of curious people followed the caravan. And so it happened, the gazebo found its new location. Community businesses helped, too. Mr. Richards, President of Northern States Power Company, donated their services as well as Cemstone Company, who provided free cement. The Collins Electrical Company generously donated half of the labor costs to install the wiring.

The sun shone brightly on an exuberant throng on June 30, 1974 for the dedication of the completed gazebo. The music of the Mariner High School band filled the air. The Girl Scouts performed their flag ceremony as dignitaries praised the work of the Women's Club. The club president handed over the deed to the mayor. Residents took advantage of the near perfect weather to sprawl on the grass in Matoska Park. Following the ceremony the Women's Club served pink lemonade. For the persevering members, it was a dream come true!

During the next twenty-five years, social gatherings, musical concerts, and weddings took place at the gazebo. But by 1999, the beloved landmark was again in danger of being demolished. The wooden stairs, columns, railing, and ceiling started to rot. Afraid of a possible accident, city maintenance workers took it apart. Upon seeing the gazebo dismantled and lying on the ground, a group of alarmed citizens organized a Gazebo Restoration Committee. Headed by Jan Holtz and Vicky Cox, they received estimates that its reconstruction would cost around $59,000. Even though the city voted to donate $20,000 as seed money, the project was in jeopardy as the remaining money was not forthcoming. But thanks to a $40,000 contribution by Ted Glasrud, a long time resident and attorney in White Bear Lake, the Gazebo's future is assured. At the meeting of the City Council in May, 1999, council members and advocates in the chambers enthusiastically accepted the donation. Spokesman Dave Pary said, "It's unusual because we're looking at a structure that's more than 100 years old, and everything was done by hand—scrolls, intricacy. It's unique. How many two-story gazebos do you see?" Brian Hanson, a local architect, drew up a design that preserves as much of the original structure as possible but will include some steel and a new plastic coated material. "The new construction should last another 100 years without much maintenance," he stated.

A visible connection with our town's past, the gazebo, once described as a "sparkling jewel," will remind present and future generations of White Bear's golden age as a major resort town west of the Mississippi River. It will, once again, be a favorite location for community events, musical concerts and weddings.

# THE OLD BACK YARD
by
A. J. Dunlap

The old back yard was the finest spot
    We had in the Old Home Town—
A private place back of bush and vine
    And fence that was tumbling down.
The sand pile under the cherry tree,
    Our nest in the sycamore,
The chopping block and the old work bench
    That stood by the hen house door—
All have a place in my memory
    That time has not dimmed or marred;
And often fancy recalls the days
    We played in the old back yard.

*Courtesy of White Bear Press.*

# Auntie May

*As Remembered by*
*Helen Lindbeck Peterson*

I was so lucky to have an Auntie May. She never married, but stayed home on the farm to "take care of Pa and the boys." Two of her brothers still lived on the farm and worked elsewhere when I was a preteen youth.

On Friday after school when I was in the elementary grades, I would start my campaign to go out to Auntie May's for the weekend. Sometimes Daddy would take me out there, just three miles north of our house, and sometimes I would ride my bike, weather permitting. Usually I had to go home Saturday night to be ready to go to Sunday School the following morning. Once in a while I could stay until Sunday afternoon or evening. I dreaded the ride home on my bike after having enjoyed the farm for a day or two. I had a great home life, but being on the farm was such a special treat.

Auntie May did much of her shopping by mail order or over the telephone, so she always had those fat Sears Roebuck and Montgomery Ward catalogs. As fall deepened into winter, more and more of the corners were turned down. It was such fun to search through the dog-eared pages looking for the things Auntie May might have chosen for Christmas surprises. When the new catalogs came to the mailbox in the spring, I could cut paper dolls from the old ones. Eventually, the old books went to the outhouse to be used a last time!

My thick hair was parted in a cross on the top of my head and braided, the two at the top worked into the lower two. It was a simple and neat way to control it, but difficult and sometimes painful to comb. Auntie May couldn't braid with any neatness or efficiency, so she'd brush the loose hairs around my face up and into the rest, and tell me no one would be the wiser. Yes, I sure am glad I had an Auntie May.

On the cold winter days I read nearly all of my uncle's Zane Gray books along with a big pile of Popular Mechanics. There were some National Geographics in the attic, and I got through most of them, too. The National Geographic had been put away to protect my young eyes from some possible nudity. A Victrola and a big pile of 78 R.P.M. records also kept me busy. Most of the records were polkas or schottisches, and many songs had Swedish words.

About once a week there would be enough cream from the single cow to merit churning. The raw cream had been lowered in jars into the well pit to keep it cool enough in the summer and warm enough in the winter to prevent spoilage or freezing. The churn was a large glass container and the lid had paddles on it. The crank on top turned the paddles, and, after much turning, *Violá!*, butter. If the jar was quite full, the task was even more tiring. Auntie May would bargain with me, "You turn it (X) times, and then I'll turn it (same number) times, and when we get butter, we'll make popcorn or fudge." And so we did. The newly churned butter had to be 'washed'. The buttermilk was poured off and saved, and cool water added to the butter in the churn. This was mixed and changed over and over, until the water was clear. Then the butter was salted.

Auntie May had a few chickens in the coop. In the warm seasons during the day they roamed free, but at night they always went back to the coop. There were several nesting boxes along one wall where they laid their eggs. Each day, the eggs were gathered. In spring, a good 'setting' hen was selected and given a few eggs. She'd 'set' and soon she had a brood following her around the yard. One hen was named Pepita. She was so tame she would come when called. Often I fed her big fat spiders I caught near the outhouse.

Many Sundays, Daddy would go out to the farm to get Auntie May for church, and on several occasions, she'd also stay for dinner at noon. Once in awhile as a special treat, she would take me to a movie at the only theater in town, the Avalon. I have no memory of the movies, but that didn't matter for I was with my dear Auntie May. After the show was over, we would walk to Zwerenz's drug store and have either a fifteen-cent soda or a sundae before walking home. It was always a difficult choice for me. Occasionally there was enough money for a banana split, my favorite! Yes, I really was lucky to have an Auntie May!

*Could this be your Auntie May?*
*Photo courtesy of Dot Magnuson.*

# Woodpile Lake

*As Remembered by*
*C. M. Ingham*

**M**olly and Mike McKlosky moved onto the old Shetland place after Cal Shetland died. His wife Martha went to live with her daughter, Sarah.

The land was not great, a little sandy and swampy in places, but Mike scrambled and fought the horrible winters and blistering summers as best he could. However, there was a nice spot near the road along the Burlington tracks. It was a tiny lake; more like a large pond with an island in the middle. On this island a profusion of wildflowers surrounded a few blue spruce and scotch pines. The lake was fed by a fresh water spring that kept it free of scum, clean and clear. The general appearance was that of a garden and was visible to Molly from her kitchen window. She loved to watch the island in bloom in the summer and crisply etched in snow during the winters. It became known in the family as Molly's Garden, and was a fond memory to them after they grew and left home.

During the Depression Mike needed some cash money so he decided to cut down the pine trees in Molly's Garden and sell the timber for firewood.

Molly was horrified and heartbroken when she saw the devastation Mike had done. As he cut up the trees and stacked the wood, getting it ready to cart away, he suddenly dropped dead! The wood never left the island, and in time the lake became known as Woodpile Lake.

Molly's will called for her to be buried on the island with her Garden when she died.

The last time I drove past Woodpile Lake Island a lone pine tree had grown up beside the rotting timbers.

# Lake Washington

*As Remembered by*
*C. M. Ingham*

On the west boundary of Willernie is an extension of White Bear Lake that is about a mile long and half a mile wide at its narrowest. Receding glaciers, leaving a band of higher ground that now separates the two lakes, closed it off. Prior to the Great Depression, Lake Washington dried up and became a peat bog, so many said.

At any rate, Dad thought we could save a bundle of money by burning peat instead of coal in our furnace. He enlisted Bob, my brother, and me, with the aid of a wagon and a wheelbarrow, to haul peat up Weinrich's Hill and two blocks to our house. The peat was then stacked like blocks of concrete (and was nearly as heavy) in our basement ready to burn. When it finally came time to use it, we found that it was more dirt than burnable stuff, so we had heat-producing dirt— somewhat. It had been a lot of work for little benefit, and was going to be more work to get rid of all the dirt. Another lost benefit was that the coal produced clinkers, which were used to make the traction better on walks and driveways. The dirt simply turned to mud.

Clinkers, which were found along with ashes in our furnace after shaking the grates, were very useful in many ways. Generally, we used them to prevent slipping and sliding. Unfortunately for us kids, Mr. Klein, who lived in a hollow down from one of our town water pumps, sometimes also used ashes and clinkers to cover the iced surface of Weinrich's Hill.

*Ad courtesy of White Bear Press.*

We used to pump water down the Hill, let it freeze, and invite our friends to slide. The Hill had a slight curve in the middle and if you didn't steer your sleds, boxes, or cardboard pieces just right, you could run into Weinrich's house or bushes.

Jim Palmer built a so-called bobsled that held four people and was steered by the driver in front using a T-bar stuck through the plank seat. If the iced surface was just right you could go about 30 mph down that hill, wide open, and shoot out onto dried-up Lake Washington for about a block—if you were lucky.

A road ran along the bottom of the Hill and across Lake Washington at an angle from Weinrich's house. When sliding down the hill, if you saw a car or truck coming, you bailed out by hitting the ditch. Why no one was killed I don't know, but we did have a couple of broken legs and arms from riding Palmer's bobsled— mostly when he steered into trees and telephone poles!

Lake Washington was also a source of fun for some of the kids who would set the swamp on fire to watch the cattails explode and burn. The Volunteer Fire Department had a 1926 Willis-Knight fire truck. It was parked in the Village Hall, which was next door to Bob's store, across from Kraxner's Meat Market. If cars were parked in front of the Fire Barn door or in front of Kraxner's, there was a big hoop-de-doo to clear the street for the fire truck. The truck went out so infrequently that it usually had a dead battery. They then hooked a chain on it and pulled it to the fire with a pickup truck or a wrecker. Usually by the time they got to the swamp, the fire had burned itself out.

At the north end of Lake Washington was a solid landmass about 1/2 mile wide that included the highway into Willernie and Mahtomedi, the streetcar tracks, and, between 1890 and 1940, Wildwood Amusement Park.

The Twin City Rapit Transit Companies established two amusement parks; Wildwood on the shores of White Bear Lake and one called Excelsior, at Lake Minnetonka, 60 miles to the east. These two parks were built to enhance travel by streetcar and open the adjacent areas for settlement.

Across from Wildwood Park, the company built an automobile parking lot. They made the lot by staking down old railroad ties in a field. The cars were then parked with their front wheels against the ties. While the people were enjoying themselves in the amusement park, one of the local garages would send down a tow truck to bump the cars over the ties. When the people came out, their cars would be stuck and they'd have to call a tow truck for a lift out, for which the towing company would charge two dollars!

The streetcar line ran from Stillwater to Mahtomedi and Willernie, then on into St. Paul. It was the major mode of transport if you had no car. We used to ride over to North St. Paul, five miles away, to see a movie. The cost of the ride was five cents each way. If you missed the last streetcar at 1:00 A.M., you had to walk home. There were many nights that my brother Bob or I missed the last car and had a spooky walk home.

*Wildwood Park was established by the Twin City Rapid Transit Company in 1889 and was a favorite destination until the 1930s. Photo courtesy of Lawrence R. (Bob) and Eileen Whitaker.*

Riding the streetcar back to Willernie was a great thrill! Coming into the end of the Lake Washington area was a three-mile downhill run called Long Lake Hill. Sometimes the motormen were bored and would open it up full throttle! The car would rock and sway and once in a while jump the tracks, but it never overturned!

Other times some of our young men, Bob included, would pull the trolley off the overhead line while it was tearing down Long Lake Hill. Then it was completely out of control, no lights, and no brakes, going about 60 mph, the foot bell clanging. Eventually it would slow to a stop in Willernie. Everyone would jump off and scatter while the motorman yelled, cursed, and put the trolley back on the line.

The streetcar system was always being sued by one of our neighbors. Nearly every time she could, she would fall inside the streetcar, either getting on or off. She did this so often, they finally banned her from riding.

During the Depression when St. Paul and its environs was a haven for bank robbers, gangsters, kidnappers, and killers, Wildwood Amusement Park figured in one episode. The treasurer of the amusement park lived in a lovely home about three blocks north of the Park. One night, three men knocked on his door and when he answered, they entered and demanded the day's receipts. He accompanied two of the robbers to the office in his bare feet to open the safe. The third man stayed with the wife and their daughter to guard against them calling the police. The treasurer's feet were so cut and burned from his ordeal that he said he almost didn't care whether they shot him!

Of course, the police were called to investigate after the robbers left, but could find no clues. The Park Association hired their own private investigator. According to him, the thieves were suspected by the FBI to be in league with Dillinger and the Barker-Karpis gangs.

Eventually, the rise of the automobile put the streetcar company and Wildwood Park out of business. Water began to once again fill in Lake Washington.

*Other ill-reputed activity linked to gangsters. Photo courtesy of White Bear Press, circa 1932.*

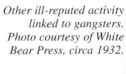

## LONE BANDIT GETS AWAY WITH $653; CHASED BY POSSE OF 100 ARMED MEN

Warner Bears His Shock and Pain Heroically; Lying on Floor, Gives Orders in Detail After Bullet Passed Through Body and Stuck in Wall; No Trace of Bandit; Wounded Man's Condition Favorable.

Top picture shows a part of the posse of 100 men who, armed with shotguns and pistols, combed the woods southwest of White Bear along the Labore and Goose Lake roads for five hours Thursday afternoon searching for the lone bandit who robbed the First State Bank of White Bear.

Lower—The car used by the bandit. Found by Francis Parenteau, Frank Diesi, Martin Fournelle and Henry Marcotte in the dense woods beside Goose Lake road. These cuts are furnished by and with the compliments of The Pioneer Press.

# The Playhouse

*As Remembered by*
*Helen Lindbeck Peterson*

During a Spring storm in 1940 or 1941, high winds destroyed many trees and buildings in and around White Bear Lake. Among the structures flattened was a one-car garage belonging to C. H. Christianson, our superintendent of schools. He asked Daddy if he had a trailer and if Daddy would remove the twisted and broken wood. Daddy told him he would remove it if he could have it. And so it came to our yard in irregular and unrecognizable pieces. Each evening and on Saturdays, Daddy laboriously pulled rusty, screaming nails from every board and sorted the pieces. Finally he began to reassemble a building.

As a floor began to take shape, I remember asking him what he was building. He pushed his ever-present fedora back from his forehead with a thumb and told me he was building his dream house. I had no idea what he was talking about and went off to play. Some time later, a rectangular building became apparent. He was putting up a playhouse! With little but salvaged scraps and hand-me-downs, ingenuity and love, he built a three room playhouse with a screened porch. I remember that all he bought was the screen for the porch. He cut some numbers from an old license plate (which fit into the chronological order on the street) for a house number. Bill Sandahl, the mailman, brought mail to us thereafter. He would even read the penny postcards sent by my Auntie May.

There was a little sink in the kitchen with water piped from the house. Daddy put up cabinets discarded from someone's remodeling project. There was a cleverly designed table that folded up in front of the sink where we often ate breakfast. The bedroom had bunk beds and a three-cornered wall cabinet. In the living room we had an old wind-up Victrola and a pile of equally old 78-rpm records, where we danced. On the porch hung a two-seat swing where my parents sat in the evenings until we were quiet and asleep. Even the dog slept out there with us. Often at sundown, neighborhood friends came dragging their pillows and other bedding to spend the night. In the morning, my mother brought a huge tray loaded with home-made bread—toasted, dripping with butter, and oatmeal and cocoa.

Eventually the day came when we moved to another house in town. Daddy hired Maurice Burroughs to move the playhouse the half mile or so to the new location. By this time I was more interested in driving than the playhouse, so, after a year or two, he managed to turn the building a quarter turn and redo it again into a garage.

*Ad appearing in White Bear Press, 1917.*

# Bridge in the Shallows

*As Remembered by*
*Debora L. Houdek*

In the mid-fifties the summers were a long collection of sensations; blue jays in the woods providing the services of the morning alarm clock, hot tar on the streets as we danced down to the neighborhood beach, lake smells from derelict weeds baking at the waters' edge, and gasoline floating in rainbow patterns on the water. We kids spent more time in the water than out. Mom called me "Fish," among other things.

When we were younger, the moms felt it their responsibility to come down to the lake and watch after us. We'd be making havoc in the water, shouting, racing, and cannon-balling off the end of the dock, while the moms sat together toward the other end in swimsuits or shorts, feet dangling in the shallows, talking endlessly about whatever moms talk about.

They were a creative bunch, though. One day they arrived with equipment and supplies. They set the pitchers of ice tea and lemonade on the dock and waded into the shallows to unfold a card table and some lawn chairs. Someone brought the cards out. There they sat in their swimsuits, like they were in someone's den, sipping at glasses, making bids and playing bridge, all the while doing their duty to watch that their children didn't drown one another.

*One of the early Manitou Island Bridges, circa 1920s. Photo courtesy of Lawrence R. (Bob) and Eileen Whitaker.*

# Summer Dating

*As Remembered by*
*C. M. Ingham*

A friend of mine, Howie, who was the same age as I was, and myself were discussing women. Actually we were discussing how we could meet some girls. Howie lived in Willernie but went to a Catholic military school in St. Paul. My older brother, Bob, who was listening, suggested we go to the Barn Dance in Withrow some Saturday night with him. We agreed and set the date for the next week. We rode up there, about eight miles from home, to an old long barn-type building surrounded by parked cars.

We paid our fifty cents, had our hands stamped and entered a cavernous dance hall. A large floor surrounded by tables and chairs covered an area half the size of a football field. At one end there was an old-time band on a stage and at the other end was a bar. People were milling around grabbing tables, establishing their territory for the evening. Bob suggested we do likewise.

Howie and I were too young to drink beer and didn't like the taste anyway, so we had Cokes. Soon Bob meandered off and took up with some young lady on the dance floor. I had never seen him dance before, so I was impressed. I had seen him play football, fight, lift unbelievably heavy things, but never saw him in action with a girl.

I thought I was strong and in good shape, but that was before Howie and I met two dance partners, Maisy and Daisy. My partner, Daisy, flung me around that floor teaching me things I never thought my feet could do. It was a terpsichorean nightmare or a whirling dervish.

After two courses of this kind of workout Howie and I staggered to the table for a rest and a drink, but not the girls. They proceeded to dance without us! As we wet our whistles and compared notes, Howie suggested we trade partners at the next set.

Half an hour later we were sweating like hogs and panting like running dogs. We finally dragged the girls to the table and had a chance to talk. Our partners were a couple of sisters who were farm girls. They had no brothers but four more sisters whose father felt they could and should do the work of sons. That day they had driven the tractors plowing for nine hours, milked 50 cows, cleaned the barn, helped their mother do laundry, iron and bake bread. If they had told me they moved the hog barn from one side of the farm to the other I'd have believed them. They were not even sweating a drop.

I had spent several years at football practices that usually didn't last over 2 1/2 hours, but this workout was tougher than anything I'd ever tried.

*A typical teenaged couple out for a date in the 1930s. Red Langhorn and unknown girl. Photo courtesy of Dot Magnuson.*

After three hours when Howie and I tried to change our partners for some new ones, they said, "No! You're ours for the night." When I asked Bob what we could do he said we were stuck and the only thing we could do was sneak out. But he didn't want to leave, so we said we'd head for home, walking. Anything to get away from those taskmaster farm girls Maisy and Daisy.

As Howie and I stole off into the dark, we compared notes. Neither of us had ever danced with partners that picked us off the floor and proceeded to carry us through the steps. What strength!

We waited about two weeks before going back, but this time we drove in Howie's Dad's car so if we had to leave early we wouldn't have to walk home.

Daisy and Maisy were there with a couple of guys twice our size and we didn't think they saw us. Wrong! They brought two of their BIG sisters for us to dance with. We valiantly hung in there for an hour, then crawled out to the car and disappeared.

The next time I went back to Withrow was to play tuba in the band. I saw the girls there but they didn't see me. No one ever looks at a band member. We sure could have used those girls on our football team.

Late that summer Howie and I decided that kind of dancing was too strenuous, but we would like to try some regular ballroom dancing. We had the best dance floor in the whole area in the Plantation Club on the west shore of White Bear Lake. It was a remnant of the wild gangster era of the 20's and 30's.

We asked a couple of nice "summer girls" and were accepted. Summer girls were ones whose family rented a cottage at the lake for a couple of weeks or months or had a summer home.

We hit a snag the night of the date because neither of us could get a car to use. Howie produced a romantic alternative, a canoe. It was up to me to sell the girls on the deal, which I did. We were all dressed up pretty, on a lovely calm evening and it was only 3-1/2 miles across the lake. We arrived at the Plantation, danced, had Cokes, snacks, and fun.

We watched the clock because we had promised the girls' parents that we'd have them home by midnight, so we left the dance pavilion at 11:00.

The first thing we noticed was that it was pitch dark out, no moon, no street lights by the lake. We had cut straight across the lake coming, but there was breeze against us going home. We decided to follow the south shore around the lake and try to avoid running into the 600 docks sticking out into the lake. It made the trip about three miles further so we paddled hard and fast. The girls gave us a lot of flack all the way because we were splashing them on the back stroke of the paddles.

Somehow we found the right dock, pulled into it and landed the girls. As one of them climbed out of the canoe, she caught her foot in the gunnel and jerked it loose. This was just enough to flip the canoe and Howie and I took a quick dip. Fortunately, the water there was only four feet deep but we were as wet as if it had been 12 feet.

We rushed the girls home, squishing all the way, and barely made the deadline. We never dated them again, for some reason.

Howie and I had one more big adventure that summer. Howie discovered Marge Anderson, but I had no date. However, I had promoted the use of Dad's car so Howie produced his older sister Phyllis as my date.

We decided to drive to Lake Minnetonka Amusement Park, fifty miles west of Willernie. We had a wonderful time riding all the rides, eating, and dancing in the Pavilion, and finally headed home.

As we were streaming along on Highway 7 through St. Louis Park, the speed limit went from 65 miles per hour to 30 in one block, with no 45 zone in between.

There were three cars in line, a '28 Essex, me in a '37 Chev, and a '39 Buick behind me. The St. Louis Park police pulled us all over together and ticketed us all for speeding 80 mph in a 30 zone. It was a somber trip home with everyone offering to "divvy up" the fine I expected to get the next week when I was scheduled to be in court.

I told my mother the next day but feared telling Dad, with the short-fused temper he had. I had to have a parent along when I went to court on Friday. Mother said she would be useless and wouldn't want to not tell Dad. Soooo, I sat Dad down on Wednesday and told him the whole story. He took it quite coolly and asked only 100 questions.

Dad and I appeared in the court. I was read my offense again and was assessed a fine of $300 and confiscation of my driving license for six months. When the judge asked if I had anything to say I deferred to Dad. Dad was working for the Minnesota Highway Department at the time and had done some homework investigating the situation at work on Thursday and Friday.

It seems many local municipalities had removed their 45 mph signs and set up speed-traps to catch such suckers as me. Dad informed the judge and the police they were in violation of State Highway Department laws so their fine was invalid. He ended his discussion by saying he doubted a '28 Essex could go 80 mph, but he would be glad to contact the owner to try it. He also didn't think his '37 Chev could go 80.

The judge agreed with Dad but said I should be found guilty of something and should be fined court costs at least. Dad compromised and said, "OK. Fine $3, $1 for the cop, $1 for the clerk and $1 for you, Judge, plus a 90-day suspension of my son's license for driving through such a stupid town!" That was the whole criminal deal.

Next day Bob told me that the '37 Chev could go 80 mph because he had done it several times on that same road. Also, the police had been looking for that very same '37 Chev for six months because it had outrun the police car several times. I then remembered that Bob had been seeing a girl in Minnetonka for the last six months.

# Not for Me By the Sea

*Written by*
*Margaret M. Manship*

Soldiers deal
within their
"spheres"
of world conflict.
Photo courtesy
of Dot
Magnuson.

World War I
soldiers at
work...

...and at play.

Twice I saw the sea
beloved of so many
but I never loved the sea.

Too vast it was
and mighty
with its rushing breakers
pulling my gaze
up and out with
their crest and over
the sails in the
middle space, to be
stopped by ships
seemingly motionless
on the far horizon
thankfully hiding
the infinite sea
beyond.

No, not for me, by the sea.
For me, let there be
the lake, bounded by
trees and houses on
prescribed perimeters,
easy waves against
the shore, and laughter
reflected from beaches.

All of us on the lake
and in its sharing
companionship
the warmth of the sun,
and the water,
but each in his
own sphere
relaxing contented.

That's how it was
before I went
to see the sea,
first from one coast,
and then the other,
during WWII, the
conflict of the
nations.

That's how it was
when I came back
to the embrace of
the lake, the
Great White Bear,
firmly encircling
the Spirit of Peace
the world had been so
desperately seeking.

# Adventures and Turning Points

*As Remembered by*
*Stan Hill*

### First Impressions

Late in April 1923, my mother, father, 13-year old brother and I arrived in White Bear Lake by train in the midst of a roaring blizzard. I was 9 years old then. The driver of the horse and cutter (sleigh), which was used as a taxi in the winter, told us he couldn't make it through the drifts to our new home (across the street from where Lincoln school is today). So, instead, he took us to the Lake Shore Inn, one of the last remaining resort hotels that had been built 40

*Looking south on Washington Avenue, known in the early 1900s as Railroad Avenue.*
*Photo courtesy of Lawrence R. (Bob) and Eileen Whitaker.*

or 50 years earlier. It was located in the northwest corner of what is now Cottage Park. The Inn was our temporary home for the next 4 days. We waited until the cold wind packed the snow so hard that the cutter could make the trip to our house by driving on top of the drifts.

The 13 Northern Pacific railroad tracks divided the city geographically and also socio-economically. We lived "on the wrong side of the tracks." We had barely enough money to buy groceries and make the modest house payments, but it wasn't hard to "keep up with the Jones's": the Jones's didn't have much either.

In the winter we lived in the kitchen — except for sleeping in unheated bedrooms. We couldn't afford to heat the rest of the house.

I went to Washington School, which stood where the Washington Square apartments are today, and graduated in 1929 from high school in what is now the old part of Central Middle School.

### An Exciting and Risky Adventure

I went to work full time in St. Paul at the age of 14, to support my parents. The bus fare for a week would have been $3.00 ($30.00 in today's dollars)—one third of my meager gross pay; so I hitchhiked both ways, winter and summer.

One morning, as we approached downtown St. Paul, the driver who had picked me up said, "I'm late for work; can you drive my car to the service station?" The service station was about a mile away through the downtown traffic. I had dearly wanted to drive a car, but never had the opportunity, since my folks didn't own one. So I simply said, "Yes."

I had never driven before, but I had watched many drivers and felt I would be able to make it just one mile. I never ever remember being so excited or nervous as when I slid across the front seat and under the steering wheel of that beautiful convertible.

My left leg shook violently as I tried to let the clutch out slowly, and the car bucked and jerked in unison with my leg. But eventually the car did pick up speed and, miraculously, I did make that mile without mishap, and drove into the service station. I turned the keys over to the attendant and walked away, realizing how fortunate I was to have completed that foolish mission without serious consequences.

### The Turning Point in My Life

It's a beautiful Sunday evening in September 1934. An 18-year-old-woman named Doris, new to the community, walks to the First Presbyterian Church (then located where the parking lot of the US Bank is today) to attend the young people's meeting. A kind woman comes along, explains that the meeting is at "the Manse" (the house where the minister lives), and offers to drive her there. She accepts.

The meeting is already in progress. A 20 year-old man is quick to notice her beauty and to realize she needs a ride home. After the meeting, he offers the invitation and she accepts. He is totally smitten!

We drove for a long time that night. It was entirely different from previous drives with other girls. I wanted to know as much as I could about this wonderful person. (Her recollection: "He asked so many questions!") The mere thought of physical advances seemed totally inappropriate. I just wanted to be near this person who thrilled me so with her mere presence. I did most of the talking (things haven't changed!)

Finally, it had to end, but not before I asked if I could see her again. The answer (gloriously) was a simple "Yes!"

### The Pinch of Poverty

In 1936, my brother was unemployed and had moved back home. My 1928 Essex (the Edsel of the 1920's) was ailing, and my $85 a month income wouldn't support four people, the Essex, the mortgage payments and the taxes. So I sold the Essex, turned the house over to the mortgage-holder and rented a cheap house in a poor neighborhood on the East side of St. Paul.

### Real Love

I walked the three miles to and from work. In the morning I would take the route which Doris and her father drove to work. When he saw me, he would let her off, and she and I would walk the rest of the way to work (usually a mile or so). On "date nights" (a couple of times during the week) I would ride all the way to her home in White Bear and have dinner there. Her CPA employer required Doris to study bookkeeping. So we would spend the evening studying her textbook. What a marvelous way to learn bookkeeping! At 11:00 P.M. I would catch the last bus back to St. Paul and walk the remaining mile back home.

Saturday night was our "big date" night, I would take the bus or hitchhike to her house. Her generous dad would lend us his car. The last bus to St. Paul was entirely too early to end the evening; so I would take a Stillwater bus that went by her house about 1:30 A.M., get off in Mahtomedi and catch the 2:00 A.M. owl streetcar back to St. Paul. That's real love!

### Marriage

We were married in 1938. I credit Doris with a great deal of the success I've had. I began to take the preparation for my Fellowship in the Society of Actuaries (insurance mathematicians) much more seriously. I felt that life now had a real purpose. We lived in St. Paul for 15 years, moved to Mahtomedi in 1953, and back to White Bear in 1987. Our roots are deep here. It's a wonderful, friendly community, and we enjoy living and serving in it. We don't expect to move ever again.

Butter

# The Good Life Around Beautiful White Bear Lake

*As remembered by*
*Harry M. Turgeon*

I am 93 years young as of March 1999 and can remember quite well the happenings, people and doings in and around White Bear Lake in the early part of this century.

In 1915, when I was 9 years old, my Uncle Louie La Bore and my Aunt Mary came for a visit to our house in North Minneapolis. They came by horse and buggy, quite a long journey in those days. Uncle Louie, then about 50 years old with a handlebar mustache and a gold chain across his expansive belly, was probably the biggest B.S.er in Ramsey County. Aunt Mary was my Ma's oldest sister. They proposed that I go with them to their farm near White Bear Lake where there would be more to eat.

Those were lean times. The war in Europe was raging and food was very expensive. For instance, potatoes, our main staple, were a dollar a peck. The equivalent today would be at least a hundred dollars a bushel.

Their farm was on what was later called Schuneman Road, which was then the main highway between White Bear Lake and St. Paul. Nowadays the site of the farm is near the Gem Lake Golf Course. The house is still there, greatly enlarged, but without the outbuildings.

## International Delivery

**A Big Day in White Bear When Fourteen Manure Spreaders Are Delivered**

### WHITE BEAR IMPLEMENT COMPANY

Distributing Agents for the Locality Make an Excellent Showing—See Picture Below

There were many little jobs to do there, and I enjoyed the whole thing. I would go up the ladder in the buggy shed to collect fresh eggs. The hens would poop on the buggy and it was my job to clean it up with water from the pump. There was weeding to do in the large onion patch across the road by the tracks, and hoeing in the corn, cabbage and potato fields.

*View of International Delivery Day. Photo circa 1914, courtesy of White Bear Press.*

There was no running water in the house, no telephone, nor electricity. An outhouse, a two-holer that stunk to high heaven, was in the back facing the plum orchard. There was a square board hanging in there with a deer hide nailed to it (something like a removable toilet seat to sit on). I was sternly ordered not to use it!

But it was not all work. On rainy days and at night, there was fishing on Goose Lake. There was an island in the middle covered with a fascinating jungle of chokecherries, gooseberries and bushes. An old wooden boat was tethered on shore, and my cousins and I would spend hours exploring the island. Now with Highway 61 going across, the island has disappeared.

Several of the women at our house and I had a special job—cleaning the one-room town hall. It was situated on the shore of Goose Lake. The filthy wooden floor had to be scrubbed. My job was to clean the spittoons. They were four or five large brass ones. I would carry them out, one at a time, across the road and dunk them into the lake and then polish them. I was paid 10 cents for my work, and I promptly spent it on slingshot rubbers and candy.

It seems that most of the men had the tobacco habit—chaws of tobacco, snuff, corncob pipe or roll-your-own (tailor-made were too expensive at 15 cents a pack). I was offered snuff once. I chewed it like gum, then swallowed the juice. It made me terribly sick behind the barn. That did it. Never again!

The folks up and down the road were of Canadian French descent, as was I, and all seemed to know each other. They spoke to each other in French, interspersed with a few English words. For example: one very old man called Monoak (my uncle), with reddish sandy hair and a mustache of the same color, hardly ever talked, mostly because he didn't know the English language well. But he sure could swear in English! He slept on a cot upstairs in the big room where I also slept. He would communicate with me somehow. He wanted small, live frogs to go fishing for bass on White Bear Lake. The frogs were numerous on the shore of the pond near where the golf course now is. By the way, that pond, now greatly shrunk in size, was at that time a vibrant 7-foot deep lake with muskrat houses, ducks and fish. I know about the fish because I planted some bullheads in there myself.

*Ad courtesy of White Bear Press. Circa 1914.*

*The LaBore family circa 1910. Grandmother LaBore, center, was 104 years old at the time of this photo. Photo courtesy of Dot Magnuson.*

I would go over there sometimes with the dog. I would lift him up high so he could see the ducks and he would yelp and swim out there, then rise up and look at me. When I would wave to go this way or that, yelping eagerly, he would swim after them. But he never caught a one. By the way, my Uncle Louie used to say, with a twinkle in his eye, that we could eat coots and mud hens on Fridays, as they were more fish than fowl.

There was one day that I can remember with great pleasure. It was hot, very hot, and cousin Jim LaBore and I were working in the hay field on the far end of the farm. Big Jim, as he was known, was big, very big, and I was a skinny little kid. He was cutting hay with the heavy mower and I was gathering some to be put into shocks. Later in the day, Big Jim called to me, "Arry, do you want to go swimming?" Somehow he couldn't or wouldn't pronounce the "H". When I eagerly said yes—(Aunt Mary had forbidden it)—Big Jim unhitched the horses and dropped the harness to the ground. The horses just stood there, breathing hard and looking tired. Their shoulders were galled red, and they were drenched with sweat. Big Jim pointed them toward a lake a few hundred yards away, later called Gem Lake. They plodded over there and then broke into a clumsy trot when they smelled the water. Big Jim shouted "Come on Arry" as he dashed past me, tearing off his clothes and straw hat as he ran. With a whoop he belly flopped into the water with a great splash and he hollered and hooted as he swam around. Then he called to me to come out and ride on his back, but I was afraid. Then he called to send the horses out, but they wouldn't go until I hit one with a stick. Jim grabbed the horse by the ears and swung onto his back, then soon slid off. Whooping and hollering and holding him by the tail, they'd go around the lake and I swear that the horse enjoyed it as much as Jim did. Later, after he had lifted me onto the wet horse on the way home, he said that we shouldn't tell Aunt Mary about our fun in the water. He was later drafted and went to France.

On occasion Aunt Mary, Uncle Louie and I would go to town in the buggy. We would park by the depot near the town square. It had a bandstand in the middle of the square. I held the horse while the band played. Auntie would visit with some neighbors and Uncle would walk across the park to a saloon. He'd come back smelling like a brewery. On the way home I would drive Lady, our white buggy horse. Without urging she would break into a smart trot and turn into our yard all by herself, anticipating, I guess, a measure of oats awaiting her.

*Railroad Park and town square with the original bandstand.*
*Photo courtesy of Lawrence R. (Bob) and Eileen Whitaker.*

I remember a house call a doctor made to treat Auntie. He came by horse and buggy and I would hold the horse for him. Afterward, when he came out, he discussed his fee with Uncle. If Uncle didn't have a dollar, the doctor would take a chicken. When Uncle pointed out the young rooster Doc wanted, I would shoot it in the head with my slingshot, then quickly wring its neck and put it in a gunnysack in the back of the buggy.

More interesting was when the animal doctor came. The sick horse was led out and the vet had a gizmo, which I found out years later, was called a twitch. He put the loop over the horse's lower lip and twisted it, which must have been very painful. When the horse quieted down he then poured a bottle of medicine down his throat and said he would stay all night. I went into the barn early the next morning, and he said that the horse would be fine. He had me lead the horse to the trough to drink and then around the woodpile.

The horse would walk slower, sniffing the ground, then with a grunt would lay down and nicker with pleasure as he attempted to roll over on the gravel and chicken poop that covered the yard. Later, I helped the vet brush and currycomb him, which the horse seemed to enjoy.

I spent the next five enjoyable summers at White Bear Lake. The last year, 1920, I got a paying job doing farm work for a man named Ratte. He was considered rich! He had a job in St. Paul and had a brand new Model T Ford. I worked there all summer doing a man's work. Mr. Ratte, his wife and two children liked me and later toward fall suggested that I stay there and do the chores. They would pay me a little and I could go to the new high school on Bald Eagle Avenue. I was sorely tempted.

The decision was resolved when I got a letter from Ma back in Minneapolis saying that she was starting housekeeping again. My Pa had died suddenly the year before and I was needed to help support Ma and my younger brother and sister. It was 1920 and I was 14. I got a job as errand boy at a printing company and stayed there for 16 years. Later, during the depression, I became a Minneapolis fireman. I stayed at that job for the next 31 years.

My thoughts continually go back to those good years. My first ride on a truck was on one that delivered beer around Bald Eagle and White Bear Lakes. I also remember the walks on the way to church on Sunday mornings with my sling shot ready. Rides around Goose Lake to St. Mary of the Lake Catholic Church and the trips by street car to Wildwood Park on the other side of the lake were memorable, too.

Occasionally there would be a party. Word would go out, up and down the road and as far away as White Bear Lake, Hugo and Little Canada. The big kitchen table would be removed and the floor scrubbed. There would be someone playing the fiddle, and someone with a high singsong voice would call the do-si-dos and the allemande left. Oatmeal would be sprinkled on the floor and they would square dance. The lamp was put high up on the kitchen stove and everyone would have a good time.

The nights were pitch black, and the ladies would go out to the biffy always two or three at a time. One would go in and the rest would stand guard. The men mostly peed on the manure pile by the barn. They would stand around out there and maybe pass around a pint bottle of moonshine or drink a bottle of beer. Sometimes the guests would stay all night and sleep two or three to a bed.

When I was eleven or twelve, I was allowed to milk our three cows. I would get about a half pail of milk. While it was still warm I would pour it into our new DeLaval cream separator in the kitchen. I would turn the crank handle faster and faster, then open the spigot and the cream would pour out of one spout and the skim out the other. The skim at that time was considered not fit to drink and was poured into the slop barrel for the pigs.

When one of the cows went dry Uncle would hitch the team to the hay wagon and then tie the cow in back. He would give me elaborate instructions on driving the team over the gravel road to the Tessier's farm, about two miles away. He would tell me to give the reins to one of the boys, and go into their kitchen and have a glass of milk and a cookie. It never worked out that way. When I got there, the boys said never mind what Uncle Louie said, just drive the damn wagon through the wide open gate in back.

The bull and some cows were some distance away and when the boys called, the huge bull came thundering over and I was scared. The boys said not to worry, because the bull had only one thing on his mind. So we just sat in the wagon and watched that curious performance.

Over the years I'd acquired many pets. One was the cutest little owl, only about 6 inches high, that I named Hootie. We rigged up a branch stand in the nook behind the kitchen stove. He would sleep most of the day and at night I would feed him angle worms or grubs or meat snatched from the table. I remember once I caught a live mouse and dangled it in

*Ad courtesy of White Bear Press. Circa 1914.*

front of him. Hootie became extremely excited, made a grab and caught the struggling young mouse by the head, held him for a long time, then gulped a little of the mouse, then gulped again until the mouse gradually disappeared and just the tail was sticking out. Then Hootie went to sleep. I suspect that one of the women of our household finally let Hootie out an open door. She was continually complaining about Hootie flying around her clean kitchen.

Another pet I had was a crow. I had watched several crows circling over a high tree near Goose Lake for a long time. One day, when the time was right, I climbed up that tree and found the nest far up on a precarious branch. I was in luck because there were 3 baby crows in there. I took the biggest, put him in my shirt, and with the crows dive-bombing me, got down safely. I named him Blackie and put him in the empty corncrib. Uncle Louie, jokingly, said that I could teach Blackie to talk when he got older. I would drop kernels of corn and angleworms into his gaping mouth. All went well until one day I showed a visiting young boy, about 3 or 4, how to feed Blackie. When I went away for a while the young boy fed Blackie some small rocks from the yard and that was the end of Blackie.

Since I was barefooted most of that time, I had to wash my feet at the pump or at the slightly warmer water in the leaky wooden horse-trough. Sometimes I was given a sliver of homemade soap and went over to the lake by the present golf course to wash all over. But let me tell about the soap making. A big fire was built early in the morning over by the woodpile and I helped keep it going all day. A giant iron pot was suspended over it. Then Uncle or someone would dump in the residue of a recent pig killing (the feet, head, tail and, yes, the insides, etc.). Sometimes an odoriferous pailful or two, of questionable age and smell, would be brought over by a neighbor and dumped in the pot. Uncle would come and shove in some wood-ashes and then stir that noxious brew, which was a dark brown-orange color with a long paddle. When it was cold and congealed the top would be cut into squares for soap. I don't remember where the rest went.

Every year or so I would go to town for a few days and visit some of my cousins, the LaBores and the Bibeaus. Cousin Maurice was exactly my age, knew the area very well, and we would explore the downtown. We went swimming at the public beach and we would watch a horse being shod at the blacksmith shop. I had my first ride on a motor vehicle and saw my first moving picture show in White Bear Lake, because Maurice's sister Irene had free passes.

I recently went for a nostalgic drive with my son Don, and my daughter Ione around the area of White Bear Lake. The central park has disappeared and everything has been changed so much that I could hardly find my way around. The house where Maurice lived is still there (on Fourth between Highway 61 and Bald Eagle Avenue) with the window above the front porch. It was that very same window that his mom warned us boys not to pee through the screen at night because then it would get rusty.

The Vincent's house across from the golf course is still the same. I remember playing "Run sheep run" and "Last couple out" with the numerous Vincent girls on their big front yard. At about 9 o'clock their mom would come out and clap her hands and say that it was time to go in. She would point her finger at me and tell me that I should go home now because it was getting late.

I have fond memories of those carefree days of long ago and they remind me of that poem by John Greenleaf Whittier:

*"Barefoot Boy" painting by Harry Turgeon*

*Blessings on thee, little man,*
*Barefoot boy with cheek of tan!*
*With thy turned-up pantaloons,*
*And thy merry whistled tunes;*
*With thy red lip, redder still*
*Kissed by strawberries on the hill;*
*With the sunshine on thy face,*
*Through thy torn brim's jaunty grace;*
*From my heart I give thee joy—*
*I was once that barefoot boy!*

# Remembering White Bear Lake

*As Remembered by*
*Jack Herzog*

I grew up in White Bear in the 20's and 30's when we still had dirt roads… My grandfather owned and operated Cook's Jewelry Store, just kiddy-corner from the old park, now housing the U.S. Post Office. The streets were being named after some local residents, and we've been told "Cook Avenue" was one named after my grandfather. Many of my friends had streets named after their parents. Downtown was small then. The Avalon Theater, Williams Drug Store, Parenteau's Department Store were just a few of the stores. Remember Kohler's Soda Bar? That was the hangout for all the kids. We attended St. Mary's of the Lake grade school. The stockyard was only a block away, near the railroad tracks. Every day after school, we would meet at the stockyard, climb the fence, and watched kids with disagreements fight.

*Looking north on Washington Avenue. Photo courtesy of Lawrence R. (Bob) and Eileen Whitaker.*

My brother and I owned our first business at ages 8 and 6. We sold frogs for 10 cents a dozen to fishermen from St. Paul. One time about four in the morning, some men came to buy frogs. Dad was awakened, and went to the garage where we kept the frogs in a cardboard box. The box was 3 feet square. Dad was trying to catch the frogs and ended up inside the box! We went out of business that same night!

Our days were never without things to do. Mom got many a gray hair hearing about things we did. One day a boat drifted into our dock area. It was full of water, so we dragged it up on land, emptied it, and let it dry out. Then we scraped, puttied, and painted it. On launching though, it leaked like a sieve, and while one of us rowed, the other bailed: but, it was OUR own boat!

Even in the winter we seemed to attract trouble. Skating on the lake was fun when it first froze. Playing follow the leader early one season, the leader went through the ice. All behind followed right in. Fortunately, the water was shallow, and home was only a block away. We came in with icicles all over our bodies. Poor Mom!

I can remember the rig that was put on the lake to cut the ice for the next summer. That was fun to watch. There was a big barn in town where the ice was stored.

I also remember the local junk man who would go up and down the street with his horse-driven wagon, hollering, "Rags, rags!" We'd follow with, "What does your mother eat?" "Rags, rags." So many memories: so much fun! I still make many trips to White Bear, reminiscing. It really doesn't seem like so long ago!!

# Cars, Gas and the War

*As remembered by*
*Helen Lindbeck Peterson*

We always had a car. The first one I remember was a 1932 panel truck. It was a Chevrolet. Daddy had fashioned a bench in the back for us to sit on, and the rest of the floor was for play. Often on a Sunday afternoon we would have a ride in the country, then a picnic lunch in a quiet place. Seldom did our family go alone, but most often we had our little friends with, or friends of my folks, or both.

I think the next car we got was a 1938 black Chev sedan. All cars had standard transmissions in those days, and the gearshift lever was on the floor. From my seat behind Daddy, I had watched the shift patterns and the use of the clutch with eager anticipation of the day when I could drive. That day came in 1943 on a Sunday when we went to see some friends in Ham Lake. The roads were two-lane asphalt with little room for error when approaching another car. I was a tall 13 years old. I remember especially overcompensating when I went too far left or right. It was harder than it looked when Daddy drove. Needless to say, every trip after that I pleaded with him to drive. And many times he let me.

When I turned 15, my driver's license came in the mail as one of the few presents Daddy ever gave me.

One Saturday morning I asked Daddy for the car to go to a friend's house. When he said, "No", I couldn't believe it. He so seldom denied me anything. Then he explained that there was very little gas left and we were all going on a family outing Sunday. Gasoline was rationed during WW II. He told me to call my friend and explain. I reminded him they had no telephone, so he told me I could go, but that he would "check the odometer". I went to my friend's house, disconnected the speedometer cable behind the dashboard and off we went to pick up another girlfriend. This friend had a gasoline pump in the yard, since farmers got all the gas they needed to run their tractors in order to feed the nation.

We pumped the glass top full and let gravity feed it into the car's gas tank. It took us a good long time and a lot of driving to use up the whole tank of gas, but when the needle on the gauge came down near the empty mark, we went back to the first house. I reconnected the cable and went home.

The artist has drawn a caricature here, but it fits the point of the text. Read and see if you don't think so.

The hardest thing in this world is actually to do things—to work.

It seems to be the bane of human nature to talk and talk and talk and then fail to execute.

Work, work, work—that's the only sure road to success in anything.

If this is so for the individual it is a hundred times more so for the people as a town whole.

Getting up steam for a town booming campaign is easy. It's the going ahead that's hard—the actual work of arriving somewhere.

We have a splendid opportunity in this town to go ahead.

You know that.

Are we going to do it ?

*Ad courtesy of White Bear Press.*

The following day my family set out on our outing. The needle on the speedometer bounced all over the dial. My mother asked Daddy what was wrong with it and his reply was that often cables froze up in the winter and that must have happened to this one. I tapped him on the shoulder and said, "No, Daddy, this is what happened." I then told him about getting a tank full of gas, having a hard time getting rid of it, disconnecting and reconnecting the cable, and all the places we'd been and the fun we'd had. He didn't get angry with me, but laughed and thought it rather clever. I think he was a scamp as a youth, too!

In 1947, the summer between my junior and senior years in high school, Daddy bought me a car. It was a 1932 Plymouth in mint condition. It had belonged to H. L. Phillips, who regularly took it to Reed's garage on Fourth Street and Washington Avenue for servicing. It had probably never got so far as the city limits. The windshield was flat and vertical and hinged at the top so it swung out for ventilation. The gas gauge didn't work, so I carried a clean stick to dip into the tank. The upholstery was a drab brownish color and made of fuzzy frieze that stuck to bare skin and itched. One soon found out how many friends one had when there was a car available. We saw nearly every road in our county and several surrounding counties. Nearly everyone who rode had a shot at driving, as well. It was a great time!

That summer, Daddy's sister came home from her missionary assignment in Africa with her new husband and their son. Daddy handed the keys to my Plymouth to his new brother-in-law with the remark that they would see a lot more relatives if they could get around. I don't recall how long they were here and used my car, but I do remember being very angry that I didn't have the use of it.

Daddy didn't buy and wrap presents. He gave of himself every day.

*Ad courtesy of White Bear Press.*

# Living on the Lake

*As Remembered by*
*C. M. Ingham*

We lived on shore of White Bear Lake for twenty-five years. This was the same lake my grandfather relished so much and fished with such zeal. It is the same lake on which he tried to teach me to fish. In reality, he taught me how to row a 400-pound rowboat from which he trolled two lines, one for each of us. I never caught anything bigger than my thumb, while he caught lots of sunfish, crappies, and rock bass. I did learn, however, the topography and wind patterns of the lake at age ten.

*The dock of the White Bear Yacht Club.*
*Photo courtesy of Lawrence R. (Bob) and Eileen Whitaker.*

My grandfather told me wild stories of the lake and its history. He even showed me the hoops of a sunken covered wagon, seen through the ice off the east side of the Peninsula in 60 feet of water. I never found out why some nut would be trying to drive a covered wagon across the lake with a team of horses in the winter, but years later, saw several nuts try the same thing—driving cars, pickup trucks and dump trucks—with the same results. With all these things going into the water you wonder how there was room for the fish—and how the oil and gas from these machines affected the fish.

*Sailboat at Williams House on the shores*
*of White Bear Lake in the late 1800s. Photo courtesy*
*of Lawrence R. (Bob) and Eileen Whitaker.*

When I became a resident of the Peninsula in 1960, I found what carnage and garbage the fishing fraternity inflicts upon our lake. Each spring I found the spiked bottoms of ice fishing houses floating onto my beach along with hundreds of beer cans, whiskey bottles and broken glass littering the shallow water where my children played and swam.

White Bear Lake is noted for fine fishing, sailing, water skiing, ice boating, ice fishing and just pleasure boat riding. Not all of these people believe the others should be allowed to do their thing. Fishermen, for instance, scream when water skiers pass over their 100-foot trolling lines. Sailors scream when fishermen anchor at the racing buoys during a sailboat race. Water skiers yell at the sailors and fishermen to get out of the way. The pleasure boaters are all busy dodging everyone else while avoiding docks.

One day I was repairing the carpet on my dock when I heard a moan out on the lake behind me. There was much activity on this nice day with many water skiers out, but I was not watching them. As I turned, I saw a man lying on his back in the water, fortunately wearing a lifejacket, gasping for air, about 10 yards off the end of my dock. I asked if he needed help. When he gasped out, "Yes!" I told him to stand up since he was in only five feet of water. He sheepishly rolled over, stood and waded to my dock. I saw that one of his water skis had floated onto my shore so I retrieved it and offered him a beer. As we sat on the bench of my dock I heard his story.

He had been skiing behind a boat that carried two friends—one of whom was supposed to be watching behind while the driver watched out front. Apparently, both were looking to the front and never saw him fall off his skis. As we sat there for about ten minutes, he became madder and madder at his idiot buddies who had left him. When he fell, the tip of one ski had hit him in the chest, knocking the wind out of him; the lifejacket rolled him onto his back, saving his life.

About 15 minutes later we saw a boat roar around the point of the Peninsula, race past us and disappear around another point, only to return very slowly searching, searching, with two scared guys holding one empty ski. My visitor finally stood up and yelled at them and, with great relief, they joined forces with much swearing and apologizing.

Several times I have discovered strange things on my beach, such as 8 or 10 bras of various sizes and colors, a few bottoms of swimsuits, (men's and women's), planks and sections of someone else's dock, which must have come loose in a storm or perhaps was poorly put together and floated over to visit us. I found a whole Class C sailboat with no sail, bouncing on the rocks one morning. I tied it up to the end of my dock thinking whomever lost it might come looking for it. Three days later I called Johnson Boat Works and asked if anyone had reported a boat lost or stolen. No, but they would come get it and keep it until someone did. Two months later I saw Buster Johnson, who told me the guy who owned the boat had reported it stolen, collected from the insurance company, sold the one I found, and bought a new one!

The city of White Bear Lake had a lovely public beach directly across the lake from me, which was very well attended—but not so busy that it didn't grow weeds. The city decided to cut the weeds, which they left to drift into all the shores across the lake. The weeds piled up on our side and proceeded to ROT and STINK! Calls to the city government met with little response so we offered to return the refuse, but were turned down. So we raked it up and transported it to the park in the center of town one midnight in our village dump truck. There was no more weed cutting done, but there was the formation of the White Bear Lake Conservation District. It consisted of two members from each of the five communities around the lake. Its job was to patrol and keep the lake clean for the enjoyment of all who loved and used the lake—with some stringent laws and fines for the lawbreakers.

One of our annual problems was the ice-fishing season. Invariably someone would spot ice formed on the lake and immediately race home to tow his icehouse out on the lake. Also, inevitably, we had several cars and trucks sink through the too-thin ice. The ordinance we had required anyone to remove said vehicle within 24 hours and pay a $150 fine.

All went well until one young man left his car, which was worth less than $150, in the lake and joined the Army. His father told us we could not collect from him in the service, but he was wrong. We had his Army pay garnisheed to cover the cost of the fine and recovery tow.

We even had an embarrassed White Bear Lake City snow removal truck driver who fell through the ice trying to dump his load of snow on the lake. The city paid the fine—but did get the truck back in one day and hired a new driver.

A friend of mine was so enamored of snowmobiles that he bought two of them. As soon as he saw ice on the lake he tested it by walking on it so he felt he would be safe on his snowmobile. He and his vehicle sank 25 feet from shore. He waded in, backed up the second machine to rescue the first one, but failed to stop soon enough. Two down! Undaunted, he backed his Bronco pickup down, fixed a cable to the snowmobile. Not having 4-wheel drive, the weight and steep bank were too much for the Bronco so it joined the two snowmobiles. He finally hired a tow truck to retrieve all his toys.

*Winter scene on White Bear Lake, ice boating. Courtesy of White Bear Press, circa 1900.*

Another friend, Lam, loved to ice boat and he had made one from a kit, which worked well when there was little snow on the lake. One day Lam was streaking up from his house toward the Peninsula when he hit open water over the deep hole there. He had heavy hunting gear on, but luckily didn't let go of the iceboat when he hit the water. Maneuvering it over to solid ice, he slid the boat and himself out of the water, set up the sail and went home. By the time he reached his beach his clothing was frozen stiff on him. He rolled off the boat, rolled across his front yard to the door, kicked at it until Janet, his wife, opened it to see what the noise was. She towed him in front of the ever-present fire until she could uncover him. A couple of shots of brandy and coffee and he was ready to go again.

# The Barge

*As Remembered by*
*C. Allen Lindholm*

Mr. Davidson, who used to live on the end of Clark Street in White Bear Lake, had a swimming raft made of galvanized water tanks. The lake was shallow there, so he put a 5-hp motor on the raft to push it out into deeper water, whenever he used it. That raft gave me the idea to build my barge on Bald Eagle Lake.

My dock was on the east shore with the prevailing winds out of the west. The water was often wavy and not the best for water skiing or surfboarding. I thought it would be nice to have a raft large enough to hold the entire club members and equipment so we could move to calmer waters and not trespass on other people's docks. It would have no railings, an upper deck to dive from, and enough flotation so if everyone went to one side, it would not tip or roll. I wanted the Water Club to pay for it but I didn't get any backing so I decided to build it myself. I got Irwin (Slim) Flaten, who worked for NSP, to get me two 30' cedar utility poles. The beauty of using cedar poles was they could bend, which would make the raft stronger. Tom Chapin was tearing down a water tower, so he got the 2 x 8's and 4 x 6's I needed, plus a lot of salvage lumber. Bill Johnson's dad was tearing down his cottage on the back of his property so he gave me the fir flooring from it. I needed 40–55 gallon barrels. Harry Robbins, Vice President of Rayette, gave me twelve from Rayette Labs. I got six more from Vadnais Motors and I paid $16 for sixteen from Archer Daniel's Midland Company in Minneapolis. Terry Rooney found the rest. We used Terry Rooney's dump truck to haul all the materials.

I built the main frame in our lower yard. I had a lot of help from my brother, Jim and some of his friends (Dick Roeder, Bill Johnson, Bob Lorentzen, Gary Olinger and others) and my friend, Jerry Fasching. We cut the 2 x 8's onto the utility poles and attached the bumper plates on the ends. When the frame was built we loaded it on two utility trailers and walked it down to Collette's boathouse (a boat livery on Hugo Road). We launched it and floated it on six barrels back to my dock where we finished building it. It was really something to see take shape since there wasn't anything like it anywhere. The main deck ended up 30' 6" long x 12' 6" wide. The upper deck was 14' x 11'. It would only take about 4" of draft. The motor well was about 7' in from the back. I did not know how much power I would need to move it. I started out using my Dad's 5-hp motor. I soon found out I could not control it in a wind (or even a slight breeze). Pete Peltier added his 4.5-hp Martin but it still wasn't powerful enough. I still needed a bigger motor! I bought a new motor for my runabout because the pinion gear was slipping on my old 25-hp Evinrude. I decided to take this old motor and try it on the barge. I found it was big enough to move and control the barge, and the pinion gear did not seem to slip when shifting gears as it had done on the runabout. Also, I now had a reverse gear for docking.

About two years later I enclosed the motor well to prevent people from falling into it and also to cut down on the sound from the motor. I built shelves above the well, which I used for storing gas cans and other equipment. My brother Jim made me 12 wooden chairs. Bill (Wimpy) Rundquist gave me his old pop cooler and I added several charcoal burners. All of this equipment fit easily on the barge.

That barge held a lot of memories for a lot of people from 1955 to 1976. Ralph Solberg (Solie), who played a lot of ukulele, named it "The Barge" and that name stuck for its entire life. It was rebuilt only once during this time. BARGE PARTIES!!! We had many barge parties, (Water Club parties, Airport parties, Neighbor parties, Office parties, Uller Snowski Club parties, Muskrat parties, Family Reunion parties etc.) They were all great.

Of all the barge parties we had, one of the highlights was when we had the Cypress Garden water skiers on board in 1956. These skiers were in town for an 8-day ski show sponsored by WCCO. The show was held on the Mississippi River for the Minneapolis Aquatennial. Nancy and Don Harding had gone to see the show. Afterwards they started talking with the skiers and invited them out to Bald Eagle Lake for a barge party on Saturday night. Their usual amusement at night, so they told us, was dying their hair. Some of the great skiers that were in town were Willa McGuire, the reigning female world champion (and was for 8 years) and Nancy Rideout, a champion jumper. Scotty Scott, one of the best Cypress jumpers, was also here. The night of the party he was a blond. No one knows what his real hair color was. It was a perfect night for the party, with a full moon. We gathered at the Harding's. Tom Chapin asked Hamm's to donate the party favors and the beer. We provided the steaks. Terry Rooney tied his pontoon alongside the barge for "fish house" runs. The Cyprus Gardens' boat driver, Jack, originally from Australia, wanted to know the specifics on how I had built the barge. He was planning to go back to Florida and buy up all the barrels he could find to build one, too. At a later date, when Sue Crocher (a Cyprus Gardens skier) was questioned at a "Man on the Street" interview as to what she liked best about the Minneapolis Aquatennial, she emphatically said, "The barge party on Bald Eagle Lake." This was printed in the Star newspaper. Dick Nesbit also mentioned Sue's reaction on one of his TV sports program interviews.

There were many other parties and outings that were memorable. Katie Ruff, who lived on the south shore of the take, was a senior airline hostess for Northwest Airlines (at that time we called them stewardesses). She used to have a summer picnic for all her co-hostesses at her house. One time she called me and asked if I would bring the barge down for the picnic. I not only brought the barge, but also my runabout. I asked John Benson to bring the floatplane. I taught a lot of those pretty girls how to water ski that day. It was the largest number of people I ever had on the barge, 87 passengers! Can you imagine Johnny Benson giving airline hostesses airplane rides! But they really enjoyed it. He dropped the door so it was quite an experience for those girls to be flying in a breeze. There were 77 girls that day and just ten guys. Wow!!!

We used The Barge for cruising the fishing area with the game warden on the upper deck during the Kids' Fishing Contest. The Bald Eagle Sportsman's Club sponsored the contest. We used it as a portable dock for skiers to ski from during ski shows. The Water Club held meetings on board. The White Bear Chamber used it, so did the VFW and the Legion. There were family reunions, office parties and other parties. It was also used as a workhorse to transport boat lifts and move docks around the lake. It was the first love boat as many of my friends met their wives on board. But the best time of all was when I rigged up a way to steer it from the top deck. I would cruise around the lake in the early mornings when the lake was still. When my friends would see me, they would come out and tie their boats to the back of The Barge and join me enjoying the morning sun. We always wondered what the rich people were doing that was better than this.

The Barge was also a camper. Jerry Fasching, or my brothers and I, would rig up our jungle hammocks, anchor and spend the night in the middle of the lake. The airport gang used to spend hours at night looking for the Russian Sputnik as it passed overhead. Johnny Benson was always the first to spot it. It went over every ninety minutes. One night Johnny spotted it four times!

And of course, The Barge was a great fishing vessel. My dad, brothers, neighbors and friends caught many northern and pan fish from the deck of the barge, over the years. Often the fish would be cleaned on the spot and cooked. Fish never tasted so good. One summer, my good friend Lee Countryman, who had moved to California years before, visited Red Murnane and I, wanted to go fishing. I fired up The Barge and he and I fished off the front deck. Red Murnane cleaned them at the middle deck, and our wives, Joyce and Lois, fried them at the stem. Lee could not believe how wonderful Minnesota fishing had become since he was a boy living here in the 40's.

"Breakfast on The Barge" was an annual event. On the morning of the 4th of July, we would go out to the island, hide from the wind and have bacon and eggs and pancakes. My folks would always invite a few neighbors and friends to join us. The fishermen trolling by would always comment on how good that bacon smelled. In later years, other pontoon boats would tie up to us and join in the fun.

*Single-deck barge built by Tom Chapin.*
*Photo courtesy of Paul Chapin.*

# Hogan's Grocery Store

*As Remembered by*
*Lorraine Billingsley (Hogan)*

My parents, Julius and Gertrude Hogan, moved to White Bear Lake in 1921. They rented a house at first, and then bought a house at Fourth Street and Miller Avenue. (It is the only house still standing that's located on the block where Washington Square is now located.) My father operated a small garage to repair cars. This was connected to the house at that location.

On January 23, 1935, they opened a small grocery store at 810 Fourth Street, which continued until 1955 when they retired. It was located just to the east of Bloom Avenue (which was then known as White Bear Avenue) where it intersected with Fourth Street. It was next to what is now known as Cup-n-Cone. The store was named Hogan's Grocery and was open 7:00 A.M. to 9:00 P.M. Monday through Saturday and 7:00 A.M. to 2:00 P.M. on Sunday. Because we lived in a house connected to the store, people would call us in cases of unexpected company when the store was closed. These were the days of ice boxes and poor refrigerators, so most people shopped every day or two.

This is where I grew up and worked, and I can still picture the store in my mind's eye. As you came in the door to your right were all the cleaning supplies; Oxydol, Ivory, Fels Naptha, Old Dutch Cleanser, and Lifebuoy soap. There was a little aisle for us to walk, and in front of the cleaning supplies was the cookie case. There were 1' x 1' deep boxes that were covered by glass covers where bulk cookies were sold. The cases were about 4 boxes wide and 4 boxes deep. Next to the cookies was the meat counter where we sold lunchmeat, cheese, wieners, bologna, milk, etc. If a person wanted steak or the like, they went to a butcher shop. At the back wall were the canned fruits and vegetables, and crackers. Directly in front of that was the counter. The counter had large, heavy, pullout drawers where brown sugar, powdered sugar, navy beans, rice and peas were stored and sold in bulk amounts. On top of the counter was the cash register, the scale, meat slicer for lunchmeat and open counter space. During Lent there would be a large box of smoked fish on the counter.

The clerks at the store waited on people and put the purchases on the counter until the order was complete. Then the purchases were added up and put in bags. Customers had the option of paying with cash or charging their goods. The left side wall of the store had a cabinet for fruits and vegetables. The fruits came in wooden boxes, and each piece of fruit was wrapped in tissue. Then came the miscellaneous. There were the school supplies; pencils, pens, pen points, bottles of ink, paper colors. There were penny valentines, Fourth of July fireworks and Christmas cards all in their season. We had needles and thread, cigarettes, tobacco, cigars, cigarette rollers and papers to roll your own cigarettes.

Then came the things that the children loved. There was a very large candy case with the nickel candy bars on the top shelf and the penny candy on the bottom shelf. Lots of variety! We also had an ice cream case that had pints and quarts, if you really wanted a large amount of ice cream. There were also Popsicles, Cheerios, Fudgesicles, and Dreamsicles that had a "free" stick every once in awhile. If you found a free stick, you could turn it in for another nickel ice cream of your choice. There were also cones: two dips for a nickel.

*Greengard's (1912), another local grocery, noted for waiting on the customers with personal attention.*
*Photo courtesy of C. Jane Jackson*

Another popular item was the pop cooler. It was a large metal box that had a refrigeration unit in it that circulated cooled water. Glass bottles of pop were put into the cold water, and people were able to buy a cold bottle of pop for a nickel.

Right in the middle of the store was the bread case and shelves for potato chips, etc. Do you remember the twin loaves of bread and cans of potato chips?

During the school year, when students still had one hour for lunch, many of them would walk from the junior-senior high school, bring their lunch, buy a bottle of pop, some potato chips or a candy bar, and stand around and eat their lunch. The store was always full of kids during the noon hour.

During World War II years, there were food coupons and red and blue tokens, about the size of a dime, that were given in change. If people heard you had sugar or cocoa, there was a rush to buy it. My parents took packages of cigarettes and divided them in half so there would be two packages of ten cigarettes. Cigarettes were very hard to get during World War II. People didn't care what brand they were, they were thankful to get any cigarettes. These are some of my memories of Hogan's Grocery.

# A Walk Down Memory Lane

*As Remembered by*
*Delores Bloom Kulkey*

I have lived in White Bear Lake all of my life except for three years. During that time I was with my husband, who was in the army, stationed at Camp Haan, California. He went into the army with the White Bear National Guard in 1941.

I was born on February 13, 1913, in a house on the corner of Sixth and Division, a block and a half away from the railroad tracks. The noise from the trains put me to sleep every night. My grandparents built the house. My brother, sister, and Dad were all born in this house, which is still standing. My Dad was born in 1891. When one of his brothers, Carl, was three months old, in 1880, my grandparents moved and built the house. The city of White Bear Lake now owns it, though they were planning on destroying it and some of the other houses nearby. We are hoping they change their minds.

This is the big American-LaFrance pumper, of 1,000 gallons per minute capacity, which was recently purchaser at a cost of $14,000. It is known as "The Metropolitan" model, weights eight tons and is the last word in fire-fighting equipment. There is none better anywhere. It is one of the big fellows which do heavy work in the big cities.

*Photo courtesy of White Bear Press*

My Dad worked for the city of White Bear Lake as Superintendent of the Water and Sewer Department for 45 years. He was also a volunteer fireman for about that long. He and Mr. Wallin, who lived down the street from us, were the drivers of the fire truck. When the fire siren went off, it was quite a race to see who could get there first, because the one who got there first got to drive the truck!

As to the railroad, my Mother told me a story from when I was about four years old. My Dad was working at his brother's grocery store, The Mercantile, where Ciresi's liquor store is now. Well, this one evening, I wanted to go outside and wait for my Daddy to come home from work. I was supposed to stay in our yard, but I disobeyed. I walked down to Fourth Street where there were quite a number of railroad tracks and many trains. The switchman for the railroad lived across the street from us. When he saw me, he asked what I was doing there. I said I was waiting for my Daddy. He knew my Dad would be coming by soon, so he took me by the hand, and that evening I helped him switch trains until my Dad came along. Dad almost passed out when he saw me. I thought it was a lot of fun. As you can imagine, I got quite a talking to and was told never to do that again.

Another time, my uncle, my Dad's oldest brother, was coming home from work one night and as he was crossing the railroad tracks, he heard a whining. He looked and noticed one of the boxcars was slightly open. He peeked in and opened the door a little more and there was a St. Bernard puppy. He took it home and gave it to my Dad. They were never separated. My Dad sure loved it. He used to hitch the dog up to a wagon or a sled and go down to the lake and haul water back for his mother's wash, as there wasn't any water softener at that time.

It was simply wonderful when doctors made house calls. I don't think we thought much about it. It was just expected. It was so nice to call up the doctor and in a very short while he was at our house. No waiting in line! I can't remember what they charged for a house call, but I do know it was very inexpensive.

*Railroad Park with the original bandstand, circa 1920. Photo courtesy of Lawrence R. (Bob) and Eileen Whitaker.*

When we were children and teenagers, we always found something to do. We played a lot of games of hide-and-seek; pom-pom pullaway; and some I can't remember by name. In the summer we played a lot of softball and we went swimming every day, regardless of the weather. We had quite long walks but we didn't mind it at all. Sometimes we went to the movie theater, which used to be next to the White Bear Armory. There was no colored film and no talking or sound but some lady would play the piano during the whole movie. There was a bowling alley down below the theater. On Friday nights during the summer, there was always a band concert in the park. There used to be a bandstand in the middle of the park and a sidewalk all around it. So all of the girls would walk around the park and all the boys would stand around and watch.

In the winter, we would go ice skating at an outdoor rink at the Webster School. When the Hippodrome was built, we went skating there. Open skating was Wednesday, Friday, and Saturday nights, as well as Sunday afternoons. I think it was $1.50 for a season ticket. I never missed it; I loved to skate. We also went tobogganing at the Dellwood Golf Course. We used to walk all the way up and back, but we thought nothing about it. No one had cars, so we walked everywhere. Why, I even walked with my date to our senior prom, which was held at the White Bear High School, in the old gym, which we called the pit.

As I take my walks today these memories walk beside me.

*Lake Avenue (circa 1910); Beautiful and memorable today as well as yesterday. Photo courtesy of Lawrence R. (Bob) and Eileen Whitaker.*

# Solheim Farm

*As Remembered by*
*Virginia Zollner Terry Merrill*

My family moved to White Bear Lake in 1941. We lived on Solheim Farm, which was located on the west side of Bald Eagle Lake. On the farm was a huge barn with a magnificent hayloft, which was used by many of the neighbor kids to play basketball. There was a majestic oak tree in the yard, and the last time I visited the site, it still stood, more beautiful than I had remembered!

Another part of the farm consisted of property known as the Girl Scout Camp, which is in the vicinity of Hobe Lane, just north of the stream running from Bald Eagle to Otter Lake. During my years on Solheim, the camp was seldom used, at least not by the Girl Scouts. However, I understand that many other things did go on in those woods!

*Ad courtesy of White Bear Press.*

We had a great hill behind the house that was perfect for skiing. The only problem was that once you got down it, you had to carry your skis back up. (No tow rope for us.)

About a half mile south of us on Bald Eagle was a place called Keiffer's. Mr. Keiffer rented boats to people who would come out from the Twin Cities to fish. One of my first moneymaking endeavors was to dig angleworms for bait and sell them to Mr. Keiffer. The only problem was that we turned around and spent all the money on candy, etc., which Mr. Keiffer had for sale.

We went to school at St. Mary's, and in those days, school buses were not available. Each morning and evening, Mom or Dad had to chauffeur us to school.

Also connected with Solheim Farm was a very large home, built by Mr. Hobe, who was, we were told, the first Consul to Norway. This home was situated on a beautiful piece of lakeshore, with many acres surrounding it. My memories of it were as a child, but I think they are fairly accurate.

Some of the unique features of the property included a solarium or greenhouse; elaborately tiled bathrooms; a beautiful front porch; a paneled dining room; a built-in exercise unit in the hall, consisting of rope pulls to build up biceps; a huge kitchen; and a carriage house with an apartment above.

In the yard, where trees had been removed, the parts remaining in the ground had been made into chairs using woven vines as the back rests. It made a very unique, interesting chair out of what would have otherwise been the stump of a tree.

The Solheim Farm is now part of the Ramsey County Open Space, I am told, and though the large Hobe house still stands, the property has been divided. It now has a number of homes on it, but the memories remain as things were then.

# The Den Mother

*As Remembered by*
*Phyllis DeLonais*

My Dad owned and operated Long's Ice Company. For fun things to do in the wintertime he would put up a toboggan slide using the ice slides. It was next to the house and utilized the gently sloping hill the house sat on. We would really go shooting far down into the pasture. In the pasture there was a pond, originally excavated to catch rainwater for the cattle. It was, perhaps, twice the size of a normal skating rink. It was the first body of water to freeze in the fall and be safe. It drew a lot of kids from around the neighborhood for skating. My Mother received many calls from mothers saying how relieved they were that their kids weren't skating on the lake.

In the Good Old
*Summer Time*
if White Bear can't
keep you *Cool,*
Try
**THE EAST SIDE ICE CO.**
Louis Rohlfing, Prop.

Daily deliveries made to all parts of the Lake.

Phone your order today.

*Long's Ice Co. and the East Side Ice Company were just two of the many ice companies harvesting on White Bear Lake. Ad courtesy of White Bear Press.*

When we were outside there were always two time clocks. One was the passenger mail train to Duluth. It always went past on the Northern Pacific tracks at 9:15 A.M. And then, of course, there was the noon whistle from the fire station for many years.

I was a den mother for 21 years with Pack 112, sponsored by the First Lutheran Church. I had many experiences doing this. One snowy winter, my son, who was in high school, kept busy by blowing the snow into a huge pile in the back yard. He then hollowed it out. There was so much room inside, we had a den meeting in it and studied things about Alaska.

Then there was the time someone told me that cow horns made a beautiful tie slide. It sounded intriguing, so I called South St. Paul stockyards to get information. Oh yes, it'd be a nice project, and they'd be happy to save around 50 of them for me. When I went to pick them up, a great big guy who easily could be a tackle on the Vikings, came out carrying them. The bag was the size of a double gunnysack, and he could barely get his arms around it. His face was hardly visible over the top and his arms were stretched to the limit around this stinking sack dripping blood all the way. I wondered what in #%@ he was going to do with these @#%! He then dropped them into the trunk of my car and said, "NEVER AGAIN! I was told that in order to get the horns off, you boiled the skull, hair and all. It was early spring, so I set up our Coleman stove outside on the picnic table and got a tub and started boiling them. After boiling a couple of them, I decided I was not going to mess with all of them that way. I used the table saw and cut the horns off first. Much less garbage to work with! In the process of sawing the horns, the saw spewed blood and bone pieces in a straight line down my front. I was into this but good! I thought I might as well keep at it. This time, after boiling the horns, the inside popped out easily. I was still in the process of doing this when school let out. My oldest son wouldn't even come home into the backyard. He was so embarrassed he walked all the way around out front. It really was quite a stinking mess.

Eventually, the cub scouts got to work on them and made really nice unique tie slides that they were proud of. That wasn't the end of it. A den leader in an instruction course wanted a couple of black ones to make a buffalo mask for skits. Then one of the mothers, who was Latvian, asked for one to stuff sausage in, as in the old country! So, it was quite a time!

*Ads courtesy of White Bear Press.*

One day in March, the entire pack went on a trip to Red Wing to go through the pottery plant. We went to the Union Depot and took the train. When we were ready to come home we found the train was delayed. The weather here was nice, but there was a blizzard out east, which had delayed the train. When that train pulled in, even I, with many Minnesota winters, was amazed at how snow-packed that engine was. Quite a sight for those kids, and what a relief for us den mothers who had to keep a pack of boys occupied for over an hour.

# On the East Shore of White Bear Lake

*Excerpts from the book to be published in January 2000:*
*Healy Families from County Mayo, Ireland and Minnesota*
*By Hope Healy Koontz*

We moved into our new home at Mahtomedi in the fall of 1923, just before school started. I can remember as a child, nearly four years of age, asking Mother if this was really going to be our home. It was on the border of Mahtomedi and Dellwood.

Our home on the lake was the type of home that still has wonderful memories for my brother, Charles, and me. Built in 1894 by a Mr. Dampier, of the Dampier Funeral Home in St. Paul, it was in the Victorian style with dormers on both sides of the two-story house and a large outside-inside chimney. This home was demolished a few years ago and a new home built on the site.

The full basement held the wood-coal furnace, the washing tubs and sinks, a tool work table, and a storage closet for Mother's preserves, Dad's homemade brew and our homemade root beer. Coal brought in by sleigh or truck was poured down an outside chute into the coal bin next to the furnace.

The kitchen, had three windows, many cupboards and a large pantry. In those days, we had a kerosene stove in which wood was also used. A few years later Dad bought mother a Hotpoint electric stove. The new stove contained a warming oven and three flat top burners. The other burner was a deep well for making stews and soups.

This kitchen held an icebox. It was not just a box sitting by itself; it was of solid stained oak built into the kitchen wall. Summertime required that a hundred pound block of ice be stored in the little box every week. An opening on the back side of the icebox on the back porch held the ice. It was not a very large box; in fact, it was very small by today's standards. That faithful old icebox helped feed us and provided for many parties. The icebox was a little demanding in that it required one to clean out the drain and pan underneath the ice, which was a smelly and disgusting chore.

The ice company furnished the ice for a very small fee, provided you hung your ice card out on your back door with the number of pounds you wanted. The driver of the ice truck deposited a hundred-pounder into the back door of the box. He had to carry it on his back with immense pointed tongs crimping the ice. There was a leather pad on his back to protect him from the cold and wet ice.

We had ice for our drinks, ice to keep the food from spoiling, and ice to suck on. Many a time we spotted an ice truck at someone's home and would try to pick off a piece to suck. It was sparkling blue ice that tasted wonderful on a warm day.

Dad brought home a marble slab measuring 5 feet x 3 feet and installed it on one side of the kitchen upon which Mother put her Saturday breads, cinnamon sticky rolls, cookies, candy and Sunday pies. I did not learn until many, many years later that the slab came from the demolition of the St. Paul Union Depot men's urinal! Dad's firm, the Healy Plumbing and Heating Corporation in St. Paul, had installed the plumbing and heating in the depot years before.

Mother used the kitchen for her ironing mangle. She used to iron all the clothes for her family of eight. She was skillful with it and worked wonders sitting at that mangle instead of standing up and ironing.

The dining room, held a Tiffany-style lamp which hung over the dining room table. There was a large buffet to match the dining room set; a two-leaf table and ten chairs. Mother's teacart on wheels held a nice tea set. Mother, who was from England, enjoyed her "nice cup of tea" late in the afternoon.

On one side of the dining room, underneath the steps, leading upstairs, was an alcove holding mother's sewing machine. Mother made a great deal of our clothing. I can remember asking her if I couldn't just once have something new from the store. The alcove was also a voluminous secret place to put toys or hide from one another. Window seats with cushions and deep cupboards held more toys and games. The window seats were also placed in the one end of the living room for more storage of music, books, or whatever we needed.

The dining room table was not only used for dining three times a day. It was the space for Dad's estimating plans for the cost of the plumbing jobs for his Healy Plumbing firm. It was the working place for all material and patterns of all kinds for Mother to cut out patterns. Our school homework was done alongside Dad's plans. There were two very wide table extensions we could use to lengthen it.

At Christmas time, that dining room table held batches and batches of Mother's breads and fudge. The fudge: divinity, maple and chocolate, was dropped by teaspoonfuls onto waxed paper for which she won first prize at the Minnesota State Fair in 1938. Boxes and boxes of Mother's candy were given to relatives, deliverymen, neighbors, and friends. The iceman delivering ice, the man bringing our groceries from Schock's Grocery in St. Paul, and most anyone who came by, all helped drop the quantity of the beautiful candy. Mother taught us all how to make pull taffy. She had hooks on the kitchen doors just for hanging the taffy and pulling it over and over the hook.

We wrapped Christmas presents on that old table. Christmas turkeys, Easter hams, leg of lamb and Thanksgiving dinners found the table extended with extra card tables at the end for guests. Many a Sunday night ended on that table with some type of a card game or any other game we had.

Our home was famous for hospitality, with relatives, friends and neighbors from around the lake, and for giving Sunday kidney stew breakfasts! This was another occasion for Mother to use her English ways. The beef kidneys were boiled in water, then the water was poured off and the kidneys boiled again, and one more throw-out. This had to be completed the day before we ate them. After the kidneys were soft, they were salted and thick gravy was made from the last boiling. This stew was then put on toast for our Sunday breakfast. All winter long, we had the stew on Sunday. We never tired of it and still make it to this day.

Our living room held eight windows with French doors leading into the front porch and sliding doors leading into the ballroom. Placed on the sides of the wall were individual fancy lights. The fireplace and mantelpiece held pictures and flowers. We used the fireplace constantly for heat, but best of all were the wiener and marshmallow roasts. The ashes dropped into the coal bin in the basement. When we moved in, there was a full bathroom off the living room. Dad had the bathroom closed up and changed into a small room for a maid and put in a small bathroom where the pantry had been. Mother had many maids throughout our childhood.

For many years we had furnace heat coming through large grills in the floors. In the winter, as young children, we would take our clothes downstairs and dress on top of the warm grills. The heat did not rise into our bedrooms as early as we needed it to dress. Later on, we had steam heat from hanging radiators in every room of the house.

At one end of the living room were glazed-in bookcases holding all types of wonderful journeys for me. We had Stoddard's Lectures that told of the ancient wonders of the world and far-off civilizations, which contained photos of people and places I had never imagined. There was my favorite ten-volume Book of Knowledge that I must have devoured over and over again. I read all of the Oz books and many others too numerous to mention here. My love of reading stood me well in life, because I was a librarian in a high school for nineteen years.

Separating the dining room and living room were painted ivory wooden pillars. The floors throughout the house were hardwoods and for years we had carpets in all the downstairs rooms. They were not wall to wall carpets. There were always three to five varnished rows of floor, which had to be shined.

The ballroom was most unusual. There were sliding doors from the living room and from the dining room. The room measured 14 by 16 feet. At various times it held a player piano, a baby grand piano and a Victrola that spun 78-rpm records if you wound it up. When the spring ran down, you had to wind it up to hear the end of the records. If there was to be dancing, the carpet was rolled up.

Many were the dancers who wound up the Victrola and gazed at a sidewall that held a mural of a young man and girl. The young man was helping her over a stream and they were dressed in costumes of the Victorian Age.

**SMART FOOTWEAR**

Covering nearly the entire ceiling of the ballroom was a hand-painted scene of cupids shooting arrows through pastel clouds. To make a border for the oval painting, flowers were painted around it and also formed a square on each corner. The painting had been on the ceiling long before we lived there, and eventually, it began coming loose. Mother and the local handyman, a Mr. Sheldrup, decided he would re-paste the part

*Ad courtesy of
White Bear Press.*

that had become loose and that Mother would touch up the flowers of the border. After it dried, Mother had to use a high ladder and pretend she was Michelangelo.

Little did Mother know that she would be gazing at the painting flat on her back, because of her various illnesses. After each operation or illness she had a bed brought downstairs and ran her household from the ballroom.

The ballroom was interchangeable as a party room, writing room, an extra living room, a family room, a game room or whatever one could dream up as the years went on and we all became older. I put a nickelodeon in this room when my son was very young. I bought it from a cousin, Eugene Liedl, our Mahtomedi dentist.

A memorable part of living in this home when my father was the Mayor of Mahtomedi (in 1934–1943) was our slot machine! Slot machines were banned sometime in the 1930s, and all of the machines were confiscated by the Sheriff (or whoever was in charge). All machines were picked up but my father managed to have one delivered to our home. In those days the slots could only hold a nickel.

Whenever we had a party, a picnic or friends and relatives for breakfast or dinner, the slot machine was the great attraction, even surpassing swimming in the lake. The machine was placed in the ballroom and everyone had his or her turn. Mother's bridge-playing friends coming out from St. Paul would stay overnight. Nickels were put in all day long, in between hands or by whoever was "dummy." Screams would be heard if they won as much as fifty cents. Often, there was a line of people taking turns by dropping in one nickel. Sometimes, a jackpot would rustle out about ten dollars or so and they would start in again. However, if the jackpot was not achieved, and after the guests would leave, my mother knew how to trip the lever in the back of the machine to make it pay off! She would then take the streetcar into St. Paul and spend her ill-gotten money! But oh, what fun we had with that old slot machine!

Mother loved to have the furniture changed around about every six months. Often the piano was in the larger living room, sometimes at one end and sometimes at the other. Before we had the baby grand piano, we had a player piano with rolls of music. There were pedals underneath which one had to pump in order for the music to be heard. Some wonderful songs were on those old rolls of music and we knew them by heart. Mother could play the baby grand piano and we stood around her singing those songs. We sang Scottish and Irish ballads, World War I songs, and popular songs. Mother was a convert from the Episcopalian religion to Catholicism. We knew the Episcopalian hymns as well as our own.

A screened-in side porch, with a long oval table, served as a congenial place to eat summer lunches and dinners. There was usually a breeze from the lake. Life and dining was less formal than in the winter. While we were children, it was our custom to swim three times a day. We could come to the table for lunch in our bathing suit if we wore a shirt over it. For dinner we had to be dressed cleanly and neatly. Blue Jays and thrushes built their nests in the vines on the outside of the screens. None of us escaped being bombed or pecked on the head when we ran out the door.

The front porch overlooking the front lawns and lake was screened and had sixteen windows. In it were the ever-lasting pieces of reed furniture which Mother painted numerous times to freshen them up. Along with other women in Mahtomedi, she took lessons on making some of the reed furniture and made many a useful urn, table, or whatever.

The sleeping porch upstairs was the width of the house, with eleven single beds filled to capacity with children and our guests during the summer. The sixteen windows were easily slipped open or shut and screens were a must. The windows were similar to the windows on the streetcars with a belt and pulley and a board to slam down and hold the window shut.

During the hot, hot month of August, my father and brothers would place huge laundry tubs on the sleeping porch. They then placed a 50 pound or 100 pound block of ice in the tub with a fan behind to blow cool air on us so we could sleep.

Upstairs we had four good-sized bedrooms. Mother and Dad's room had a walk-in closet leading to another bedroom. The bathroom at the end of a long hall had an unfinished walk-in closet which we called the "tar closet" because it had a tarpaper ceiling. Dad made Irish poteen during the prohibition days and kept it hidden there. He and our Minnesota State Senator Sullivan would have a nip when the Senator would walk down along the lakefront from his home.

In the long hall leading to the bedrooms there was a large closet. One of our cats decided it was a nice place to have her kittens, and they were born on Dad's birthday one year.

Outside in the back of the house there were two garages. One was small and held the usual tools for gardening and fishing rods. The other had two stories with a toilet and a full basement. It was a marvelous place for us girls to play in and it was also used as a place to undress for swimming when we had lots of company, as we usually did. Chickens ran around on the dirt floor of the basement and my two brothers had to kill and pluck them. Then, for sport, they would watch the chickens run around with their heads cut off!

Next to the "big garage," an artesian well with an electric pump supplied our neighbors, the Rollin Lanphers, the Fowbles, the William Bergs and us, with clear, cold and delicious water. We charged them just a small sum for the water. It is not known if the well was there when we arrived in 1923. Rollin Lanpher, who owned the Lanpher Hat Company in St. Paul, supplied us with venison and ducks in the hunting season.

Pipes from the well led to the house and our neighbors. They were set down about ten feet into the ground to prevent the water from freezing in the winter. Occasionally a pipe would break and the leaking pipe had to be discovered. My brother's job was to dig up the right pipe—all ten feet down. In 1928 Mahtomedi installed their own water system and we stopped supplying water to the neighbors.

Mr. Fowble kept beehives and kept us supplied with honey year around. Even though we had a reserve of honey, we paid for it in the long run because the bees swarmed on one particular tree of ours every year. Mr. Fowble would put up a ladder and gather his bees, but often the tree limb had to be cut off and down came the bees. We would scatter faster than the bees. But it was a fascinating procedure to watch.

Our home with its memories sadly is no longer standing. Our friends and relatives still discuss the wonderful times we had. Often we had church socials on the lawns. We gave our home over to a group of nuns many times. My sister Dorothy's wedding reception, as well as my own, was held there. Sadly, my parents sold their home in 1951 and moved to Coronado, California. That home, our early lives, and the memories of fun and laughter, have never left us.

*Ads courtesy of White Bear Press. Circa 1914.*

# Funerals, Visitations and Wakes

*As Remembered by*
*C. M. Ingham*

Funerals are difficult times for everyone, but occasionally some strange things occur that breaks the solemnity of the affair.

My brother, Bob, holds the record, as far as I know, for having been a pallbearer the most times. That's what happens when you are everyone's friend, but it's hard on the back and knuckles. I have only had the honor about 12 times.

In our American Legion club the tradition is to have a squad stand "vigil" the day and evening of the visitation. We try to assemble a group of veteran friends of the departed and, wearing our Legion caps, stand at attention at the head and foot of the casket for half-hour stints. This means you need at least four men, but preferably more.

In selecting the guards we always had to try to determine the religious affiliation of the deceased first. If he was a Catholic we tried to get Catholic guards so they could have the honor of standing at attention during the Vigil Mass and Prayers, which could last as long as an hour. It was amazing how many Catholics disappeared when volunteers were called for.

Today the pallbearers usually do not have to carry the casket far, but in past days we had a backbreaking job getting the casket from the church to the hearse, always down a flight of steps, and to the graves. It was a Godsend when they developed those folding carts on wheels like stretchers in ambulances. The funeral director usually has someone guiding, while the pallbearers merely push it along, with little lifting and no carrying. This works well when you have level ground and a hard surface.

*Ad courtesy of White Bear Press. Circa 1914.*

I once had the misfortune of being involved as a pallbearer at a cemetery where the gravesite lay on a hillside. As we stepped away from the hearse onto the grassy slope we found that rain had left a slick surface. We were told by the funeral director to use a "shuffle" step. Each of us tried our own version and the casket started to pitch and roll as one after another of us slid, slipped, dipped and tripped and eventually went down. The casket did not stop when we did, however. It took off on the slick ground as though it was a toboggan and plowed its way down the hill, glanced off a small tree, righted its course to miss the grave by a mere three feet, coming to rest head-on against a large stone monument.

Fortunately, the funeral director got to the casket first, popped the lid, jerked the corpse back into position, closed the lid, and told everyone but the pallbearers to stay at the graveside. He called the grave attendants to come with ropes to help. As we finally worked the casket up to the grave and finished the ceremony with a carpet of fake grass covering the huge dent in the front of the casket, it was hard to keep a straight face, even the family had trouble. We were all invited back to the family home to re-live this and to relieve our jitters.

One of my most embarrassing episodes was when I went to the visitation for the mother of my brother Jack's best friend. I had known his mother for forty years, so was anxious to visit with the family. As I entered Paulsen's Funeral Home, where I had been many times before, I walked in with the local police chief, whom I also knew. We went into the first room on the left, greeted several other people I knew, and signed the guest register. I made my way through to the casket and received a shock. As I looked down at the person in the casket I realized I had never seen her before in my life and vice versa. I wheeled out of the room, entered the next visitation room and met more friends but found the man in the casket was also a stranger to me. By this time I was utterly confused, until my brother finally saw me and dragged me into the right room. I was so glad to finally find the deceased, I rushed up to the casket and hugged her, much to the surprise of her two sons.

My mother, at the age of 84, decided she wanted to pre-pay her own funeral. She had gone through the expenses at my father's funeral about nine years before and felt she did not want anyone to have to make those hard decisions on a spur of the moment like most people do. Therefore, she discussed it with her three sons and made an appointment with a funeral director for all four of us. When the time came she decided she didn't feel like making these decisions, but would defer to us. My two brothers and I met with the funeral director in his office. He explained that this was not unusual, laid out the options for us, and showed us the contracts required. Then he suggested we go to the "show room" to pick out the casket and accompaniments.

We were shown into a beautiful room full of all manner of caskets from a plain pine box to one covered and lined in denim—for the teenagers, he said—to the more elaborate, ornate bronze, silver and expensive wooden ones. Bob, the oldest, suggested we have large, comfortable handles on the sides because he had barked his knuckles too many times on those little bar handles about the size of a fountain pen. I suggested a beautiful Old English oak box to match Dad's, so they could lie in eternity as a matched couple. It was out-voted in favor of bronze. Jack was detailed to choose the interior lining and colors of the accoutrements.

We hemmed and hawed over each decision like we were buying a car or piece of furniture, in great solemnity. We were shown the required concrete vault and water-proofing and eternalizing, and were properly amazed and impressed—and were glad—Mother had decided not to come. This last part was morbid and as exciting as waterproofing a basement.

When we went home to report our decisions she seemed happy—and impressed—that we could all agree on something, but did ask if they didn't have samples of the inside lining or pictures of the caskets.

Have you ever been to a real, old-fashioned wake? It is a strenuous experience that I had the pleasure of witnessing before I was old enough to drink. A friend of mine invited me to the wake for his Uncle Mike. Uncle Mike was a brother of my friend Bill's mother, and he had many talents, none of which made him any money, but which did earn him a host of friends. He it was who taught us how to whistle, stand on our heads, swing a bat, make a willow whistle, catch leeches, and ride down "Suicide Hill" standing on a sled. Well, poor Uncle Mike, who said he had a "weakness" that prevented him from working, finally died. It was said, unkindly, by some folk that Uncle Mike's weakness was really an addiction to never working because it interfered with his drinking, sleeping and laziness.

At any rate, the wake was scheduled to be a celebration of Uncle Mike's life, and was to be held at Bill's parents' home. My dad said it really would be a celebration for his brother-in-law, Bill's dad. He wouldn't have to support Uncle Mike any longer—nor bail him out of trouble.

The casket was brought to Bill's folks' home and put on two chairs in the front room in great solemnity. Ladies and friends of the family brought mountains of food all day long. The men friends brought two barrels of beer and several bottles of something stronger.

The ceremonies began in the evening, with people dropping in to view Uncle Mike one last time, and to say "good-bye." The casket was open, so they could prove he was really dead, and as the beer and booze flowed more freely the friendliness and noise increased. Some of his friends got him to sit up in the casket, others poured him a drink and tried to feed it to him. One of the women wanted to sit on his lap "one last time," and climbed up on the casket. This upset the casket, it fell off the chairs, tipped over, Uncle Mike fell out, and they found he had no pants, socks or shoes on. The lady, undismayed, stated, "Well, it's not the first time I've seen him this way," to the concurrence of others.

Some more sober minds decided he belonged back in the casket, but found he had a broken arm from the fall. In the process of trying to stuff him back they got him in upside down. This scene was too much for some of them; they just closed the casket that way and left it on its side. The next day, when the funeral ceremony took place, the report from the pallbearers was that inside the casket they found seven bottles of booze, which they confiscated as their due, since Mike could not use it anymore, especially with a broken arm.

Then there is another side to funerals my father told me about. When he and Mother lived in the small town of Leeds, North Dakota, there were few funeral homes in the area just before World War I. The local furniture storeowner, who apparently had access to wood for coffins, usually handled this work. In a nearby town two enterprising men had a thriving, first-class funeral business with just one casket.

They had an elaborate bronze casket with lace and silk or satin interior, and priced their funerals very reasonably. No other funeral home in the area could compare price-wise. This upset the competition so much they sent out spies to see how the pair did it. The report was astounding but was kept a secret that several other funeral directors copied. A very nice, elaborate, expensive casket was purchased, and then enhanced by removing the bottom and replacing it with a series of clips, clamps and levers. This allowed a wooden coffin to be placed inside the casket with the top of the coffin attached to the bottom of the casket. After the funeral at the graveside, when the spectators had gone, the wooden top was slid out of position, the casket lowered into the grave where the levers released the wooden coffin, and the casket then retrieved. The wooden top was placed in position and covered with dirt and the grave was closed. The ornate casket was covered with cloths and returned to the mortuary where it was cleaned and ready for the next prospective customer.

This procedure was adopted by others, and may have spread throughout the profession. Look carefully the next time you are involved with a funeral.

# Memories Are Made of This

*As Remembered by*
*Pauline Jackson Hollen*

**M**y first memory was when I was five and I lived in a little white house at Hoffman's Corners on Highway 61. I would walk across a little bridge that went over the railroad tracks in order to get to school. Hoffman's Corners was a store and vegetable stand. The house is still there, along with a few of the other homes I remember going to as a child.

The school I walked to was called Zuercher's, and it was across from another grocery store named Fischer's Corner. The school had an outhouse toilet, so the trips to it were as few as possible. I still remember the time when I was seven years old and the boy in front of me wet his pants and it ran down my legs! He cried and I did too.

When I was almost eight years old we moved to a big house on a road by the railroad tracks near Birch Lake and Centerville Road. We had a barn, a big windmill, and a chicken coop with a couple of chickens and a cow. The train tracks were directly behind our house. My brother Marvin and my sister Marvel would sit on top of a hill and wave to the engineer. They would always wave back as well as an occasional wave from a free rider.

One day our cow got loose and ran down the tracks. When we saw the train coming we were ready to assume the worst, but the train passed and there, on the other side of the tracks, was our very contented cow, munching on grass.

In those days there were farms all around us. Today, the pastures are gone and the landscape is filled with apartment buildings and a Cub Foods store. Oh, the house is still there, but the view of the barn, the silo, and the pastures are gone.

From there, we moved into town. We bought a house located just off Highway 61. Mom still wanted her cow and chickens and we sold eggs, milk, bread and rolls. Rich people came from the other side of town just to buy Mama's goodies. I would do deliveries in the morning before school. I remember the cream coming halfway down the bottle. We charged a whole 5 to 10 cents a quart.

When I was ten years old I went to Washington School on 4th Street, where now stands a large apartment type building. I attended the White Bear High School. I rode to school on my bike, which I earned picking berries and digging weeds for farmers. After a hard day's work we would ride down to Preibe's Boat Dock on the corner of Highway 61 and the south side of the lake. There was a little store where we could buy five-cent ice cream cones or popsicles. Once in a while we'd get a popsicle stick that would win us a free one. The owner would let us swim off his dock on hot days of the summer. He sure was nice to us kids.

Our house was now located on a dirt road at 1402 Florence Street. It was two blocks west of Bald Eagle Avenue. We loved to go to the little grocery store across the street from the Catholic school, called Berg's Store.

From the time I was ten years old until I was thirteen, I was on an acrobatic team. We would travel all over to schools and county fairs, as well as to Wisconsin and lots of amateur programs at Lyceum Theatre in St. Paul. The theatre would host contests held between the movie showings. We actually won a few times! We were

# NEIGHBORS REFUSE WATER; HOUSE BURNS

### Neighbors Reek Revenge on Robert O'Leary, Refusing To Allow Firemen to Have Water

When the White Bear fire department answered a call to White Bear Beach, Monday forenoon, where the home of Robert O'Leary was on fire, they met with an experience which for down-right dammeanness beat anything they have ever heard of. It was the positive refusal of a neighbors to allow the department a few gallons of water, thereby causing Mr. O'Leary's home to be completely destroyed.

For some time there has been an inharmonious condition existing among the neighbors, and O'Leary was disliked by some. When the firemen arrived it was necessary to use the booster tank on the truck, as this secion being outside the city limits and far from hydrants, no hose connection could be made. The firemen soon had the flames under control when the water was exhausted. An attempt was made to get a few pails of water from the neighbors. One after another refused.

The firemen then used the hand pumps and chemicals, but they too were soon exhausted. Chief Campbell rushed to the old Soo Line well, now abandoned, but the water was so far from the surface that 42 feet of suction hose would not reach it. There was nothing left to do but give up and watch the house go up in flames.

That section of White Bear Beach is commonly known as "Hells Half Acre", and judging from such a condition it must be properly named.

Most of the furniture was saved. Loss is placed at $2,500; with $1,100 insurance.

Mr. O'Leary was home at the time and the first he knew of the fire was when he discovered the roof on fire. The origin is undetermined.

*Real fires in White Bear.*
*Courtesy of White Bear Press.*
*Circa 1930.*

also in the St. Paul Winter Carnival parades, marching past the Capitol to the old auditorium. Bernice and Bernard Benson taught me everything and even made our costumes, including some bear suits. I still have two that I wore on stage.

*Ad courtesy of White Bear Press. Circa 1914.*

My father's aunt and uncle owned the White Bear Lumber Company. I would love to go there and to their house by the little Lutheran Church where I was confirmed. I sang in the church choir and some days I even got to ring the bell on Sunday mornings.

One time there was something going on at the Armory. Tables and booths were set up all around the building. We did our acrobatic show and were then free to walk around. I watched a lady decorate breads with cream cheese. I learned how to do it by watching her and to this day I still enjoy decorating sandwiches and breads.

Two bachelor brothers lived next door to us. One was a simple-minded man. He rode a blue girl's bike to work every day, smoking a curved pipe. He worked for the city. He would go up to the fire hall and blow the whistle at 8:00 A.M. and then again at noon and 5:00 P.M. It was the town signal to go to work, eat lunch, and quit work, I guess. He was always on time. He cleaned the library. One day I took a picture of him there. Kids were always making fun of him and calling him names. He was always very kind to us, though.

One day the fire department staged a fire in town. They brought in an old house and set it in the street next to Highway 61, a block north of the fire department. Everyone gathered around. It was dark and the firemen acted as though this was a real fire. The firemen had one of their own dressed in a nightgown and cap holding a doll in an upper window, calling for help. The house was set on fire and began to blaze. The fire alarm went off and the truck came with sirens blowing. The rescuers climbed a ladder, removed the mother and baby, and put the fire out. I was very young and the whole thing scared me.

One day at school our class got to go to Kohler's Ice Cream Parlor on Main Street. They took the entire class on a tour through the factory where we got to see how they made ice cream. They gave each child a cone as we left.

*Ad courtesy of White Bear Press.*

There was a little lady who lived next to us. She always wore black, like a nun, even in her garden. Her name was Clara Hays. She was very kind and I sure loved her.

And my last memory is of the trains of course. I remember riding uptown on the steamers. I would jump on and off the cars as they gathered steam—DUMB!! Then came the first diesel engines, but my love was always for the old ones. So each Christmas I set up my little toy train to run around the Christmas tree and remind me of the things I hope never to forget.

# My Boyhood Memories

*As Remembered by*
*Jack Vadnais*

**M**y name is John (Jack) R. Vadnais. I was born in a home at 1979 Fourth Street, White Bear Lake, Minnesota on February 19, 1925. I had five sisters and six brothers: George, Charles, Florence, Dick, Mona, Leona, Marguerite, Gordy, and Anna Mae. One brother, Lawrence, died at five years of age and another brother died at the age of nineteen months.

We lived in a one and a half story home with a kitchen, front room, bedroom and a porch. The second floor had two bedrooms and a small sun porch. My five sisters slept in one bedroom. My older brother had his own separate room. Charles was away at a school for the deaf in Faribault. Three of us brothers slept in the sun porch, which was large enough for one bed.

The heating of our home was with a pot-bellied stove located in the front room and a wood burning cooking stove in the kitchen. Railroad ties were used for fuel in both stoves. The ties were used and discarded by the railroad. We had mountains of them stacked in the back yard by the time fall would roll around. The saw we used to cut them down to size was called a luger. It had a blade approximately two feet in diameter and was run by gas. My older brothers and father would cut the ties into stove size pieces. The stoves would be stoked up before bed, but by many a morning they would be nearly cold.

One morning when I was about five years old, the temperature in the house was extremely cold. We had no heating on the second story except that which came through the vents in the floor. This particular morning, I grabbed my underwear in one hand and headed downstairs. My mother was already getting breakfast and baking bread in the stove. To warm up quickly I ran into the kitchen and sat down on the warm oven door which mother had just opened! Boy, oh boy! I really burned my bottom!

We had an outhouse in the backyard. Most of the time we used catalogs for toilet tissue. On Halloween it was a great fun prank to tip over the outhouses. Some Halloweens the joke would be on us, for the outhouse owners would remove the houses before we got there.

In the late winter, a butchered pig was put on the front porch. This was always covered up with a sheet. When meat was needed, my mother would take a meat saw and cut what was required for supper. Potatoes were stored on the dirt floor of the basement in bushels, enough to last the entire winter.

In the summer time games like ani ani over would be played. We would throw a ball over the garage for the other team to catch. We would play other games like cops and robbers, too. Our guns were made out of apple box ends, with cut rubber binders fitted over the ends. We were then able to shoot the binders at one another. There was always a game of softball going on. Both boys and girls would participate in these games. Marble games were played where the kids with the "good" shooters cleaned up in the game of "for keeps." The winner of that game got to keep the loser's marbles. Even old tires were quite the novelty. We'd have a great time rolling them up and down the street.

While attending St. Mary's School, we were, unknowingly, in the back yard of White Bear Lake history. The big round train turntable building was directly behind our playground. The turntable could turn the trains around in order to send them back up or down the tracks. Today North Star Bank stands in the turntable's place.

It was surprising to me, the number of people who worked for the railroad. My father, Adlore Vadnais, spent twenty years as a clerk. Two of my uncles were engineers. I can still remember the big steam locomotives pulling into the depot. I will always remember the sulfur smell from the coal and the spinning of those huge wheels as the trains began to move.

On the other side of Second Street, where the fire department now stands, were the old stockyards. If, heaven forbid, you were challenged to a fight, the routine was to "meet me in the stockyards."

Where Ramsey County Beach now stands were the "Ice Slides." There, the ice was cut into three hundred-pound blocks, which then went onto slides and into boxcars for shipping. The Citizens Ice Company hauled the ice to St. Paul, where it was stored in sawdust until summer. White Bear Lake also had its own ice company. They would deliver ice for your icebox right to your door. It was always great to get a piece of ice to lick on from the driver on those hot summer days. On Sundays, you could buy ice from filling stations. The station worker would put 25 or 50 pound blocks on the bumpers of your car. The ice would melt into the bumper and be very secure until it reached its destination. As a teen I loaded ice that I would cut from 300-pound blocks, using an ice saw. The ice saw looks very much like a crosscut saw used to cut large trees. I would cut ice blocks fitted to the customer's request. Most of the time the bumper dictated the size of the blocks. To this day, I still have the ice scale used to weigh the ice!

In the winter, after we had safe ice, we would go to Clark Avenue to play hockey. This meant walking to the lake, taking off your shoes, lacing on cold skates, and afterwards putting on those same freezing shoes to walk home.

Later in the winter, the hippodrome was opened to the public. We would bring our girlfriends there to skate to the Skater Waltz. After we finished skating, we would hike to the White Bear Drug Store. They had a beautiful fountain with malts, sarsaparilla, and, of course, ice cream cones. I can't forget Greengard's Store either. Old Phil Greengard would sit in the back of the store smoking his pipe. All we had to do was tell him how much money we had to spend and he would always say, "Help yourself." I never could figure out if he made money. I guess that trust worked both ways in this case.

One of our other winter sports was "hitching" onto cars. This wasn't seemingly dangerous to me. Streets were not sanded as they are today and there were not nearly as many cars. We would hold onto those big bumpers, squat down and take a ride. In some instances there were too many kids hanging on to the bumpers and the car could not get going. A few would have to leave and drop off in order to let the car move.

Etched deep into my memory is that of Charlie Clark, the local blacksmith. For fifty cents he would run a hot steel rod over his tongue. This was quite a sum of money in those days. I can still hear the sizzle as it passed over his damp tongue! Charlie's shop was on the northwest corner of Fourth Street and Murray Avenue. The old house is still there but the smithy shop is long gone. Another local blacksmith was Billy Bear. His shop was located next to the Total gas station on Fourth Street and Washington Avenue. Pete Hugger ran the last blacksmith shop, in what is now my back yard on Fifth Street and Campbell Avenue. His shop was burned down by an arson. His barn was later given to the fire department and moved to the county fairgrounds for fire practice. A poem was written and published in the White Bear Press. The poem was appropriately named "The Old Blacksmith Shop".

*White Bear Lake Blacksmith Shop of the early 1900s.*

# Caddy Shack

*As Remembered by*
*Bill Patterson*

During the summers in my early years I spent a good deal of time at the lake and learned to swim when I was six or seven. My father had been encouraging me to learn and finally threw me off the dock so I had to swim. Our neighborhood included the Johnsons right behind us at 904 First Street. Mrs. Johnson (Zelda) remained in the house until her death in 1985.

Glenn Johnson and I did a lot of reading. In the hot summer months we'd go up to the old library (donated by Andrew Carnegie, AD 1914). We were strong on westerns—Zane Grey, probably. The librarian intimidated me more than any

*Interior of Carnegie Library, early 1900s.*
*Photo courtesy of*
*Lawrence R. (Bob) and Eileen Whitaker.*

other person with whom I've come in contact. She made us feel as though even breathing in HER library was against the law and a crime punishable by immediate eviction. But we gradually became conditioned to her and managed to get considerable use of the place.

A lot of our reading, as I have said, took place in the hottest times of the summer—like in 1936 when the temperature stayed in the 90's and 100's for

weeks, without any rain. At that time of the year, White Bear Lake—then and now—became full of something known only as "the itch." We could no longer spend most of the day in the lake. The itch was a form of hives caused by a microscopic parasite, which I have been told was the result of ducks and snails inhabiting the lake. It didn't bother us in the cooler parts of the summer, but in late July and early August, it made swimming on our side of the lake taboo! So, instead of swimming, we put on our bathing suits, ran through the lawn sprinkler to cool off, and settled down in the shade to read.

Glenn and I also played golf. He started caddying at the White Bear Yacht Club in about 1931. He talked me into starting in 1933. We hitchhiked the four miles to Dellwood—most of the people who gave us rides were golfers on their way to the course. Sometimes we rode our bikes. It was a pleasant ride and I look back on it with great pleasure. The hill right after entering Dellwood was a little steep—especially since there was no such thing as multi-speed bikes. Sometimes when the hitchhiking was bad we would walk.

The Depression years left little else for young boys to do to earn money, so there was an abundant supply of caddies. Before being admitted to the group of qualified caddies we had to pass an oral test, and caddy for the caddy master, to prove we could do the job. The test included knowing the rules of golf, the terms of the game, the length of all the holes (I still remember some of them) and, most certainly, knowing the etiquette and behavior expected of a caddy. The members of the Yacht Club were among the elite of St. Paul. Many lived in Dellwood only in the summer. More and more, as the automobile made it convenient to commute, people abandoned their homes in St. Paul and converted their summer dwelling to year-round homes. They included well-known names such as Ordway, Archer, Mairs, Schuneman, Lilly, Graves and Ridder, along with J. F. Patterson of Patterson Dental Supply. Many times over the years I was asked if I was from that family.

My first time "out" (which was the term for getting to carry someone's bag around the course) was on Memorial Day 1933. I not only got out; I got to carry two bags for a few holes. The golfers were Mr. and Mrs. Bob Fobes. I survived the round without getting marked 'unsat' and made eighty cents. I was quite proud of having earned what for then, was a lot of money. When I went to St. Joseph's Hospital to

*Streetside (above) and lakeside (below) views of White Bear Yacht Club, 1935. Photos courtesy of Lawrence R. (Bob) and Eileen Whitaker.*

visit Dad, I was eager to tell him. It was one of the greatest let-downs of my life, for his response was, "It will take a lot of eighty cents to pay for this surgery." I'm sure that his concern was for the great burden he had to bear; without having insurance, without a way for him to run his business, and still he had to maintain his family.

The rest of the summer I labored at being a caddy, did what I could to help around the house and started to learn to play golf—which I am still doing. We played on Monday mornings at the Yacht Club and had a caddy tournament at the end of the year. One year I won thirty-five dollars—enough for spending money for the school year.

Caddying brought me into contact with many interesting people. One was a quite influential man who was in his eighties, when I caddied for him. He would come to the course late in the day and play four holes—10, 11, 17, and 18. He needed to be pushed up the hills, which his caddy was required to do. We would place a hand in the small of his back and push to his commands of, "push harder, Caddy." Our reward for this was a ten-cent tip, on top of the twenty cents we received for caddying the four holes.

Shreve Archer (Archer Daniels Midland Co.) was the favorite of us all. His standard tip was a shiny fifty-cent piece, which he gave the caddy as they walked down the 18th fairway. He was a fine gentleman and talked with us on a real "man-to-man" basis. His usual foursome included Sam Mairs (a curler), Ted Moles, Shreve's son-in-law and H. L Donahower. Among others I remember were Bill Fobes—a long hitter—Bobby Graves, who was state amateur champ one year—and Ted Fields, who later was the insurer for W.A. Patterson Co.

When I started caddying, the standard rate for eighteen holes was sixty cents, with twenty cents an hour for overtime over three hours. We got a five-cent raise that year and the following year the older caddies decided we should strike for higher wages. Glenn and I were not aware of the planned strike, as we were friends of the caddy master. So when we arrived at the course on the chosen Saturday, the strikers dragged us into the dismal hole that served as a caddy shack. Negotiations got along fast and we were given fifteen cents a round raise and twenty-five cents/hour for overtime (over three hours for a round).

I caddied for most of six summers and made spending money, learned a little about playing golf and met some interesting people. Tom Vardon was the head professional. He was the brother of the famed Harry Vardon and had a thick Scottish accent. We would go out on the 18th fairway and shag the balls being hit. We used baseball gloves and got pretty good at getting the balls on the fly. I recall Tom giving a lesson to one of the lady golfers and hearing him tell her "You've got to get your 'arse' into it."

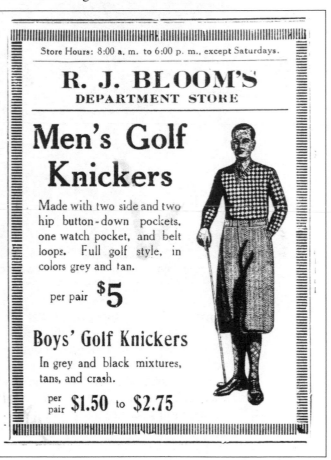

*Ad courtesy of White Bear Press. Circa 1914.*

# No Computers, No TV

*As Remembered by*
*Helen Lindbeck Peterson*

Growing up in a small town in the 1930s was a full and fulfilling life. Some of us had bicycles and clamp-on roller skates, ice skates and sleds. Some of us had toboggans, or a swing in the willow tree or maybe a sandbox. Most of us had chores, and some had odd jobs such as baby-sitting. There was often wood and ashes to be hauled in and out, a garden to be tended, grass to be mowed, snow to be moved, and other chores we took for granted to be part of everyday living.

When the responsibilities of the day were finished, there usually was time for fun and games. In the warm summer evenings, we played Run-Sheep-Run, Captain-May-I, kick-the-can or hopscotch. Sometimes we roller-skated or rode our bikes, but whatever the activity we always slept well and hard. Nearly everyone had a bag of marbles and another bag for jacks and a ball.

*Children at play, Lucille and Rich Bazille.*
*Photo courtesy of Dot Magnuson.*

We had several orange crates, which we used to build an office or a store. Daddy had salvaged an old cash register we used with the Monopoly money to play store outside in the summer. Those crates, along with a couple of planks, became whatever our imaginations could create.

There was a pump in the back yard about halfway to the garage and outhouse. Every Sunday night we pumped water for the laundry the following day. I never knew that the pump water was superior to that which ran so freely from the faucet, but my mother thought there was a difference. Pails of water had to be pumped on the eve of wash day to allow the temperature to rise from the icy cold. It was heated in a copper boiler on two or three burners of the kerosene stove, then dipped into the wringer washer that had been wheeled into the big kitchen. In the winter the water was heated on the cook stove. Two washtubs were set on a plank between kitchen chairs and filled with rinse water. In good weather, the clothes were hung outside year around, and in inclement weather they were hung on racks in the house, boosting the humidity in the winter to a point where the frost on the windows was quite thick.

Without central heat, the kitchen was the only room that was heated to a comfortable temperature in the winter, unless we had company. The kitchen stove had a reservoir at one end where the teakettle steamed on top, so we generally had hot water, though not from the tap. At the back of the stove and above it, was a warming oven where we kept the matches, soda crackers, and other goods that needed to stay dry. The kitchen was the hub of the house. We did homework at the

kitchen table, wrote letters, ate there, played cards, Parcheesi, Monopoly, Pick-Up-Sticks and other games. Coffee was poured there at 10:00 A.M., 3:00 P.M., and again at 10:00 P.M.—always with homemade doughnuts, cake or cookies.

One spring day, Daddy brought a newborn lamb home for us to raise. He had stopped at Hogan's Grocery store on Fourth Street and bought a bottle of Coca-Cola and a nipple. We drank the Coke, and filled the bottle with milk for the lamb, who was named Jippy. Then we dressed up in our stash of finery—old hats and long dresses, beads, earrings, and high heels—and played house. We took Jippy along for walks, as we pushed the doll buggy. He was our fancy French poodle. In the fall when he began to sprout horns, he went to live with the other animals at Herman Hansen's farm. Mr. Hansen was our milkman, who delivered raw milk about twice a week.

In the fall, the leaves were raked to the dirt street and were burned there. Sometimes we toasted marshmallows over those pleasant, pungent fires. When the siren was blown at 9:00 P.M. (10:00 P.M. in later years) for curfew, everyone under 16 ran for home.

In the early 1930s, there was but one law enforcement officer in town. His name was Art Long, and he drove a black roadster with a rumble seat (maybe his own vehicle) at first. Later, he had a white squad car. His office and the jail were located in a foreboding brick building on Clark Avenue and Second Street. Here, too, was the equipment for the volunteer fire department: one square-looking truck. The siren that shrieked for the volunteers when there was a fire was also blown once as the noon whistle and it sounded one time again as the curfew in the evening. The siren could be activated from the jail/firehouse or Northwestern Bell Telephone office, which was housed on the second floor of the Getty Building located on Third Street at the corner of Clark Avenue. When someone called in to report a fire, the call had to go through the chief operator, who noted the details, informed the operators, and turned on the siren. The telephone drops for the homes of the firemen were painted red, so the operators could give those calls priority. Off the men would race, either to the fire or the station, whichever was closest to them once they knew the location.

We had two deliveries of mail each day except Saturday, which had only one. Stamped postcards cost a penny, and a first class letter was three cents. There was a weekly paper published called the White Bear Press, owned by a dignified looking Civil War veteran named Captain Stickley. He strode about town wearing a brown campaign hat and sporting a goatee. The Twin City Lines buses ran between White Bear Lake and St. Paul several times a day. The two drivers to and from White Bear were Eddie Dufresne and Joe Ryder, and the fare was twenty-five cents one way.

These were the days of steam-engine trains. Many went through White Bear, most of them carrying freight, but at least one or two were passenger trains. There was a large structure by the depot with an extension that swung out over the engine to fill the boiler with water. A tiny flagman's house was located on the north side of Fourth Street—just big enough for a small stove and a chair for the flagman to go into in bad weather. When a train approached, he would come out and hold up a stop sign for the east-west traffic until it was again safe for traffic and pedestrians to cross the tracks. In the depot were benches for those waiting for travelers or for a ride. A telegraph operator, Evar Peterson, had his niche there as well. Here telegrams could be sent or were received.

There were several grocery stores and meat markets. There was a feed store, a bank, a library, a beauty shop, a bus depot, a department store and a dry goods store, two public grade schools and a public high school, doctors and dentists, an ice cream parlor, a movie theater, gas stations and garages. Whatever could not be found in town could usually be found in St. Paul.

The annual Ramsey County Fair was held for four days near the north end of what is now Bloom Avenue. In the relative cool of the hippodrome, where there had been ice all winter for the city skating rink, long tables were lined up to display the baked and canned goods, handicrafts, and other entries. One entered on the street side, walked through the colorful displays and out the other end to the midway with its noise and crowds, sideshows and the smells of animals—a most exciting experience. We saved our dimes and nickels for the thrill rides and junk foods and savored it all. By Sunday afternoon, roustabouts were starting to take machinery apart, displays of entries were disassembled, animals were taken home, and the show was over for another year.

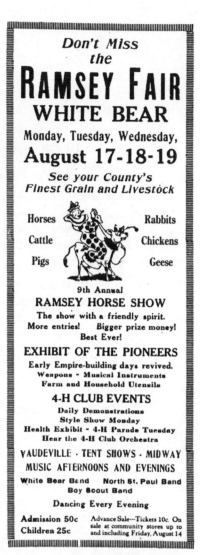

*Ad courtesy of White Bear Press.*

*Washington Square, circa 1940. Photo courtesy of Lawrence R. (Bob) and Eileen Whitaker.*

# Memories of Hoffman's Corners

*As Remembered by*
*Donald Charles Hoffman*

One couldn't ask for a better location to start a business than at the corners of County Road E and Highway 61. Just about every car going between St. Paul and White Bear had to pass that way. Charles Hoffmann Sr. (2 N's before 1917) bought land there in the 1890's and did what most Luxembourgers do well…grow things. Charley was born in 1867 in the small town of Muhlenbach, which was the center of greenhouse growing in Luxembourg. Since most Luxembourgers speak French, as well as German and their own language, he settled between the areas of Little Canada and White Bear where a lot of Frenchmen lived. On his nearly 20 acres of land at Hoffman's Corners, he grew produce for his own store as well as some contract growing for Gedney. Charley Hoffman Sr. had married Mary Sprunck, who was born just a few miles from Charley's hometown in Luxembourg. Over time, the two would raise a family of ten children.

A large new house was built around the turn of the century, which had modern indoor plumbing and central heating. This house was converted to the "Hilltop" restaurant after Charley Sr. retired in the late twenties. The "Hilltop" was a popular watering hole during the thirties. It burned to the ground in 1937. Behind this first homestead was the Hoffman barn, which, up until the mid-fifties, still had two stanchions and horse cribs. It is now the site of Tousley's Sports Center, and the concrete floor there is that of the old barn.

Charley Sr. served as president of the Minnesota Growers Association for many years. Charley returned to Luxembourg for a "short" visit from 1926 to 1927, then moved to California with his second son, Victor, where he operated a ranch in Van Nuys. Charley Hoffman Sr. died there in 1953 at the age of 86.

In the twenties, Charley's oldest son, Henry, took over the business and built a large new store complete with a short-lived soda fountain. The whole outside storefront was covered with bushels of red tomatoes and vegetables of every type, their prices chalked in large white letters on big black signs reaching to the ground. The smell of fresh dill tied in bundles and ripe fruit greeted the many customers going through the screen doors, which slammed behind them as they went into the store. On the east end of the store were the big barrels of vinegar with their wooden spigots. On the west end, Anyrine scooped ice cream for five-cent cones. In front, cars parked on the cement apron between the store and Highway 61.

Henry lived in the back of the store with his wife Anyrine Nadeau Hoffman and their children until they built, in 1939, the big, grand, square, flat top California style house on the hill, very close to where the old homestead had been and where Henry had grown up. This house stood until it was demolished in 1997.

Around 1932, Henry sent his younger brother, Robert Hoffman, to Texas to arrange to buy land to grow grapefruit for the store trade. Robert saved the train fare and rode the rails instead to Mission, Texas. The land was purchased, grapefruit was grown, and Charley's second youngest son Joe Hoffman and Joe's wife Jeanette Auer Hoffman, went there and managed the fruit orchard from about 1934 to 1944. Here they grew TEXAS JIM brand grapefruit, named after Jim Hoffman, Joe's oldest son. TEXAS JIM grapefruit was also sold in the West Seventh Street St. Paul fruit store, which was run by Lucille Hoffman Till, Charley's youngest daughter and her husband, Tom Till.

Around 1945, Joe Hoffman came back from Texas and ran the Hoffman's Corners market with Oliver Tessier until around 1950, while Henry sold fruit in the side garage until his semi-retirement. Then, Dick Arcand and his wife, Shirley Hoffman Arcand (Henry's oldest daughter), ran the new store, which was built around 1951 as a sort of small strip mall.

Henry Hoffman served as mayor of Gem Lake, a new community that incorporated Hoffman's Corners. He served in this capacity for many years while still selling fruits and fresh produce. He retired in California, but came back to Hoffman's Corners in the summers to man the fruit stand. He died in 1986.

Robert, the youngest of the ten Hoffman children, opened the first drive-in restaurant in the area in 1933 and ran it with his wife, Ruth, until it was torn down in the mid-fifties and a new all-season restaurant was built on the west end of the strip mall. This unique small hexagon drive-in (called curb service then) restaurant was called "Robert's", officially, but also went by the names "Stand," the "Round House," and the "Barrel." Robert served the best hamburgers and barbecue ribs anywhere, as anyone around the White Bear area will attest. On any summer holiday, the lot around the drive-in had cars lined up more than ten deep, which kept the carhops very busy and the cooks busier. The big barrel of "Richo" root beer was capped into heavy faceted glass mugs and the hamburgers, "regular" fifteen cents, and the "jumbo", with lettuce, tomato, relish, and onion on a toasted bun for twenty cents, were double wrapped in tissue. Ribs, ham, beef and pork were slow smoked in a small brick pit where Robert burned hickory logs that he brought back from Wisconsin. Fries were cut from big fresh white potatoes, deep fried and sold for fifteen cents an order.

The carhops would put the orders on the metal trays with little rubber covered feet that fit against the car doors. Car lights would be flashed or horns blown for the tray pick-up. There was a lot of activity including flying gravel from cars peeling out on hot summer nights.

Around the early 1940s, George Welch, who was managing the Tavern across the street from the store (now the Country Lounge), would put a sheet up on Henry's garage. After a short commercial slide show, he would show movies which people could view from their cars, providing he could keep the kids out from in front of the projector.

In the late twenties or early thirties, a new Cities Service station was built on the east end of the store. This station was operated by Robert Hoffman and others for a few years, then later by Lloyd "Shorty" Urban from 1942 on. In 1946–47 he expanded the station business to include the sale of Admiral Appliances and had the first television sales showroom in the area. At times, twenty to thirty people packed the station showroom to watch Kukla, Fran and Ollie on the little seven-inch television sets.

In 1950, Cities Service was changed to D.X. Sunray. Eventually, this one station's business expanded to twenty-six HCO (Hoffman's Corners' Oil) service station stores around the Twin Cities area.

In the early twenties, on the site across Highway 61 from the store and station, a chicken coop from Charlie Sr.'s farmstead was moved. It was remodeled into a fruit and vegetable stand, then a boxing gym, and later into a tavern. In the mid-1920s Charlie Hoffman Jr., the third youngest son, and his wife Carol Auer Hoffman, built a new attached house and operated the fruit and vegetable stand until about 1935, when it became a tavern and restaurant. There was a little orange Blommer's ice cream stand just to the east, selling two scoop side-by-side cones for a nickel.

Mrs. Rivard, the cook for the restaurant, said that if the price for a chicken dinner consisting of two pieces of chicken, fries, toast, salad and beverage was raised from thirty to thirty-five cents, the customers would complain. She was right! During the late 1930s, Roy Shipstead of the Ice Follies ran the restaurant. Next, Mr. Valelli who had an Italian restaurant ran it. Later, George Welch ran it until the early 1940s. During the Second World War, it was closed and used to store grapefruit. After the war, Mr. Paddleford ran it as "Pad's Place", after which it became the "Burlap Lounge". In 1964, Art Birklund tore down the building and built the present "Country Lounge."

To the west of the Country Lounge is the White Bear Floral Company. Prior to 1932, Henry Wohletz grew wholesale celery in St. Paul, which he sold to Henry Hoffman in 1932. Mr. Wohletz purchased seven acres from Henry Hoffman west of Charlie Hoffman Jr.'s place. Mr. Wohletz built one glass greenhouse, and with his wife Elizabeth and two daughters, Esther and Lorraine, developed the White Bear Floral Co. which grew into thirteen greenhouses. Lorraine Wohletz Birklund and her sister Esther still work at the flower shop.

Across Highway 61 from the greenhouse stood a small building called the Chicken Shack. After the Hilltop Tavern burned down in 1937, Henry Hoffman moved that building to the north side of County Rd. E., where the present HCO station and car wash stands. He leased it to Mike and Minnie Domeski, who ran it until the late thirties as a tavern. Freddie Roth operated it as a tavern and dance hall for more than twenty years. A large mural on the walls depicted a group of frolicking elves by a cave over the words "Yeorge's Beer it's cave aged". This building is now located on Goose Lake Road along with a few other buildings from Hoffman's Corners.

On the other side of the Blommer's ice cream stand, there stood a large block building built in the late 20's or early 30's. This was a Phillips 66 station and auto repair business run by Hector and Elmer Arcand, until the Second World War began. Then the ubiquitous sign "closed for the duration" was put on the door and the place was closed and boarded up. It later became the home of the Mosquito Control Co. and was torn down in the mid 50's. An Eddie Arnold's Chicken Shack was built on the site. This would eventually become a Tasty Freeze and now is a coffee shop managed, since 1995, by Greg Rick.

On the northeast corner of Schunemann Road and County Rd. E, Augie and Charley Schunemann ran a grocery store for many years in mostly friendly competition with Henry Hoffman. There was a small tavern run by Mr. and Mrs. Garner to the east of the store, which is now a pottery outlet. Behind Freddie Roth's and across the road from Shunemann's store was a small one-room brick schoolhouse. Henry Hoffman later bought this land, now Barnett Chrysler, but could not move the brick building. It was the only building he did not move. The other buildings from Hoffman's Corners have been relocated, some up to five times. Most of them are on Goose Lake Road, and Charlie Hoffman Sr.'s descendants occupy them.

Last and least is a ravine behind the floral shop along side of the railroad tracks. The Hoffman's, the Wohletz's, and others have used this ravine as a dumpsite for over one hundred years. Down near the bottom has got to be what is left of the old 1917 Studebaker Touring Car. In the winter, the older Hoffman children had to take off their coats and put them over its hood while they attended Mass at St. Mary's

Church in White Bear Lake, so the water in the radiator would not freeze. A 1911 Kissell truck and assorted Model T Fords and more recent vehicles and appliances joined it as time went by. Sadly, but "progressively", many of these buildings will soon be demolished to make way for a new development. Only the memories will live on.

*A 1914 Studebaker Touring Car.*
*Photo courtesy of Lawrence R. (Bob) and Eileen Whitaker.*

# STUDEBAKER

Electrically Started
Electrically Lighted
Two-passenger

## $1050 00

**"Buy It Because It is a Studebaker",**
Not because of the price mark, but because of the Trade Mark
Not because of the good looks, but because of the Good Name
Not because of the outside, but because of the Inside

*Ad courtesy of White Bear Press. Circa 1914.*

# A Mink Ranch or Three

*As Remembered by*
*Marjorie (Weaver) Bednarek*

n the early summer of 1947, my parents, Daisy and Walter "Sonny" Weaver, moved to White Bear Lake with the sole intent of raising mink.

I never knew what prompted Dad take on such a venture. Perhaps he fell in love with the thought of wealth associated with the raising of fur products. This was laughable, at best, as for years afterward he referred to himself as being "mink poor."

Certainly, Mom would have chosen another vocation. Sky diving or hunting in the wilds of Africa comes to mind, for raising vicious little animals with a propensity for biting the hands that feed them is not for the faint of heart. At the slightest provocation they have been known to produce a skunk-like scent or, if stressed to any extent, will eat their own babies.

Mom came away from the mink-raising experience unscathed, unless of course one counts the sheer determination in her voice ever after as she declared, "I never want to own a mink garment of any kind!" I am certain that decision was not born of a desire to please the animal rights movement.

They purchased a home and three adjoining acres from the Van Grossman's, who had already built their new home just to the north of us.

Dad set about preparing for the arrival of his "stock" by building cages out of army surplus ammunition boxes and chicken wire. As the stock grew, he built a fenced mink yard and placed the cages in long rows under some shade trees. In the spring, the cages were set on the ground so the "kits" would not fall through the holes in the chicken wire.

I remember one particularly wet spring when the mink yard flooded. Kits were trapped in the flooded cages and we had to gather them up and warm them on the oven door in the kitchen. Mom rubbed them down with a soft towel before putting them back in their straw-filled ammunition boxes.

At one point, Dad noticed that one of his mink had a purple or lavender cast to its fur. This mutation, born on Dad's ranch, created a new fur color for products thereafter called amethyst. That mutation also carried an uncommon, more docile nature, which allowed Dad to cuddle it like a pet. He named it "Pete" and when old Pete died, he was given a tearful farewell and buried with honors in the meadow behind the mink yard rather than becoming a part of someone's coat or scarf.

Our nearest neighbors were Nichols', near County Road F (who later started a small grocery store on that corner); Doty's, who had a small farm and sold delicious tomatoes and corn in the late summer months (Mrs. Doty always added more than the required 12 ears of corn to our sack.); Orville and Vivian King, who moved to the town of White Bear; Howard and Louise Seifred, who moved into the King home; Petraks, who lived on a farm located on White Bear Avenue near the corner of what is now Birch Street; and Strassers, whose property met ours in lowlands of the back meadow. All were neighbors too.

By 1958, Dad had induced the Seifreds, the Petraks and the Jim Masters' family on Highway 61 to go into the mink business.

When progress, in the form of new housing, took over the area, it was apparent that three mink ranches in a row on White Bear Avenue could not survive the urban push. The mink had grown from six, to upwards of 400 by then. Mom and Dad decided it was time to sell out and they subsequently moved into the town of White Bear Lake.

Today, "Nichols Drive" off White Bear Avenue, runs through the middle of (what was once) Van Grossman's back yard. The Doty Family remains immortalized as "Doty Drive" begins an eastward direction just a few feet south of their old farm site. Doubtless, few are left to recall a time when three mink ranches existed between County Road F and Birch Street, or that once a woman lived there who declared with determination, "I never want to own a mink garment of any kind!"

My father and his brother, John, in the Healy Plumbing and Heating Corporation, received a United States Patent for eighteen years for inventing the pipe and holder to "hang" a radiator on a wall off the floor. Formerly, the radiator was placed on the floor.

*Ads courtesy of White Bear Press, 1914.*

# Flour

# The Early History of White Bear Lake

*Story circa 1881, retold by F. J. Whitaker in 1936*
*Submitted by Lawrence R. (Bob) and Eileen Whitaker*

## Foreword

The task of writing about the history of a small city such as White Bear Lake is rather complicated. Many books and articles contradict each other, and the true one must be ferreted out. I have had a difficult time finding the truth for some of my statements, but early settlers can confirm most. I have made use of the material collected by the White Bear Lake Historical Society. I admit that some of the people will find errors, either in dates or other details, but errors are found in most history books. I hope that the reader will obtain as much pleasure by reading this thesis as I had in writing it.

F. J. W.

## Early Settlers

Little is known about White Bear before 1851. In spite of the fact that St. Paul was a short distance away, no roads led to this spot. There were no dwellings except the tepees of the Indians.

We hear of the first settlers arriving at White Bear Lake in the spring of 1851. Probably the first one was Hugh J. Vance, who did not settle in White Bear, but located at Bald Eagle Lake. He may have been the first man to drive a plowshare into the soil in this locality. He lived at Bald Eagle until 1861, then along with his two sons, enlisted with the Union Army. They were killed in Missouri the following year.

This same spring also brought V. B. Barnum, who settled on the present site of the old automobile club. In this grove

*The first house built in Cottage Park, 1857. Photo courtesy of Lawrence R. (Bob) and Eileen Whitaker.*

of nice trees, Barnum erected his cabin, and as shingles were unobtainable, he covered his cabin with elm bark. Barnum created a hotel on this spot and later built numerous cabins to accommodate his many guests. He later sold the hotel and grounds to John Lamb, but the property reverted back to Barnum. William Liep appeared on the scene in 1866 and bought the property from Mr. Barnum. Under Mr. Liep's management the hotel became known all over the country.

James F. Murray came in with the settlers about this time. Mr. Murray purchased a tract of land, which extended from the Lake Shore depot and included the Island. He divided his land among his three sons. He built his own cabin near where the Markoe cottage stands, and it was in this cabin that the four-year-old daughter of Mr. and Mrs. J. C. Murray died. A visiting clergyman, J. G. Riheldaffer, preached the funeral service. This was the first sermon in the community. In 1857 Mr. Murray sold the Island to George Burson for $80.00 while in 1881 it was sold to a syndicate for $20,000.00.

Other settlers were coming in to cast their fortunes with the little bit of struggling humanity. Among these were James R. Clewett, Thomas Milner, William Markoe, G. N. Schnabel, and J. L. Fisk.

W. W. Webber, Senior bought a 160 acre tract which now includes the present approach to the city by Highway 61.

Daniel Getty opened the first store in 1870 in a small building, which stood opposite the depot in what is now Washington Park. Barnum sold cigars and liquors next to it, while Porter Long opened the second store and sold groceries. Mr. Getty and his sons were very successful in business and erected the present Getty Block. Mr. Getty allied himself with every movement for the betterment of the community.

*Daniel Getty soon found his original small store inadequate for the growing village's needs. Within a few years he built the Getty Building, shown here with its original facade.*
*Photo courtesy of Lawrence R. (Bob) and Eileen Whitaker.*

I cannot continue without giving an account of the Aubreys. In England they were Sir Arthur Aubrey and Lady Paul, but to the people of White Bear they were Mr. and Mrs. John Aubrey. The father of Sir Aubrey was Sir John Dean Paul, who was a dignified banker whose bank had failed. He was sentenced to exile in Australia for fourteen years. The son, feeling his father's disgrace, decided to leave England and go to another country where he would not be known. Upon arriving in this country he became John Aubrey and with his wife, came to the frontier in Minnesota. They settled on the isthmus between White Bear and Goose Lake.

Mr. Aubrey became one of the best hunters and trappers in this locality, and the sight of Mr. Aubrey roaming the countryside accompanied by his two hunting dogs became very common. His wife soon became one of the most influential people of the settlement. She became a teacher in the log schoolhouse, and later organized a church, named St. John's in the Wilderness. In the meantime, back in England, Sir John regained his title and possessions. The Aubreys received word of Sir John's death, and with many misgivings, returned to England and assumed the Barony. At this time the residents of White Bear learned that for ten years they had been associating with members of the English nobility.

## Schools

In 1857, who could foresee the educational system that White Bear would have eighty years hence? The small log cabin served the community well in the early years. Mrs. John Aubrey was the first teacher, and it was mainly through her efforts that the school was built. The early settlers sent their children to this little cabin to be educated. In those days a little education was better than none at all. At no time do we hear of complaints against attending school. At times, friendly Indians would peer through the windows and watch the children as they learned their three R's.

In 1868 the little log cabin was unsuited for the purpose of a school as the number of enrolled pupils had increased. On the corner of Murray Avenue and Second Street, another building was erected and maintained as the

*Washington School, after its expansion, housed grades K–8. Photo courtesy of C. Jane Jackson*

*The Division Street side of White Bear Lake High School, 1935. Photo courtesy of Lawrence R. (Bob) and Eileen Whitaker.*

school. This was known as the West Side School. The number of pupils increased rapidly and in 1878 another story was added to the structure.

However, by the year 1887, the number of pupils had increased to such an extent that an independent school district was organized. The district built the Webster School on the corner of Fifth Street and Stewart Avenue. This building was erected at the cost of $13,000.00 and was fitted with all the modern improvements. I may also say that this was the first schoolhouse in Minnesota to furl the American Flag from its peak. The school system of the town now consisted of two buildings—the West Side School and the Webster School— which provided six rooms for educational purposes.

*St. Mary's Catholic School on the corner*
*of Bald Eagle Avenue and Second Street.*
*Photo courtesy of Lawrence R. (Bob) and Eileen Whitaker.*

Today,* White Bear maintains the Washington and Webster Schools as the public grade schools, and they are filled to capacity. There is also a Catholic grade school. Besides these three grade schools, there is a modern high school that has become quite inadequate. At the present time, work is being rushed for the completion of an addition to the high school that will also serve as a junior high.

*Editor's note: "Today" refers to the time when the author wrote this, circa 1930s.

## Churches

### St. Mary's of the Lake

Before 1873, the Catholic people of White Bear Lake were obliged to go to Little Canada to attend Mass. In 1873, Rev. J. L. Koop, obtained permission to say Mass in the log schoolhouse. He was a friend of the late William F. Markoe; the choir from St. Mary's Church in St. Paul assisted.

In 1874, the Rev. Father Othmar O.S.B. of the Assumption Church in St. Paul celebrated the Feast of the Nativity of the Blessed Virgin Mary by saying Mass in the parlor of the Markoe cottage, known as the "Mound" cottage because of its nearness to the large Indian mound. This cottage became the center of Catholic activities in White Bear. A large number of visiting priests and missionaries were welcome to partake of the Markoe hospitality and to say Mass for the Catholics of the community.

*First St. Mary of the Lake Church, 1880, was a wooden building erected on Second and Bald Eagle Avenues for a cost of $1,000. Photo courtesy of Lawrence R. (Bob) and Eileen Whitaker.*

*James J. Hill's daughters built St. Mary of the Lake Stone Church in 1926. Photo courtesy of Lawrence R. (Bob) and Eileen Whitaker.*

White Bear became a mission of Little Canada and, under the care of Rev. Father Goiffon, the spiritual needs of the people were looked after. Many visiting priests said Mass, which relieved Father Goiffon of making the trip to White Bear. With his own hands he helped the people build the first Catholic Church, which was completed about 1880.

On the Feast of the Assumption, Rev. Bishop Grace of St. Paul blessed the edifice and dedicated it to God. Evergreens from the tamarack swamp west of Goose Lake were used to decorate it. Besides the assembled parishioners, there were many visitors from nearby parishes.

### St. John's in the Wilderness

The very first religious services were held in the log schoolhouse. Lady Paul, better known as Mrs. Aubrey, desired to have an Episcopal church built. In 1861, a building was erected facing Goose Lake on the present site of the Episcopal cemetery. Bishop Whipple consecrated it. The parish was organized in 1868 with Messrs. Fitzburgh and William Freeman as wardens and Messrs. Milner, Webber, Sr., Joseph Freeman, and Smith as vestrymen.

This site was quite removed from the homes of most of the settlers, so in 1874 the building was moved across the ice to the site of the present building. This first building was quite aristocratic in appearance.

*St. John's in the Wilderness Episcopal Church, 1861–1926. Photo courtesy of Lawrence R. (Bob) and Eileen Whitaker.*

### Presbyterian Church

The first services were held in the log schoolhouse with Rev. J. G. Riheldoffer officiating. The church was organized in 1869 and was composed of eight members. J. R. Murray and Daniel Getty were appointed as ruling elders. A lot was purchased at what is now Cottage Park, but later the lot was considered too much out of the way. In 1871, Dr. J. H. Stewart of St. Paul donated the present lot. In 1873, the cornerstone of the present building was laid, and the building was completed the next year. The church building was decorated with evergreens and flowers at the dedication ceremony.

*The First Presbyterian Church of White Bear Lake, 1871–1958, built at a cost of $2,500. Photo courtesy of Lawrence R. (Bob) and Eileen Whitaker.*

### German Lutheran Church

West Side School held the first services. In 1888, the services were transferred to the Webster School, and in 1891 a lot was purchased at Seventh Street and Stewart Avenue. On November 15, 1891 Rev. H. Volkert dedicated the building. The first officers were William Goesch, William Boesel, and Otto Luedke, as trustees, while Theodore Hanson was secretary and William Goesch was treasurer.

### First Lutheran Church

This church was originally the Swedish Lutheran, but in 1925 it adopted its present name and in 1929 it accepted the congregation of the German Lutheran. The meetings were first held in the Chateaugay Hotel in 1888. Later, Mr. and Mrs. Carl Sandahl allowed the meeting to be held in their residence. During the fall of 1888, work was started on the building of a church on the corner of Sixth Street and Stewart Avenue. In June 1889, Rev. Gus Wahlund dedicated the building.

*First Lutheran Church. Photo courtesy of Lawrence R. (Bob) and Eileen Whitaker.*

## White Bear Lake in the Nineties

It must not be supposed that the popularity of White Bear Lake as a resort grew up suddenly. The first settlers arrived in 1851, and for nearly twenty years many had to walk to St. Paul for supplies. During the nineties, White Bear Lake as a resort, became second in interest only to Lake Minnetonka.

*The White Bear Lake post office, 1913. Photo courtesy of C. Jane Jackson*

The post office of White Bear Lake was established in 1859 with James C. Murray as postmaster. In 1881, the state legislature incorporated the Village of White Bear Lake with the following officers: Daniel Getty, chairman of the council, James C. Murray, Luke H. Bacon, Abel E. Leaman, and Fred W. Benson, councilmen; B.E. McGurok, recorder; H.H. Getty, treasurer; William Clark, village justice; Reuben Clewett, marshal.

The old Lake Superior and Mississippi Railroad Company built a railroad line to White Bear Lake in 1868, thus completing the first link of the road to Duluth. In the same year, the old red depot was built. At first, its dimensions were 24 by 60 feet, but later a baggage room of 12 by 24 feet was added. Upon the opening of this first link between White Bear Lake and St. Paul, the company gave an excursion for 500 people. It was a gala day for all. From that day, the popularity of White Bear Lake increased. As many as twenty-five trains plied between White Bear Lake and St. Paul daily. White Bear Lake became quite a division point on the railroad line, as there were branch lines to Minneapolis and Stillwater. During the summer season the railroad company would run what were called the "Theater Trains" to St. Paul, Minneapolis, and Stillwater for the benefit of those who wished to attend the theater, entertainment, lodges, or parties. The railroads played a large part in making White Bear Lake a popular resort.

The hotels of White Bear Lake were the keynote of the pleasure seekers. There were many to choose from and they were all filled to capacity during the summer season. Probably the best known hotel was that of William Liep. Mr. Liep also had quite a number of nice cabins, which were rented to his guests. Mr. Liep was a man of medium size with dark hair and whiskers, and was always pleasing to his guests. The Liep Hotel was located where the old automobile club stood.

The Williams House had a fine shady lawn, and an excellent view of the lake. The many patrons of this house found the hostess, Mrs. R. H. Williams, a very genial landlady.

The Chateaugay Hotel, operated by Fred W. Benson, also commanded a pleasing view of the lake. The landlord lost no opportunity to provide for the comfort and happiness of his guests.

The Lakeside Cottage was probably the most quiet and homelike hostelry. It stood upon the high banks north of Sixth Street on Lake Avenue. The view was one of nature and its loveliness. A guest could see Manitou Island, Dellwood,

Mahtomedi, the peninsula, and a fine view of the lake. Mrs. W. H. Drake made it pleasant and profitable for the dwellers that stayed at her house.

Ramaley's Pavilion, which was a large dancing hall, served the best in everything in the line of lunch, ice cream, and other refreshments.

The patrons of these hotels did not sit in a chair all day, for there were many things to amuse the pleasure seekers. There were hops, dances, and musicales, which were always successful. Col. Liep gave mid-summer band concerts at his hotel. The White Bear Yacht Club, which was organized in 1889, gave regattas that amused many of the pleasure seekers. Several steamers made regular trips to all points of the lake. Among the best known, the Dispatch and the Manitoba, both could be chartered for night dancing parties. Smaller launches, rowboats, and sailboats could be rented at reasonable rates. Many people found amusement in watching the baseball games that were played by crack teams from St. Paul. Other persons were amused by the tennis games.

*From Ramaley's docks one could cruise the lake in naptha-powered tour boats.*
*Photos courtesy of Lawrence R. (Bob) and Eileen Whitaker.*

*Ramaley's Pavilion opened on June 6, 1890, accommodating over 2,000 people. Photo courtesy of Lawrence R. (Bob) and Eileen Whitaker.*

# Legends of the Indians Around White Bear Lake

*As Remembered by*
*F. J. Whitaker*
*Submitted by Lawrence R. (Bob) and Eileen Whitaker*

Before beginning to speak of the Indians of the area, it might be well to look a bit at the general terrain of the countryside. It is quite well established by E. H. Winchell in his *Geology of Minnesota*, published in 1901, that a geological lake existed over the locality of White Bear, Bald Eagle, and other lakes of the vicinity. This glacial lake extended into Anoka and Washington counties.

Likewise, another glacial lake existed in the region north of White Bear Lake from near Centerville to Forest Lake. As these glacial lakes subsided, the melting craters tended to fill the existing basins, which formed the various lakes of the area. The excess waters tended to follow the natural drainage toward the east through Big Marine Lake and then to the St. Croix River, or towards the west through Rice Creek and thence to the Mississippi River. The lakes that remained covered a larger area than at present. One result of this was that a comparatively short distance separated one lake from the other. Thus, one who knew the country also knew excellent traveling routes by means of which he could travel to various places within the general area. These various lake routes served as connecting links between the main rivers bordering the general locality—the Mississippi, the St. Croix, and the Rum Rivers, which one may consider the main arteries of travel for the Indians.

The first mention of a white man in the vicinity of White Bear Lake is found in J. V. Bower's, *Members of Exploration in the Basin of the Mississippi*, published in 1900. In Volume III on page 55, he says that the Sioux who captured Father Hennepin and his companions in 1680 left their canoes near Dayton's Bluff and proceeded overland on foot directly to the Mille Lacs region. They undoubtedly traveled via White Bear Lake, thence to near where Centerville is now situated, and to the Rum River and Mille Lacs. Father Hennepin, in his account, likewise mentions leaving the canoes and walking overland, during which they waded streams. He makes no mention of travelling by canoes although it would appear natural for them to have used the waterway connection between the Mississippi and the Rum Rivers.

Be that as it may, we now return to the subject of Indians around White Bear Lake. During historic times, the first Indians to dwell in the general territory where White Bear Lake is situated were the Sioux. The Chippewas, at that time, lived in what is now Wisconsin. They were later pushed westward by other tribes who also were dispossessed of their hunting grounds by the encroaching settlers. Hence, this area lying between the main camps became a "bone of contention" with both tribes claiming the right to hunt, fish, and gather wild rice and make maple sugar in the locality. This resulted in many battles between the tribes. W.H.C. Folsom in his *Fifty Years in the Northwest*, published in 1888, says that the island in White Bear Lake was the most fought over spot in this immediate vicinity.

### Indian Legends

There are several Indian legends as to how White Bear Lake received its name. The best known is that of Kissemepa and Kagoka. Mark Twain in his *Life on the Mississippi*, tells of this legend, humorously commenting on its validity.

Another legend from the Sioux gives this account. Chingachgook, a Chippewa scout, had met Nakawisi, the daughter of the Sioux Chief, Eagle Eye, beside a spring near her camp and fell in love with her. Later, Nakawisi, learning of a council proposing war upon the Chippewa, hastened to inform her lover. Chingachgook, with others of his tribe, proceeded to the Sioux council and persuaded them that peace would exist between the tribes if he were allowed to marry Nakawisi. Chief Eagle Eye replied that the youth would first have to prove himself worthy of the maiden by performing a great feat. A short time later, the Chippewa brave crossed over to the island, eagerly leapt ashore and swiftly ran up the path to meet his beloved. Coming in sight of her, he saw a huge white bear about to strike her. He drew his knife and fearlessly attacked the bear, plunging the knife again and again into the bear until the beast was dead. Both man and beast lay motionless upon the blood stained ground while Chief Eagle Eye spoke, "Chingachgook, thou hast met the test. Nakawisi is yours." The brave warrior did not answer, for his spirit was accompanying that of the bear to the happy hunting ground. Thus, the island was called "Spirit Island."

Another version of this same legend makes no mention of the maiden being on the island. This version says that the bear inhabited the island, and that the test was that Chingachgook was to kill the bear. Neither the warrior nor the bear survived.

Still another legend states that the island was created in a single night with a great white bear roaming on it. The Indians supposed that the bear was symbolic of the Great Spirit, Manitou, and called the island, "Spirit Island." The present name of the island is "Manitou Island."

### The Mounds in White Bear Lake

Indian legends passed on from generation to generation by word of mouth may become distorted in the telling. More durable than such legends was the group of nine mounds, which once stood on the banks of White Bear Lake in the vicinity of Shady Lane and Lake Avenue. Of these mounds, there was one, large and impressive, from which a person could have an excellent view of the lake. The other eight mounds were somewhat low and rather inconspicuous in comparison to the largest so that they were seldom noticed. The "march of civilization" has wrought destruction to the mounds with one exception. This remaining small mound is located some distance from where the others once stood, and forms the elevation for the flagpole on the Dougherty property. Of these smaller mounds, nothing is known concerning their destruction.

The largest and most impressive of the mounds stood approximately where Shady Lane meets Lake Avenue upon the property of the late William Markoe. It rose to a height of about twelve feet with a base of about seventy-five feet in diameter. It stood close enough to the bank of the lake that one side merged with the bank and sloped to the water's edge. From its summit, as mentioned above, a person could obtain an excellent view of the lake and, consequently, became a show place for the community. William F. Markoe, writing about the mound in the February 1, 1935 issue of the WHITE BEAR PRESS, mentions that in about 1873 a rustic

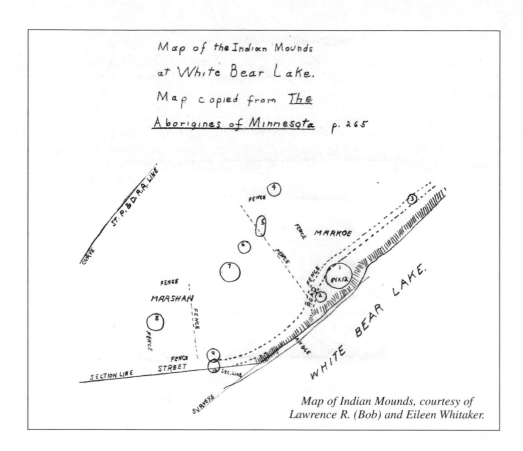

Map of Indian Mounds, courtesy of
Lawrence R. (Bob) and Eileen Whitaker.

summerhouse of split tamarack was erected on top of the mound. The casements of the windows and door of the little house were adorned with U.S. shields while the interior furnishings consisted of a round table with circular seats. During the winter months, the top of the mound served as the beginning of a toboggan slide by means of which the participants glided out onto the lake.

Lake Avenue, at that time, had to swerve away from the lake bank as it approached the mound. About 1883, an unfortunate incident occurred which aroused the feelings of many people, and caused them to condemn the mound as a public hazard. A carriage, becoming unmanageable upon striking an exposed root near the mound, careened towards the mound and upset. The occupants were thrown from the carriage; one being fatally injured while the others were less seriously injured. Because of this accident, and the demands of many people, the city council resolved to remove the mound instead of having the road moved a bit further from the mound.

For several years, Mr. Markoe protected his rights with a court injunction and, it is said, stood guard with a shotgun over the mound. Thus, this precious relic of prehistoric times was preserved for several years. The Minnesota Historical Society, as well as other interested people, beseeched the city council not to remove the mound. The city council, however, would not change its decision, and the work of demolition began on April 18, 1889.

The work was under the direction of Albert Clewett, the road commissioner at the time. As the demolition work continued, it was found that the mound was built of a rich black loam, which had most likely been scraped from the adjacent property.

Spectators picked up many relics, but neither workmen nor spectators were prepared for the gruesome sight when the workmen reached the natural level of the ground. Here they unearthed nineteen skeletons with numerous flint arrowheads, war clubs, etc. Mr. Clewett gathered up the skeletons and a number of other relics for the Minnesota Historical Society. The skeletons were not accepted, so they were brought back to White Bear Lake and buried in a single unmarked grave in the southwest corner of Union Cemetery.

Relics retained by the Society consisted of a perfect human skull, a bone scoop, a bone needle or hairpin, a curious right-angled bone, (which might have been a deformity), a cake of blue pigment, and red coloring matter in powder. N.H. Winchell, in his *Aborigines of Minnesota*, quotes the St. Paul Pioneer Press (April 28, 1889) giving the list of relics received by the Historical Society. The late Mr. Markoe, in his article cited above, states that a flintlock pistol was found in or near the mound. The ancient landmark and burial mound was now desecrated with the remains removed and placed in an unmarked grave.

The question arises as to who were these mound builders and whence did they come? Those are questions which have not been fully answered, except that we know these were prehistoric peoples. Recent studies seem to indicate that they might have been of the Hopewillian culture, which flourished from about 1500 BC to about 500 AD. These people are known to have erected mounds of many types, such as burial mounds, ceremonial mounds, effigy mounds, etc. Although centered in Ohio, they are known to have traveled the Ohio and Mississippi Rivers. Perhaps they had reached this area while on their travels.

It is known that some later tribes, coming upon burial mounds already erected, would make further burials, which are termed "intrusion" burials. This explains why there are sometimes burials of the different cultures found in the same mound. Perhaps explaining the presence of the flint lock pistol, N.H. Winchell in his *Aborigines of Minnesota*, page 266, quotes an item from the St. Paul Pioneer Press, (May 30, 1889). It stated that One-legged Jim, a brother of Old Betts, asserted that his forefathers built the large mound at White Bear Lake for the burial of a celebrated chief. Thus, the notion was formed that it was the burial place of Chief White Bear. However, Winchell on page 298 says that White Bear was a chief of the Yankton Sioux, and that his grave is a mound near Glenwood, in the western part of Minnesota.

### Indians During Settled Times

As mentioned above, both the Sioux and the Chippewa tribes claimed the territory around White Bear Lake. The Sioux, by reason of first occupancy; the Chippewa, because of their having been driven from their former lands. The Treaty of 1851, made by the Sioux and the whites, appears to have allowed them the right to hunt, fish and gather berries in the area.

In 1853, a party of Chippewa concealed themselves near the trading post in St. Paul, and opened fire upon a party of Sioux as it arrived at the post. The citizens quickly barred the doors and hid the remaining Sioux. Other citizens quickly formed a posse to pursue the fleeing Chippewa. They were able to follow the group to a point near White Bear Lake where they lost the trail, without being able to find any trace of the Chippewa.

W.H.C. Folsom in his *Fifty Years in the Northwest*, published in 1886, relates that in 1855 a group of Sioux from Kaposia (near South St. Paul) passed through White Bear Lake on a hunting trip. A few miles north, near Oneka Lake, they came upon a small band of Chippewa. They killed and scalped one. While in the fray, two of their number were wounded. The Sioux returned and camped at Goose Lake about where the Episcopal Church was first erected in the present Episcopal cemetery. They held a scalp dance for two days and nights, which also gave their wounded warriors a chance to recuperate. They then returned to their village at Kaposia.

During the time of the Civil War, the Sioux uprising began on August 17, 1862. This was confined mostly to the Minnesota River Valley, although even at White Bear Lake precautions were taken. The settlers went about in fear since they were uncertain as to the extent and the number of Indians involved. At night, blankets were hung to cover the windows, so prowling Indians were unable to learn the number of persons in the building.

*American Sioux Chief White Cap,
a member of the Minnesota band involved
in the uprisings of 1862, circa 1935.
Photo courtesy of Lynne Hagen.*

Many communities organized bands of home guards for protection in case of a raid. The Ramsey Picket Guards was organized September 1, 1862 and served until the 18th of that month when the danger had passed. Captain George W. Few's Company consisted of 35 men, of whom the following were from White Bear Lake; L. C. Dunn, 2nd Lieutenant, David Bibeau, William Freeman, William Houle, Camille Langlois, Paul Labore, and Thomas Milner. There is no record that they ever saw battle action in this area.

In the fall of 1889, just after the removal of the ancient burial mound, a group of Indians passed through White Bear on their way to harvest wild rice. They saw that the burial mound had been removed and were very much displeased; so much so, that they set up camp near the site of the old icehouses and their actions became warlike. The inhabitants became alarmed, and strict watch was kept. Finally, the Indians smoked the peace pipe and went their way. This was the last record of Indians in this locality.

# White Bear's Indian Mound

*Written by Wm. F. Markoe*
*Submitted by Lawrence R. (Bob) and Eileen Whitaker*

*William F. Markoe and the "Mound Cottage," circa 1902.*
*The first catholic church meetings were also held in the cottage.*
*Photo courtesy of Don McCormick.*

Recent interviews with a number of old settlers at White Bear Lake have brought to light a number of interesting and hitherto unpublished facts about the colossal Indian mound that used to adorn the north shore of White Bear Lake.

In the year 1873, the late William Markoe, who had sailed over the lake in his balloon in 1857, purchased an acre and a half of lakefront at what is now the corner of Lake Avenue and Shady Lane. This included the Indian mound and the riparian rights and subject only to an easement permitting pedestrians and vehicles to pass.

The mound was elliptical, rather than circular, in shape, and was estimated to be approximately 75 feet in its greatest diameter, and 18 or 20 feet high. On his return from what is now Niagara University in New York State, the writer spent much of his vacation in constructing a rustic summerhouse on top of the mound. He had to saw, split and match 480 pieces of tamarack about 15 inches long to form the walls, and the gothic mullions for the doors and windows had to be found in just the right shape and size in nearby oak trees. These doors were surrounded by U. S. Shields, and the roof was crowned with a rustic cross. The interior was furnished with circular seats and a round table. The novel structure soon became a showplace of White Bear, and hundreds of picnickers, brought to the lake daily by trains on the St. Paul & Duluth R. R., immediately rushed to the mound to eat their lunch and enjoy the beautiful view of the lake.

A scientist from New York, who was making a study of Indian mounds, assured Mr. Markoe that if his mound could be transported to Central Park in New York, as Cleopatra's Needle was transported from Egypt to America by means of a specially constructed raft, the City Council of New York would gladly sign a check for $1,000,000. He then asked if there were any more mounds in the neighborhood. Declaring knowledge of another mound in the vicinity, the scientist began breaking his way through a tangled mass of underbrush, and there, sure enough, was a single grave lying undisturbed.

In those days, there were two classes of residents in White Bear: permanent and transient. The latter included many of St. Paul's "Four Hundred" who wished to escape the clatter and din of city life and enjoy the health-giving ozone of country life. The other ambition was to build a great city and "make St. Paul its back door!" In the course of time, most of the summer residents migrated to Manitou Island or Dellwood. Before long, ominous mutterings began to be heard against the mound as a dangerous place for teams and drivers to pass. This feeling was increased by an accident which happened in front of Col. Leip's Hotel, a quarter of a mile from the mound, on the Fourth of July, 1883, in which a horse took fright at a fire cracker and ran into a tree in the middle of the street, killing a Stillwater man. The village was sued for damages. Then the late Honorable C. D. O'Brien won the case for the village. For several years, Mr. Markoe protected his rights by means of an injunction signed by the court and filled out except for the date.

Although there is nothing in the records of the village council to show the date of the destruction and desecration of the Indian Mound, the consensus of opinion seems to be that it occurred a year after the building of the first Ice Palace in St. Paul. That would make it in the winter of 1887, after the summerhouse had been blown down by a severe storm. A gang of workmen with teams, plows, picks and shovels were engaged for a whole month in removing the Mound. They replaced it by making an ugly fill like a railroad cut from a point west of the Mound along the lakeshore to Clark Avenue. One old settler is said to have stood guard with a shotgun to protect his trees in front of his property.

Strange to say, the whole mound was built with rich black loam supposed to have been scraped up from the adjoining property, and not till the workmen reached the natural level of the ground did they begin to realize the gruesome character of the work they were engaged in. They recovered 19 complete skeletons so well preserved, especially their teeth, that they were thought to have been young braves. Stranger still, there were found near every skeleton, three large cobblestones arranged in the shape of a three-leaf clover, which prompted a would-be wag to wonder if they were "Irish Indians"!

On the other hand, the finding of a flintlock pistol in or near the Mound suggested the possibility of there having been a French voyager following the trail with them, or perhaps as a prisoner. Numerous flint arrowheads, paint pots, tomahawks and war clubs were also unearthed. Many of these relics were picked up by spectators and carried off, thus making it almost impossible to comply with the promise to turn over all such relics to the Minnesota State Historical Society in St. Paul. The 19 skeletons were hauled to the museum, but the society declined to receive them, and they were hauled back to White Bear and buried in a single grave in the southwestern corner of Union Cemetery. Besides the skeletons, many skulls, thighbones, shinbones, etc. were gathered together by Mr. Markoe and his grandchildren and buried in a new grave on his property at a spot known only to them. Old settlers, judging by the size of the oak trees shown in the pictures, believe that the mound may have been from 100 to 200 years old. All regret that act of vandalism and agree that the destruction of White Bear's Indian mound was the "crime of the century!"

*The controversial Indian Mound along Lake Avenue prior to its removal in 1889.*
*Photo courtesy of Lawrence R. (Bob) and Eileen Whitaker.*

# Indians, the Fever and Fun Times

*As remembered by*
*Althea W. Rohlfing*

I am 81 years old and was asked to tell you a little about our life way back when I was about your age. I went to grade school and high school here in Mahtomedi and was graduated from high school in the first graduating class in 1934. There were only 16 graduates in our graduating class. That was 64 years ago. A lot of changes and improvements have been made in our schools and the community these last 64 years.

However, before that time I want to assure you that "Yes, we did have Indians living here."

My mother was born in the White Bear Lake area and always lived here in this area. In her ten years she lived with her grandparents about a mile up the train tracks from Mahtomedi toward Stillwater.

Her grandfather went out in the woods near their house and cut wood to keep their wood pile either replenished or complete. They always had to have a supply of wood on hand so they could prepare meals because they had only a big wood-burning stove. In about 1890, when it was beginning to get dark outside, my grandmother heard the door open and someone walking around in the kitchen and thought it was Grandpa coming in for supper. A little later, when Grandpa really did come in, my Grandma went to the kitchen to put the dinner on the table. She was surprised when the huge kettle of soup which she had been preparing all day was not there.

She knew some Indians had come in, taken it off the stove and took it home with them. They had to make a big kettle of soup at a time because they had no refrigeration with which to preserve the meat and vegetables. That night they had only creamed potatoes for supper.

However, two days later the Indians brought the kettle back, all cleaned up and they had a nice venison roast in the kettle as thanks. That was their peace offering. My great-grandparents decided that the Indians probably had not had anything to eat for maybe 2 days and were hungry and it was the only way to get something to eat. Here, I might add that they came back several times later asking for "Tukinshaw," or salt, because they liked its flavor in their food.

My father came here to live in about 1885 from the Lake Minnetonka area when he was 12 or 13 years old and lived with his sister and family in White Bear Beach. He was sure he could find more work here. About three years later he had enough money saved, with which he bought a team of horses. Several years after that, he was able to buy about ten acres of land on Echo Lake, a little lake which is on a part of the White Bear Yacht Club Golf Course and is now considered in Dellwood. When he bought this property, there were two hills with a valley in between in which some Indians had built their tepees because the hills protected them from the cold north winds and blizzards.

Occasionally the Indians would get into fights, or so-called tribal wars, with other tribes in the area until, gradually, the Indians disappeared. Many of the Indians where my mother lived died from pneumonia.

*School board budget courtesy of White Bear Press.*

In 1923, when I started school in the first grade and my oldest brother was then ten years old and in the fifth grade, there was an epidemic of scarlet fever in the Mahtomedi and White Bear area. My oldest brother got scarlet fever and died from it. My other brother and I were out of school from the day after school started in September until the new term started after Christmas, almost four months.

Like you, we had very good and caring teachers but we did not have the benefit of the good equipment you enjoy. Our football field was full of sand burrs and sometimes the boys came in from practice pretty scratched up. Regulation football pants were almost unheard of in those early years and some boys were lucky enough to get a football helmet for Christmas or on their birthday.

My parent's home on Echo Lake was typical of homes built in 1901 or 1902. There was NO electricity and NO indoor plumbing. Our pump was about twenty feet from the kitchen so we kept a clean pail of water in the kitchen for drinking and cooking. It was necessary to pump the water for washing clothes and, also, we had to keep a huge tank filled which was down near the barn with which to water the four horses and two cows.

Each of us kids had skates (the kind which had to be clamped on our shoes), a pair of skis which did not have a harness (just straps), and a sled. Also, we had a toboggan which we took turns using. For inside amusement, we had various card games and lots of books. The boys had building games or toys like Tinker Toys, Lincoln Logs and Erector Sets.

For several years between about 1912 and 1920 there was a small brick building on the corner of Juniper and Warner Road and was known as "The Ark", in which silent black and white movies were shown occasionally. Someone had to stay with the machine all the time to give the machine a push, a swat or whatever seemed necessary to keep the machine going when it got stubborn and stopped.

About this time the nice movie house named The Avalon Theater opened in White Bear and showed the latest movies to come out of Hollywood.

And, of course, there was the Wildwood Amusement Park with its many amusements such as the Ferris Wheel, Roller Coaster, Water Slide, Merry-Go-Round with its beautifully carved horses, and the Park men had a miniature golf course. Nor can we forget the many places where we could buy five-cent ice cream cones, pop or popcorn, to mention only a few. There were even row boats to rent. This was a real treat for people who did not live near the lake.

We had only dirt roads and trails here. In the spring when the snow was melting, and in the summer after a good rain, the roads were filled with deep muddy ruts and holes. Because there were almost no automobiles yet, it wasn't too hard to get around because the horses seemed to pick the easiest spots on which to walk. Anyway, there were not too many horses pulling buggies or wagons in the early 1920s. I believe, but I don't know for sure, that the state or City of Mahtomedi did not start to pave or blacktop the streets until the late 1930s or early 1940s. That was the real start of all the traffic through Mahtomedi. With this, it was necessary to name the streets.

Of course, we cannot forget those wonderful big yellow street cars. What a ride! You've never had a real ride until you have taken that one. It was a real wild ride. It was a normal ride from St. Paul until we left North St. Paul and started down what was known as the Long Lake Hill. I'm sure we went 60 miles per hour when the street car swayed from side to side. It seemed like we would never stop and considered ourselves lucky when we did stop at the very end of the line which was almost in our front yard in Mahtomedi.

As I think back on our life, it was loads of fun! This includes going down to the lake and catching a lot of six-inch long black leeches or catching crayfish and making them catch on to the critter ahead of it with its pinchers until we had a string of them, about one to two feet long. I am sad to say I have had to leave out some of the fun stuff.

I hope you have enjoyed it with me today. Now wasn't that fun?

# STREETCAR REMOVAL CASE BEFORE RAILROAD COMMISSION YESTERDAY

### White Bear Joins in With Residents of Birchwood and Bellaire in Request for Bus Service in Case Streetcar Service is Taken Off; Herbert Keller Appears for Citizens in Plea.

*Courtesy of White Bear Press.*

# R. R. COM. GRANTS STREET CAR CO'S. PETITION TO QUIT

### Sounds All Right on Paper But Doesn't Square With Facts; Rights of Citizens Disregarded

## CASE MAY GO TO COURTS

### Commission Did Not Recommend Substitute Bus Service, or Consider Scores of People and School Children Who Are to be Left Without Means of Transportation; Two Mails Affected.

The State Railroad Commission has acted in the case wherein the Streetcar Co. petitioned for permission to abandon the White Bear Wildwood line, and it has issued an order granting said petition. The "findings of facts and order" of the Commission is printed herewith on this page.

While this decision is just as was expected, yet when the fact is announced it is discomforting, for neither the Commission nor the streetcar company has ever given the patrons of the line the least consideration. There would have been no objection to the order if the Commission had provided for a bus service to take the place of the streetcars.

The residents along that line built their homes there because of the transportation facilities afforded by the car line. The Commission cites the use of private automobiles and busses as lessening the patronage. The bus service does not extend to this district. The automobiles are used by the men through the day and the women and children are without service except the car line. School children were denied a car at an hour when they could use it. This forced the purchase and use of school bus and employment taxi to transport the school children.

The company claims this condition has been coming on for the past 10 years, but they did not suggest a bus service. The company owns the bus line.

The company's manipulation of figures on income, expenditures, etc., are not true to the actual condition.

However, it is necessary that some move be made to secure transportation for the people along this line, and just what action will be taken has not been determined. Unless some arrangement can be made to help the situation, the case may be carried to the courts.

# The Cornerstone of an 1880s Village

*As Remembered by F. J. Whitaker*
*Submitted by Lawrence R. (Bob) and Eileen Whitaker.*

A fire department that may well be called first class in every particular, is one of the prominent organizations of the village, and its membership comprises the best young blood in White Bear. Our fire department has been supplied with a full compliment of apparatus, consisting of a side arm engine, two hose carts, and a hook and ladder truck. The department has always responded readily and quickly when called upon and invariably rendered good and fantastic service.

The Department is ably officered as follows:
Chas. Reif, Chief
E.F. Heller, Secretary
W.H. Jackson, Treasurer
Frank Clewett, Otto Lundke, C. W. Thompson,
Executive Committee.

A new fire hall and engine house was erected for their use in 1888, at the corner of Clark Avenue and Second Street. The department has organized and maintains a relief association to provide assistance to any of the department who may become disabled or ill from exposure while on duty.

### The Citizen's Union

The Citizen's Union, as its name implies, is an association of citizens and freeholders who have formed themselves into an organization for the better protecting, and maintaining the improving of affairs in the village, and acting in connection with the village council. They have done much good, and will continue to do so.

The members are:
D. Getty, President
D. Hanna, Vice President
J.C. Murray, Treasurer
G.H. Staehle, Secretary
C.J. Gotshall, A.H.S. Parkins, J.M. King, A.E. Leaman,
G.S. Gannett, Executive Committee
The Village was incorporated in 1881 with Daniel Getty, Chairman.
L.H. Bacon, A.E. Leaman, J.C. Murray and F. W. Benson as councilmen.
B.E. McGurk as recorder.
H.K. Getty as Treasurer.
Wm. Clark as Justice.
Reuben Clewett as Marshal.

The village was re-incorporated under the general laws of the state in 1884.

*Ads promoting "Beutification Campaign of White Bear Lake in 1914. Courtesy of White Bear Press.*

# By the Light of the Silvery Moon

*As Remembered by*
*Jeannie (Lemke) Ramsey*

*What follows are some excerpts of the lives of my relatives who were in White Bear Lake, Minnesota, or associated with the area in some way. A taped conversation with Robert Bruce Albee and Mary Ellen (Albee) Lemke provided most of the information I share here, and I added some personal remembrances of my own. I am one of the daughters of Mary Ellen and Marvin Lemke, and a great-great granddaughter of the first party mentioned below. Looking back at our family history makes White Bear Lake a very big and important place. Writing this article from California, I focus on a Minnesota map, and zero in to a place of beauty and heart-warming memories. In what follows, I will attempt to convey how some of my relatives in the years gone by have shared in its past:*

On October 9, 1858, in Gramentine, Germany, Emily Blassen Wagner and Edward Wagner had a baby girl. They named her Albertine Bertha Wagner. When she was about the age of 22, she and her parents, along with one of her two sisters, came to the United States.

Eight years before Albertine's birth, Theodore A. Hansen was born on August 20, 1850, in Schwerin, Meclanberg, Diekhof, Germany. His parents were Johan Joaechun Frederick Daniel Hansen and Katherine Elizabeth Marie Sophie Benedict …Whew! Theodore also grew up in Germany, but after he met and fell in love with "Bertha" Wagner, he followed her to America, and finally, to St. Paul. They married on August 17, 1881, in St. Paul.

The Hansens "settled down" in White Bear Lake in a house on Banning Avenue. Bertha's parents, Emily and Edward Wagner, were also included. Their "downtown" location was a block from Main Street and opposite the White Bear Lumber Company near the railroad.

Theodore and Bertha had a family of three: Marie (her additional names unknown), born in 1884, Anna Louise Theodora, "Lucy," Hansen (my grandmother), born May 17, 1886, and Ernest (Ernst—his additional names unknown), born in 1890. All of the Hansen children, Marie, Louise, and Ernest, were baptized in the German Lutheran Church. Bertha Hansen was a charter member of that Church in White Bear, and was one of the creators and organizers of the "Fraunfrine." (Translation: Lady-Friends Organization)

Mr. Hansen worked as a gardener in White Bear Lake, on "The Island," for people who had their beautiful summer homes there. He became Mayor Hansen of White Bear in the late 1800s or early 1900s. He also frequented the saloons, of course, a place for social gatherings and for more constituents.

One quiet afternoon, Bertha heard a knock on the kitchen door. A man from St. Paul was standing there; he asked her if she could make him a sandwich. With her German accent, she said, "A s-o-n-d-v-i-c-h? Vut's a sondvich?"

He explained, "You take a piece of bread, a pat of butter, and you put a piece of cheese or a slice of meat on it, and another slice of bread on top of that—you put the two slices of bread together—and that's a sandwich." She did just that, and he gave her some money for it.

That event gave her an idea: She could sell "sondviches" to the many folks who came from St. Paul to The Lake by train on weekends. From then on, she was "in the restaurant business," which she started on "The Square." Her restaurant was located almost directly opposite the present-day old post office building. It was a success, and a big business in White Bear Lake at that time. It was possibly the only restaurant there at the time.

Pies sold exceptionally well: About 20 to 25 were made for the weekend crowds. The pies were cut into quarters—which made VERY LARGE pieces. One-fourth of a pie sold for a nickel (five cents went a long way back then).

Her daughters, Marie and Louise, assisted Bertha during their pre-teen and teen years. They helped their mother by peeling bushels of apples and preparing other ingredients for the making of "those pies." They helped in the kitchen and swept the floor. Anything they could do was a great help to their hard-working mother.

The restaurant had a telephone—the only telephone in town. So Louise (Lucy) would get on her bicycle to deliver phone messages all over town. She earned lots of money, including enough money to pay for her bike.

After many years of good memories, hard work, fun, and success, the restaurant was sold around 1918. "Mayor" Theodore retired from his gardening business shortly thereafter.

Bertha's parents, Emily and Edward Wagner, lived out their lives in the Banning Avenue house. Emily was a concern because she had gone blind and was living in the house by the railroad tracks. People wondered how she could safely live by the railroad without being hit by a train. She hadn't lost her hearing however, so that was not a big concern of hers.

Forty One Shady Lane was the second address the Hansen family shared: a two-story house surrounded by a white picket fence. Shady Lane ended right at Lake Avenue. The streetcar tracks used to run within half a block from the house, but around 1930, it was abandoned. When that happened, Highway 61 was built right through the same location as the tracks. This required the removal of a house next to 41 Shady Lane, on the side by the old streetcar tracks. The lane wasn't so "shady" after that. The house then was right next to the new highway.

Two of the three Hansen children, Marie and Ernest, remained at Shady Lane after high school. Louise enrolled in a nursing school at St. Luke's Hospital in St. Paul. She started in 1904, when she was 18, and completed the program three years later.

Her first job as a nurse was at St. Luke's for Dr. Colvin, and Dr. Berch, who was an ophthalmologist. She also did private nursing for some of the wealthier families. One of her assignments was to go to Shell Lake, Wisconsin, where she unknowingly would meet her future husband, Madison Eden Albee, around 1912. Mr. Albee owned the telephone company. Mrs. Keller, whom Louise was assigned to take care of, was a boarder in the building owned by Mr. Albee. Louise and Madison married on June 4, 1913, in White Bear Lake, Minnesota.

The brother, Ernest Hanson, worked at the White Bear Lake Post Office, a job he acquired after graduating from high school. The Postmaster was Fred Campbell, who had lived on Lake Avenue during the early days of White Bear. When Ernest was nearly 30, he became inspired to move to California. He was able to trade jobs in the postal service with a young man from Long Beach. Before his move, he had met a young woman who had grown up around Hugo or Bald Eagle Lake. Her name was Mary LaBelle. When he moved to Long Beach, he sent for her to join him and to be his bride.

155

Marie Hansen met Hugh Hamilton in White Bear Lake, and they married in 1918 or 1919. They shared the Banning Avenue house with Marie's parents, "Mayor" Theodore and Bertha Hansen, along with her brother, Ernest—during the beginning of their marriage.

Hugh Hamilton was born in Nova Scotia, but ran away from home when he was still a young boy. He headed to Western Canada. Sometime around 1900, he got a job in a power plant at Baudette, Minnesota—near Lake of the Woods on the Canadian border. Around that time, he contacted his sister, Jane, who lived in White Bear Lake. Jane Hamilton Chisholm was married to Jack Chisholm, who was an electrician and worked for Northern States Power Company. When Hugh arrived in White Bear Lake, he was hired to work at "NSP" in the plant or substation. Hugh had studied and attempted to complete an electrical degree of some kind.

Around 1908–1910, he bought the hardware store on "The Square" in White Bear, opposite the present-day U.S. Post Office. He named it "Hamilton's Hardware Store," and ran it until the late 1940s or early 1950s, when it was sold.

Hugh used to replace a lot of windows. Customers would bring their broken windows in. He'd take the old glass out, put a new pane in, putty around it, and charge "just a little bit" for the work. He also cut threaded pipe, "old-fashioned" zinc-plated pipe.

Nephew Bob worked with Hugh in his hardware store every summer from 1934 to 1941. Bob sold hardware behind the counter and helped "Hughy" wherever needed. He had to climb the tall ladder, which stretched up to the ceiling, to recover hardware located anywhere it might be on those high shelves. The interior of the store was solid oak.

When Hughy let Bob drive his car, it was quite a turning point in his life. Hughy's car was a brown 1936 Dodge. Bob got to drive it and make deliveries for Uncle Hughy to Bald Eagle Lake, where a number of his customers lived. When Bob eventually went to the University, he would always try to go back to White Bear in the summertime.

Hughy's best business was during the months of April through June, and September through November. He sold lots of paint. The summer months were not as productive. Bob could only make it to White Bear during the less-productive summer months, so Hughy had to do all the work by himself.

Marie was a secretary. She later "did the books" for Hugh's hardware business. She was also a homemaker, played the piano extensively, gave piano lessons, and was the organist at the Episcopal Church. She played for weddings and church events. Some of her relatives from St. Paul would sing at the church, one of them a dentist, Dr. Paul Coch, was married to a niece of Bertha Hansen.

Around the time Highway 61 was put in, near the 41 Shady Lane house, Hugh and Marie Hamilton bought the house and property at 27 Lake Avenue. It was purchased from Cooper Fulton, who lived on the corner. Harry and Ione Green were the Hamilton's closest neighbors. Ione was a coloratura soprano who, when practicing at home, could be heard at Wildwood Park.

Mayor Theodore Hansen had died before those events. (He died September 11, 1920.) Bertha was the only family member remaining, and she joined Hugh and Marie at their Lake Avenue home. (She survived Theodore by seventeen years, and died April 29, 1937.)

Lucy and Madison Albee, who resided in Shell Lake, had a daughter and two sons: Mary Ellen, Robert (Bob), Bruce, and Theodore (Ted).

Ernest and Mary Hansen, residing in Garden Grove, California, had two daughters: Pauline and Marlene.

Marie and Hugh had no children, but shared in many happy and memorable times with their nieces and nephews.

In the early years of the next (fourth) generation, Louise and Madison Albee's children, Mary Ellen, Bob, and Ted, would go with them to White Bear Lake to "the relatives'," Grandma and Grandpa Hansen, Uncle Hugh, and Auntie "Re." ("Re" was a name she acquired when Mary Ellen was small and could only say "Re" for Marie. The name stuck, and that is what she was called for the rest of her life.)

When the Albee children were small, they would be around their German-speaking grandparents, and a few German expressions would be learned. Unfortunately, their father prohibited the teaching of German to the children. He "wouldn't allow it." Some of the expressions and German phrases Grandma Hansen would "accidentally" use rubbed off, despite their dad's wishes.

It was an exciting time. The Lake was just a block away from the house on Shady Lane. The kids got ready with their swimsuits and grabbed a towel, and ran for the lake. They couldn't wait to get in the water!

*Bernier family enjoying the lake at Clark Avenue, circa 1912.*
*Photo courtesy of Janet Greimann.*

Wildwood Amusement Park was a great attraction at White Bear. It was directly across the lake, on the south side. They used to go over there on the streetcar. The fare was 10 cents. They had so much fun on the roller coaster, merry-go-round, and bumper cars—just the best!

Auntie 'Re and Louise Albee would take the three Albee children out to the Park. They had so much fun on the high slides and all the things there for children. They had never seen so many kids before. Unfortunately, Wildwood Park was closed right around World War II. The streetcar tracks were removed around then, too, which didn't help the Park. Crowds began to dwindle.

In the summer, the Albees would drive from Shell Lake and drop the kids off for a couple of weeks, at least one or two kids at a time. Besides Wildwood, they'd take a trip into St. Paul. They would go to a show and to lunch at the Golden Rule, or one of those big stores, have a big hot roast beef sandwich with mashed potatoes and another vegetable for just 35 cents! That was a thrill. We never had that at home.

Then there was an ice cream parlor at the corner near the bus depot. After the show, they'd get back on the bus and go there to have ice cream.

The three Albee siblings were young adults by the time the Hamiltons and Grandma Hansen moved to the Lake Avenue house, and they visited less frequently. As they grew up, other interests and responsibilities were replacing those happy childhood days at Shady Lane.

As one of the next generation, I remember the wonderful Thanksgiving Holidays we would spend in White Bear with my mother, Mary Ellen Lemke, and my sister, Suzanne. (I don't remember if my dad would join us. He was often away, working on the railroad.) The gathering of family and those great dinners were wonderful times we had. We would go to St. Paul, and shop for Christmas things the day after Thanksgiving, where I would see Santa Claus. Como Park was also another great treat.

I was able to know Uncle Hugh the last few years of his life. He was special. I'll never forget his hardware store, or his personalized orange/gold accounting sheets, or the smell of his car in his garage. I watched him play cribbage and walk with a cane. I don't remember ever hearing any harsh words from his kind-looking face.

My sister, Suzanne and I would stand by the piano and sing, or just listen as my Auntie 'Re (our Great Aunt) would play the piano. We would pound or play on it ourselves, run after each other through the long hall and chase around the swinging doors inside that big, wonderful and fascinating house. Such a comfortable place where we would rock in the living room rocker over the large oriental rug covering the solid oak floors. We sat on the swing or rattan furniture on the porch. The first thing we would do when we arrived at Auntie Re's was to go directly to the phone, because we didn't have one, and dial "Time." I remember it so well. I'm sure I could draw a floor plan of the house, if I had to.

At times, my Grandma Lucy and Auntie Re would talk German together. It was nice to hear, but "funny," and of course I never understood it. They later said their conversations were intentionally in German so that we kids could not understand what they said.

We became friends with the two Ramberg girls next door. They were fun "playmates" when we visited Auntie 'Re.

We would take nice walks downtown along the tree-lined streets to go to the movies at the Avalon Theater. The Avalon was a pleasure to look at. The walls were made of boulders, with up-lights on top, which made it feel like a mysterious and comfortable cave. It wasn't until my adult life that I discovered the architectural origin of the Avalon Theater. I had taken a boat to Catalina Island off the California Coast in Los Angeles. I was surprised to see the Island of Catalina had an "Avalon Theater" as well. Upon entering the theater, my mouth dropped!

Its interior was exactly like White Bear Lake's Avalon Theater! The Catalina's theater was especially popular during the "Big Band Era," when the bands would play in the ballroom and "crooners" would sing.

To my amazement, the original owner-creator of the White Bear Avalon Theater had lived or traveled in Southern California in years prior to his building the theater in White Bear. He saw the Catalina Avalon and liked it, so he re-created it. It's a small world, indeed.

After "going to the show" in White Bear, we would go next door to the drugstore, where they had a fountain counter service. We would have something to eat or drink, conversation and laughs, before walking back to the Lake Avenue house.

White Bear was a great place—a fun place. The beauty, serenity, and quietness was like a pleasurable dream.

I can still hear the blue jays, morning doves, and little birds singing from the trees. I can see the squirrels gathering acorns and scurrying across the large lawns to run up a tree with their recent finds. I hear the fluttering leaves in the blissful breeze blowing softly across The Lake. I see the glistening water sparkle as the sunset turns crimson and pink...It is a very special place.

Thank you for those memories.

*Ad courtesy of White Bear Press.*

159

# The Reunion

*As Remembered by*
*Josephine (Howland) Morrow*

The flu epidemic of 1918 and the Cloquet fire touched our family immensely. My mother's sister, Daisy McCartney, and her husband, Claude White, fled the Cloquet fire with their two young children, aged two and four. With the four year old pushing the baby in the buggy, they carried whatever they were able to cram into two suitcases and hurried to the evacuation train. All the seats were filled, so they rode in an open gondola car to White Bear Lake to take refuge at the home of Daisy's father, William McCartney. The McCartney property bordered the now existing Clarence Avenue, Kretch Avenue and County Road G.

Claude went to work with my father in the logging industry near Stillwater for only two days when he came down with the flu. It spread throughout the family, and both Daisy and Claude were so weakened by the smoke in their lungs from the fire that neither could fight off the pneumonia that developed. Daisy died on November 1, and Claude died two days later. During the epidemic, the dead were immediately buried so as not to spread the disease. They were put hastily into pine boxes and conveyed up the street to Union Cemetery. Their four-year-old always remembered following behind his mother's coffin up the dirt road to the cemetery. Their graves remained unmarked until 1996 when their grandchildren and great-grandchildren placed a stone in their memory.

An aunt who was on the faculty of the University of Chicago adopted the two little boys. The children's names were changed and our family lost track of them, communication being quite poor in those days. During World War II, the oldest boy, married and living in California, was a ham radio operator. He and his wife took turns scanning the airwaves for messages from soldiers in the Pacific to relay to their families back home. At the same time, Bob Davies, another ham radio operator who lived on Birch Lake Avenue in White Bear Lake, was doing the same. When Bob signed off he gave his location. The name of the town "clicked" in the mind of the elder brother. He radioed back asking for information about our family, and found that we lived nearby. A date for a return call was made and we were put in touch with the long lost children.

Although the two boys are now deceased, contact between both families has continued.

# Summer Daze

*As Remembered by*
*Carol Honebrink Sawyer*

I remember summer days at White Bear Lake. I remember all the summer days of my young life being spent at the cottage my dad and mom built for themselves and their first-born daughter, located up the hill between County Road F and the old streetcar tracks in Bellaire. The small cottage was built in 1915 and Dad would tell us how he hired a farmer to bring the lumber on his horse-drawn wagon. The cottage had to be added on to, as five more children were born and a grandmother moved in for the summer months. Our family spent winters in St. Paul.

I remember that we kids never knew what would be coming up the back road with my dad. One time it was a pony which stayed with us through five lucky children. Next a log cabin play house with redwood furniture for the youngest, not to mention assorted pets—dogs, cats, chickens for the "coop," pet ducks and pheasant eggs to be hatched by the hens.

I remember all of us marching down to the lake with our mother and the neighboring families to spend the afternoon splashing, playing games and learning to swim—perfect carefree vacation days. My favorite memories are from riding the pony, named Jack. Who knows how old this dear thing was—probably retired from a circus show somewhere. A little Shetland, he was no match for the other pony who went along with us. My good friend, Alice Toresdahl from Bellaire, rode a Welch pony, about twice the size of Jack. But the competition worked wonders for us both. Jack finally broke from the accustomed trot to an actual canter! What a thrill—I fell in love with riding from that moment on! Alice and I rode together all summer days until Alice graduated to a real horse, which was a birthday present from her dad. By then Jack was too old and tired to run.

Other good memories are of the different groups of friends out at the "Lake". Friends from the town of White Bear (courtesy of Alice Toresdahl) Betty and Jean Roberts; the Mahtomedi group (courtesy of my good friend Hope Healy), too numerous to list; and then the bridge-playing neighborhood friends, Louise Clark, Margaret Murnane, and Mary Ingebrand. Evelyn Staples was a friend from Birchwood who, during a girl scout outing, showed us a plant growing by a school building. She called it 'marijuana' and told us not to touch it!

I remember one summer when the neighborhood kids, under the direction of a young teacher who rented a summerhouse nearby, put on a play in the "Little Red School House" at County Road E and White Bear Avenue. As the only one who could fake an English accent, I was selected to play the villain and had to dress as a man! I also could hold a monocle in one eye.

There are great memories of the Ingebrand family who stayed for a few summers in the "brown house" next door. They had five children, one the same age as each of us. The Monopoly board was always up on the card table in our sun porch. Every Sunday found the two families riding horses from a rental stable near the town of White Bear. There was always a badminton game in the front yard.

And, I remember the corn roasts! Every summer when the Indian corn from Rooney's farm was ripe, dad and sons would dig out a place in the front yard (up the slope from the old streetcar tracks) for a roaring bonfire. The hot fire must

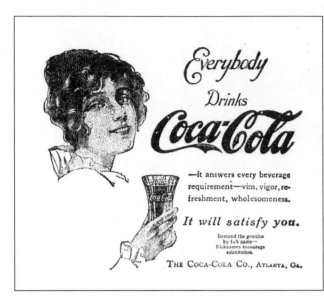

*Ad courtesy of White Bear Press.*

have been horrendous, but we had to have a corn roast! Among all the neighbors, other friends and relatives, we probably had 50 or more happy people, with butter dripping from chins, hot dogs in hand, and marshmallows roasting. Of course, there was ice-cold beer, iced tea, and Coca-Cola.

Early neighbors I remember were the Ross family in the year-round house next door to the east, the Shepherds across the streetcar tracks on Summit Lane, and the Murnanes across the way. Mother played bridge a lot. One day she was entertaining a foursome when my brother, Bud, and the neighboring Ross kids were playing by Murnane's yard. Bud and Don Ross had climbed a tree and were chopping at branches with a hatchet. I was unfortunate enough to be underneath when the hatchet missed the branch and landed embedded in my head! They got the hatchet out and sent me home with a younger Ross leading me—blood coming down across one eye! I got in the front porch and showed mother, who calmly said, "Go to the kitchen, dear, and I'll be there as soon as I finish playing this hand!" My mother was used to minor calamities by then, and anyway, she loved playing bridge! I was no worse for the wear, although there may be some who might dispute that.

I remember the Mamples who lived in Birchwood, great friends, and so hospitable. I often was allowed to play a hand or two of bridge with them. My favorite quotes of Les' were, "It's okay as long as you're thinking" (if a player took too long) and "children think you are playing" (if some opponent tried a finesse that wasn't going to work).

I remember ball games all summer long. I played center field. I think of that every time I hear the song "Put me in, coach, I'm ready to play. Look at me, I could be center field."

I remember sitting down on the dock in the evenings listening to the music drift across the water from the Wildwood dance pavilion.

My dad loved The Lake above all other places—his last day on earth was spent there. It's exactly what he would have wanted.

I still collect wonderful memories of The Lake. The "cottage" is gone now, but tradition still holds—the 4th of July and Labor Day are at The Lake. We still have picnics on the beach, where we are lucky enough to have a dock, a boat and now a pontoon. My children and grandchildren now will have their own memories to add to the summer days at White Bear Lake!

# No Electricity

*As Remembered by*
*Helen Lindbeck Peterson*

In the early 1930s we had several household appliances that were not electrified. One was the icebox. Periodically in the warm weather the iceman would rumble down the street on his route, stopping at the predetermined houses to leave his frigid load. He carried an ice pick to chop the larger pieces into the sizes he needed to sell in order to fill the ice chamber of each icebox. When we saw him coming, we would race to meet his truck and hover around him while he jabbed at a large block of ice with the pick to reduce it to the size needed. He had a heavy-duty rubber shoulder protector slung on his shoulder, and then with a pair of ice tongs, he'd hoist the block of ice to his back and trudge off to deliver it to the icebox. We children were busy at the back of his truck snatching the cold slivers of ice to eat. What an exciting and welcome treat on a hot summer day.

Another appliance we had that did not operate with the benefit of electricity was a flatiron. Actually, we had two, as I recall. While one was being heated on the stove, the other was in use on ironing day. In the winter when the cook stove in the kitchen was hot, the iron was heated there. In the summer it was heated on the kerosene stove used for cooking. Fabrics were of natural fibers then, and most everything had to be ironed—no permanent press.

Some of the other gadgets we now take for granted are hair dryers, automatic washers and dryers, electric shavers, a lamp in every corner, air conditioners and furnaces, escalators, door openers and motion lights, cordless phones and timers to run our electronic mechanical contrivances, and far too many others to list. You, dear reader, will think of many more.

*Ad courtesy of White Bear Press.*

# Forever a Drummer

*As Remembered by*
*Josephine (Howland) Morrow*

I am not sure how Uncle Jack and my paternal grandfather, Herman Howland, came to know each other, but it was a fact that they were both Civil War Veterans from Wisconsin, although in different units. Granddad Howland was in the 3rd Wisconsin Cavalry and assigned as a scout to hunt down Quantrell. Uncle Jack was in the infantry.

Returning to Wisconsin after the war, Granddad married, had a family and then, lured by the promise of free land out west, homesteaded near Carthage, S.D. in the 1880's. Maybe it was that same attraction that drew Uncle Jack to South Dakota, and maybe that was where they met. Whatever the reason, Uncle Jack met and married Herman's daughter, May, in DeSmet, South Dakota in the year 1898.

The couple moved to Minnesota, settling first in Itasca County, then moving south to White Bear Lake about the year 1916. There they bought a house on the southwest corner of Third and Miller. May's father Herman, and my family also moved into the area about the same time.

I never knew my Uncle Jack Seaman, for he died when I was six months old. Nevertheless, I heard a lot about him because, apparently, he was quite a character. He was a dapper dresser and I was told that he was also an avid hunter and fisherman. He even built his own boat! He must have also been quite artistic for he etched the head of a buck, antlers and all, into the glass of his front door and kept a stuffed pheasant in his front room.

*Jack Seaman,*
*courtesy Josephine Morrow*

I was told that he was honest, trustworthy, highly thought of and very responsible. As soon as he received his veteran's pension check he would pay his bills and give his wife enough money to run the household. With whatever money was leftover, he proceeded to spend on drink. On the occasions when there was a lot of leftover money, he would pick up his fiddle and play tirelessly. On other occasions he would practice drum rolls that could be heard throughout the neighborhood.

White Bear Lake was a perfect place for him, being the hunter and fisherman that he was, but it was the hunting that eventually did him in. One chilly November day in 1928, he went out duck hunting and caught a cold that evolved into pneumonia, and he subsequently died. His wife stayed in the family home for several years but eventually moved to the Soldiers' Home at Fort Snelling in Minneapolis.

We have proof today that Uncle Jack was very proud of his Civil War service and that seemed to be his claim to fame. I was told that he spent several years carving his upright tombstone before he died to be sure that all the facts of his service were left for posterity. The stone stands in the northeast corner of the original Union Cemetery. It can still be read as clearly as the day he carved it. It reads:

John E. Seaman
Born at
Monmouth, Ill.1846
Co. G. 32nd Reg. Wis. Vol.
3rd Brig. 1st Div.
17th Army Corps.
With W.T. SHERMAN on all his Sieges and Campaigns. Served as drummer boy.
Smallest boy in Sherman's Army
Captured the first spy in
Gen. Price's army at Memphis, Tenn.
Died Dec. 28, 1928

### Soldiers' Monument

Clark Avenue
Parkway

## Unveiled Decoration Day

May 31st, 1913
Dedicated to the Veterans of the Civil War by the Soldiers Monument Association of White Bear.

*Photo, circa 1914, courtesy of White Bear Press*

*The Civil War veterans of the E.B. Gibbs Post, chartered March 10, 1884. Photo courtesy of Lawrence R. (Bob) and Eileen Whitaker.*

*Ad, circa 1914, courtesy of White Bear Press*

# White Bear Businessmen's Association

*As Remembered by I.V. Johnson*
*Submitted by Pat Brannon*

Someone said "Great Oaks from Little Acorns Grow." That statement is apropos to the White Bear Area Chamber of Commerce. The present Chamber has had many names over the years. Unless I am mistaken, we originally started, as a Businessmen's Association. In 1955 the association elected me, I.V. Johnson, as chairman. I'll never know why. My job at the time was working for the school district in the field of elementary education. So, I asked the Superintendent of Schools if the school district might consider paying my association fee, which I believe was the total sum of $154.00. The answer I received was, "It would be a nice gesture on our part but, I'm sorry, it would be an illegal expenditure of funds." So, I paid my own way.

At that time, the Association was a small group of maybe 40–45 members. We got together periodically after that and talked about problems relative to the community of White Bear Lake. Sometime in the early 50s, a few businesswomen joined our group, namely Ruby Mullett, Helen Carlson and Reggie Bisa. It became necessary to change the name of our group to accommodate the women. I think we then became the White Bear Association.

Frank Mehlhorn, our erstwhile secretary, kept the minutes of the goings-on. It would be interesting to read those minutes, but I have been informed that they are no longer available. Too bad. They would be interesting.

At every meeting a "Lottery" was conducted. A businessperson was informed that he or she must bring a prize to the next meeting. Charley Hausner, a realtor and our official auctioneer, collected the names of everyone in attendance; put them in a hat and someone was chosen to draw the winning number. Charley was the life of the party. At one o'clock sharp, Allan Warner, bank president, moved that the meeting be adjourned.

For a little diversion, we took a few tours via bus. Some I recall, like one trip to Milwaukee for a major league baseball game; a trip to Winona to tour the J.R. Watkins plant. They are the people who make the famous Watkins Vanilla. We also had a trip to Duluth to tour the steel mills then in operation. Usually about 35 people went on these tours. Gus Mullett always saw to it that the bus was properly loaded with the necessary refreshments to keep everyone in a good mood while we toured the countryside. Those trips were lots of fun and developed great fellowship.

This is the time that White Bear Lake was considered a "bedroom" community for the Twin City area. Businesses that were interested in locating in White Bear were actually discouraged from coming here. People in White Bear prided themselves in their beautiful homes, the schools, the churches, and cultural activities that made White Bear Lake a great place to work and live. Congratulations to the present White Bear Area Chamber of Commerce. You have been successful because of the outstanding leadership provided by members who sacrifice their time and talent to work toward the goals they have set for themselves. I am pleased to have been a member of this outstanding organization.

*The White Bear Businessmen's Association, 1950s.*
*Photo courtesy of Pat Brannon, White Bear Lake Area Chamber of Commerce.*

# Reporting on White Bear Lake

*As Remembered by*
*Virginia MacKay*

As a native of Illinois, I came to White Bear Lake in 1962 with my husband and two sons. Both the adults had worked on newspapers in Bloomington, Illinois, Rapid City, South Dakota, and in Milwaukee, Wisconsin. I had also filled various other writing positions over the years. At first we rented a farmhouse on East County Line Road, and that's where we first learned that White Bear Lake still had milkmen. We had one who teased our large dog. Our dog was ill mannered with strangers, but gentle with us, a mixed pedigree, which we called a Heinz-dog. He was especially unhappy when the milkman arrived. He once bit our parish priest, too, but that's a different story.

In a couple of years we moved into one of the new houses in a new settlement known as White Bear Hills on the city's south side. The first day the milkman called upon us in our new house he insisted upon knowing if we still had that big dog. We didn't. Many of us who were new to the area were aware that many of the old timers referred to us as "the people in the developments," but that was fine—we didn't mind. We were all set to pay for half a dozen new elementary schools and at least one new high school because our growing families had created the need for them. We were also prepared to support new churches, new businesses, new art ventures and make a brand new county library not only a possibility but also a necessity. We were also prepared to run things for at least two decades. I think we did just that.

*Constructing a White Bear Lake residence.*
*Photo courtesy of Lawrence R. (Bob) and Eileen Whitaker.*

During the time, most city councilmen and many school board members were selected from the ranks of the newly arrived, many of them 3M'ers. It was a thrilling time to be in White Bear Lake. Enough of the old atmosphere was still here that we got a feeling for what should be kept and what was no longer needed here.

I recall a Saturday morning in Hayden's Hardware Store in Wildwood Shopping Center. It was then called Allabar Center, located at the corner of Highways 244 and 120. I was waiting to pay for a few little items when a serious do-it-your-selfer came to the counter and asked Mrs. Hayden about some copper tubing he was holding. "How much do you need?" she asked. "I don't know exactly," he replied. "Take the roll home and use what you need and then bring it back and pay me for what you use," she said. Copper tubing cost the earth then, as it does now, but she trusted him with it and trusted him to be honest in reporting how much he took off the roll before bringing it back. That's the part of White Bear Lake we hoped to keep forever.

At first I worked for the Sun Newspapers, a chain of 28 weeklies owned by a Twin Cities man. The chain's operation surrounded the seven-county area then and was considered a well-run operation. I covered the meetings at Willernie, Mahtomedi, White Bear Township, Grant and old Lincoln Townships. Most of those officials had never had personal coverage before and they ate it up. Covering Dellwood was more difficult as the female mayor held the council meetings in her home and generally set the meeting time to suit her schedule. Reporters were not only uninformed about the meeting date but were also unwelcome, should they turn up. Later, I took over coverage of White Bear Lake City Council and all the area school boards as well. The Sun maintained offices in White Bear Lake for several years until the chain was broken up.

It was an important period for the municipalities of the area. The newly formed Metropolitan Council was flexing its muscles, and the newly financed Metropolitan Sanitary Sewer District was beginning to buy up city sewer systems to form the giant system that takes care of today's solid wastes. Then, we all thought urban sprawl would be under control because the Metro Council was charged with planning the future and the sewer district could control where and when a sanitary sewer interceptor would be constructed, thus limiting development and restricting the leapfrogging that came no matter how much faith we put in the Metro Council and the Sewer Board.

On a brighter note, the newly arrived residents insisted upon and supported the creation of parks and open space and seemed not at all concerned that White Bear Lake had a reputation for not encouraging industry here. Washington and Ramsey Counties got together and managed to convince the legislature to build Lakewood Community College and the Special District 916 Vocational-Technical School on the border between the two counties. Lakewood came first, opting to use the then vacant Washington School, which stood on Fourth Street west of the railroad tracks, where senior citizen housing now stands. Washington School had served as a high school, a grade school and even in the early days as a normal school for the training of teachers. Lakewood moved to its present location after a couple of years and Washington School was razed, but not before local artist Frank Zeller created a fine painting of the school and campus.

Barbara Simpson, another local writer who submitted a column called "Soft Bread, Hard Butter" to the old Sun newspapers, often talked about Helen Fillebrown and her wonderful house on Lake Avenue. Finally, I went to do a story on Helen. She and her brother lived in the house known as the Red Chalet. It had a long pedigree, having been built in 1879 and designed by renowned architect Cass Gilbert. It was filled with historic furniture and wonderful memories which Helen was able to recall to the last detail. Through Barbara's persistent efforts and with the help of the resulting publicity and continuing discussion and additional feature stories through the next couple of years, the Fillebrowns decided to leave the house to the Historical Society. Without Barbara's efforts and those of Marge Schneeman, Esther Newcome, Janet Schuneman and other women in the community, the house might have gone on the market and been lost forever.

A feature story on the gazebo, done for the Sun, also helped stimulate the community, and the women named above got that structure moved from its original site on South Shore Boulevard, where it had served as a honeymoon cottage for a young couple early in the century, to the park where it now stands. It served, as the Fillebrown House did, as a grand focal point for the city's Bi-Centennial celebration in 1976.

These women and others, including many from Mahtomedi and Birchwood, and through the efforts of Sister Florentine who taught music at St. Jude's Catholic School in Mahtomedi, got the White Bear Lake Arts Council rolling in the 1960s.

*"Fair in the Fields," circa 1975.*
*Photo submitted by White Bear Center for the Arts.*

The Arts Council was responsible for art shows and exhibitions at Lakewood College and for a wonderful annual art fair. The first fairs were in a meadow in Washington County, later at the Lakewood Campus and finally at Matoska Park on the lakefront.

One day I heard about a White Bear Lake man who was building a boat in his garage, a special boat that he hoped would make him famous. Gerry Spiess was that man. After the boat, Yankee Girl, was finished he sailed it, all alone, across the Atlantic Ocean. He set a record for the era and whet his appetite for a longer trip around the whole world in the future. However, the Atlantic trip, June 1 to July 24, 1979, "was not exactly a day at the beach," Gerry said afterwards. There were some pretty frightening times, but he survived. He was honored by the City of White Bear Lake, the City of St. Paul, and by the Governor as well as in special ceremonies. The ten-foot Yankee Girl was the smallest craft to sail west to east at that time. The media called her a teacup.

Gerry Spiess wasn't our only adventurer. Ralph Plaisted was a White Bear Lake resident when he was preparing for his trek across the polar cap to the North Pole. Another White Bear Lake man, Blair Woolsey, was part of his group, too. This was also a success and was the first such trip made on snowmobiles.

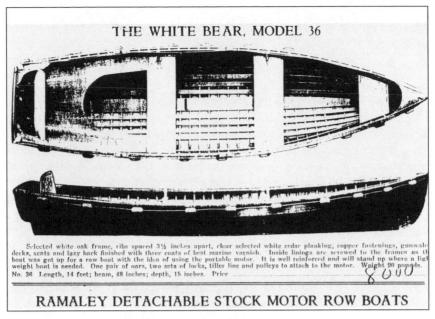

Sales brochure, courtesy of Bob Borowski.

When the old Plantation Boat Works, as it was locally known, on the western shore of White Bear Lake was closed, a group of people thought the site was fit only for a high rise dwelling for the fiscally well-endowed. One local elected official even thought she might like one of the condos being considered, where she could look across the lake and down upon her constituents. But, alas, it was not to be. There was lots of opposition and I was able to write editorial after editorial opposing such a structure. Those in the know were able, too, to produce facts and figures, including the damage the very shadow of such a building would do to fish and other wildlife in the area. And, so we won. The high rise was forgotten and Lion's Park was conceived.

Many will not recall the coming and going of another weekly newspaper in White Bear Lake, but I certainly do. It was called the Advisor. My husband, Neil, and I founded it and co-published it for three years in the 1970s. I believe it was a rallying effort that helped bring White Bear Lake, Mahtomedi and surrounding areas together. It celebrated the residents with features about everyday people and their interests. It covered the city, townships, school boards and various commissions and the county board on a week-by-week basis, the old-fashioned way, in person. In all modesty, I can say it was often quoted as a good thing in the journalism classes at the University of Minnesota. The editors were often treated to comments on special stories by the journalism professors from the University of Minnesota, and quoted by other papers and radio commentators. Lack of advertising support and competition for that ad dollar, rather than a lack of readers, caused its demise.

There's nothing like covering local news to change an ordinary person into an ordinary person everybody knows.

# An Introduction to the Theatre via the Trousdales

*By C. Andrews, Ph.D.*
*Submitted by Truly Trousdale Latchaw*

Throughout the late nineteenth century, the only forms of "culture" to reach the settlers on the Midwest prairies were traveling troupes of players and entertainers. In small towns and cities throughout the middle west, opera houses were built, not for the purpose of presenting operas as such, but to provide stages and seats for traveling performers and their audiences. On the outskirts of the town, an area of land was preserved for the circus tents. Because the opera houses were not air-cooled in the summer, the companies which presented the plays would set up tents on the circus grounds, usually for week-long stays. Although some wagon shows moved from town to town via horse-drawn vehicles, most of these entertainers traveled by railroads, which reached every city, town and hamlet.

With the advent of the filmed plays in the early part of the twentieth century, some opera houses installed screens and presented both stage entertainment— vaudeville or plays—and films. Vaudeville often served as an interlude between film presentations. In other cases, store buildings were converted to motion picture theaters. Here the film, a longer feature, shorter comedies and travel films, was the only form of entertainment. Eventually, the giant motion picture houses replaced the remodeled stores. In many of these, vaudeville still furnished an interlude between screenings. Soon, even these places presented only film programs.

Meanwhile, across the nation, companies of actors presenting stage plays and inter-act entertainment had taken to the highways, utilizing circus type tents for their auditoriums and motor trucks for their conveyances. They might stop over in a town for a week or for the whole summer. There were many reasons for these changes. The old auditoriums had been burned or torn down, were remodeled for use as stores, or else were not air-conditioned in summer. Some, if vacant, were too dirty or unkempt for use. However, in the wintertime in the north, some companies used these old houses.

Eventually, various circumstances, including the advent of radio and then of television, along with the continuing motion picture, tended to put these traveling shows out of business. Here, then, in Truly Trousdale Latchaw's excellent history, is the story of one of those traveling companies.

### Editor's Note:

*The previous introduction was included with a play submitted to this book by Truly Trousdale Latchaw. The history referred to by Dr. Andrews is of Truly's parents. It is in the tradition of Truly's heritage that she, too, became interested in the theatre. The following story is a compilation of episodes from a play that was written by Truly Trousdale for the Cities centennial celebration.*

P.T.

# White Bear Lake Centennial Pageant

*Written by Truly Trousdale Latchaw*

### Episode I: Our Primitive Past

 *Scene 1*

**L**ong ago, bands of both Sioux and Chippewa Indian Nations lived near the shores of White Bear Lake. Princess Nakawisi, daughter of the Sioux chieftain, met and fell in love with Chingachgook, a Chippewa brave. Because the Sioux and Chippewa were at war, there was little hope that anything could come of this love until Chingachgook came to the Sioux, wanting to smoke the pipe of peace and asking for Nakawisi's hand in marriage. The peace pipe was smoked and Nakawisi was promised to Chingachgook with the condition that he first prove himself worthy. The occasion soon presented itself when Nakawisi was attacked by a huge white bear. Chingachgook fought with the bear and killed him. However, in killing the bear, Chingachgook forfeited his own life also. It is claimed that one can still hear Nakawisi's mournful cries haunting Manitou (Spirit) Island. The Indians named the lake for the white bear and there was a lasting peace among them.

*Scene 2*

During the years that followed, the Indians lived happily along these shores and, when they died, they were buried in a manner common to the Indian in these parts. After a primary burial in the tops of the trees, the bones of the dead were taken down and buried in a common mound. There were five such mounds at White Bear Lake. When white settlers came, the mounds created a hazard for the buggies and wagons and so were torn down. There were protests from the women, who feared the Indian wrath, but they were to no avail. When the Indians discovered what had happened to the last resting place of their ancestors, they were very angry. They wanted to avenge themselves on the white settlers, but the Indian chief decided against it. The peace pipe was again brought out and smoked: this time, by the white settlers and the Indians.

### Episode II: The Settlers—Their Schools and Churches

Although people of many nationalities eventually came to stay in White Bear, the French Canadians were among the earliest. The first school, organized in 1853, had six pupils. Mademoiselle Eliza Lebonne taught the lessons in French. Later, classes in English were taught by Mrs. James Aubrey. Mrs. Aubrey and her husband returned to England when it was learned that Mr. Aubrey had inherited the family barony. During their ten year stay in White Bear, the Aubreys also were influential in building our first church, St. John's in the Wilderness Episcopal Church. The original site of this church was in what is now known as Cottage Park. Soon, there were several churches in the area.

### Episode III: The Organization of White Bear Lake

During the years from 1850 to 1880, many people came to White Bear, bought land, and settled down. This period saw the beginning of the resort business at the lake. These early residents represented many nationalities. One of their chief amusements was square dancing. This was done in the streets with everyone (including the Indians) joining in.

### Episode IV: The Palmy Days

The years from 1880 through the early 1890's were known as "The Palmy Days." The waters of White Bear Lake were reputed to have great healing powers and people came from far and wide to bathe in it. Business in the resort hotels boomed, and there were, at one time, 47 trains a day bringing visitors to White Bear. People from as far away as Memphis, Atlanta and New Orleans came to form the regular summer colony. In 1899, a ten-minute streetcar service was inaugurated and Wildwood Amusement Park became very popular. Huge steamers cruised the lake, taking passengers to and from Wildwood to White Bear. It was during this time that sailboat racing became popular. There were two yacht clubs at first, although they eventually merged into the present Yacht Club. Gustav Amundson was responsible for much of this popularity of water sailing. He designed and built the first sailboat on White Bear Lake. In the 30s came the depression and prohibition. Wildwood was eventually closed. White Bear and the surrounding areas were swarming with racketeers who came here to "hide out." Some of these were apprehended by the F.B.I. during their stay in White Bear.

### Episode V: Progress

White Bear is recognized as one of the towns in the United States of America that has made the most progress in recent years. We are proud of our growing community with its lovely suburban homes clustered around shining lakes. We are proud of our schools and churches where our children are being led into the paths of fulfillment. Our enterprising businessmen and loyal residents are helping keep White Bear Lake on the map.

*Truly Trousdale Latchaw*

# A Brief History of the Railroads

*As Remembered by*
*Phyllis DeLonais*

September 1868 marked the beginning of a new era for communities surrounding White Bear Lake. The dedication of rail service from St. Paul to White Bear Township by the Lake Superior and Mississippi Railroad took place. Transit time from St. Paul was reduced from over three hours by horse and buggy to less than one-half hour via the new rail system. The rail line was dedicated on September 10, 1868, with the arrival of a special train from St. Paul carrying over 500 people, including the president of the railroad, William Banning, and U. S. Senator Alexander Ramsey, among the noted dignitaries. The train consisted of ten flat cars, four passenger cars for the ladies, and was pulled by two locomotives headed by the engine, the "William R. Marshall".

*The first depot was built in 1868. Prior to this time, train transportation was a three-hour journey from St. Paul with horse and buggy. Photo courtesy of Lawrence R. (Bob) and Eileen Whitaker.*

The year 1870 marked the completion of the Lake Superior and Mississippi Rail Line to Duluth through White Bear Lake. Also completed that year was the Stillwater and St. Paul Railroad's line from White Bear Lake to Stillwater. The year 1871 brought the inaugural run of the Minneapolis and Duluth Line from St. Anthony to White Bear Lake. The town now became the major hub of rail transportation from the Twin Cities to all points north.

The continued growth in rail traffic caused the need for the railroad to build a roundhouse. In 1874, buildings for maintenance, a picnic pavilion and a restaurant near the lake shore station were built. Later in 1879, the station was rebuilt into Ramaley's Pavilion. Many existing buildings were also enlarged in 1893.

By 1935, planning was underway for the construction of Highway 61 through the center of White Bear Lake. This required the removal of the train yard, the demolition of the roundhouse and the replacement of the original 1868 depot with the current structure. The present depot was used initially by the Northern Pacific Railroad and, in turn, by Burlington Northern until it was closed during the 1980s.

As the system of highways was expanded and improved, passenger and freight rail service decreased through White Bear Lake. The passenger service was discontinued in the 1960s and, currently, only the infrequent freight train heads to the end of the track, which now extends only as far as Hugo.

The City of White Bear Lake bought the depot and the surrounding property in the fall of 1990. Upon completion of the restoration of the depot in late 1991, it became home to the White Bear Lake Area Chamber of Commerce. In June 1992, the White Bear Lake Area Historical Society opened the Depot Museum.

## FAST TRAINS

| Leave White Bear | Leave St. Paul |
|---|---|
| S   6:58 A. M. | S   6:00 A. M. |
| 7:28 A. M. | S   6:30 A. M. |
| 8:28 A. M. | 7:30 A. M. |
| 9:28 A. M. | 8:30 A. M. |
| 10:28 A. M. | 9:30 A. M. |
| 11:28 A. M. | 10:30 A. M. |
| 12:28 P. M. | 11:30 A. M. |
| 1:28 P. M. | 12:30 P. M. |
| 2:28 P. M. | 1:30 P. M. |
| 3:28 P. M. | 2:30 P. M. |
| 4:28 P. M. | 3:30 P. M. |
| 5:28 P. M. | 4:30 P. M. |
| 6:28 P. M. | 5:27 P. M. |
| 7:28 P. M. | 6:27 P. M. |
| W  12:12 A. M. | W  11:15 P. M. |

S   Except Sunday.

W   Wednesday, Saturday, Sunday only.

Complaints and suggestions always receive prompt, courteous attention.

A. W. WARNOCK,
General Passenger Agent,
Minneapolis.

*Twin City Lines, circa 1914.*
*Ad courtesy of White Bear Press.*

Spice

# Our Neighbor, Ma Barker

*As Remembered by*
*Hope Healy Koontz*

My parents, James and Lucy Healy, and all us children lived in a lakefront winter home in Mahtomedi located near the border of Dellwood, on White Bear Lake. We lived through the gangster era of the Barkers, John Dillinger, "Pretty Boy" Floyd, Al Capone, "Babyface" Nelson, and others. These underworld gunmen who robbed many of the banks in Minnesota and murdered with impunity, often headquartered in the Mahtomedi area during the 1920s and 1930s.

Our neighbors in the summer of 1932 were Ma Barker and "her boys," Fred Barker and Alvin Karpis. They rented a summer cottage from the Lambert family just four houses from us. When the dawn stole the night and the lake was still, the loons crooned their lonely tunes while these criminals took their boat out on the lake to plan another bank robbery. That bank was the State Bank and Trust Company in Redwood Falls, Minnesota. It was robbed in September of that year by our nice, quiet neighbors.

Most of us children were young and had no idea that notorious gangsters drove the cars that were coming and going to the Lambert cottage at all hours. One member of our family did become acquainted with Ma and her boys. His name was Patrick Vincent Healy. He was my first cousin, a nephew of my father. He visited us from Chicago on the pretext of visiting relatives. What he really was doing was spying on Ma Barker and all the visitors to their cottage. Patrick Healy later became the Prosecuting Attorney in Chicago who prosecuted the John Dillinger Gang. Patrick later became Head of the Vice Commission of Chicago.

In writing my family history I have inserted that my mother's "claim to fame" was that she fished with Ma Barker! She would not have liked that allegation at all for she was a lovely, refined woman who would not deem to be caught with such notorious persons!

*Story and graphics circa 1931, courtesy of White Bear Press.*

## MYSTERIOUS FIRE IN AUTO AT BIRCH LAKE MURDER SUSPECTED

### Car Evidently Stolen; License Plates Removed; Tire and Head Lights Stolen

Tuesday evening as Chief Fred Campbell and Fireman Earl Millette were in the chief's office at the fire hall, a call came in asking for deputy sheriffs, and stated that there was an automobile in the ditch near Birch Lake, off Ramaley avenue. Not knowing it was on fire they drove out. Seeing the fire they rushed back and took truck No. 2 to the scene when the blaze was extinguished.

The fire was on the interior of the car and the motor was not damaged. The license plates were gone. The cap was off the reservoir, and undoubtedly gasoline had been sprinkled on the interior to start the fire.

When Campbell and Millette returned with the truck some fast worker had taken one tire and both headlights. The car is a Franklin appears to be practically new. It now is at the Reed garage.

#### Murder Suspected

Later—This afternoon it is reported that a murder is suspected and newspaper men are assisting Deputy Sheriffs Honhorst and Leahy in searching the roadsides in all directions for a body.

It is believed the car belonged to Chicago gansters, as a Chicago license plate was found in the car— No. 445,255 for 1930. It is believed the car was fired inside to destroy any evidence of blood. The cap was off the gas tank. The license plate may have been stolen. The motor number which had been tampered with, was decyphered and telegraphed to Chicago and other cities as well as to the Franklin factory. It is possible the ownership might be traced through this means.

There is much speculation over the matter.

# Once Was Enough

*As Remembered by*
*C. Allen Lindholm*

*Segment I*

When I started the sixth grade in my new school, White Bear Junior and Senior High, I met a new friend, Daniel "Boonie" Lucas. He lived on the opposite side of Bald Eagle Lake from me. One day, I decided to visit him, and since I had swam many times out to the island, I decided to swim across the lake to his house. I didn't think it was that much further. There were not many speedboats on the lake in those days, so I didn't believe there would be any problems. I tied my tennis shoes around my neck by the laces, and jumped in. I started across, and whenever I got tired, I would roll over on my back and rest while swimming backwards. I crossed the bay, went around the point and set off across the lake for the Girl Scout swimming beach, (now the Hobe Lane area.) It was a long, long, swim, but I finally made it. When I finally reached Boonie's house, Mrs. Lucas asked how I had gotten there, since she didn't see my bicycle. When I told her I swam across, she was both surprised and disturbed, because I had done it alone. After spending some time with Boonie, Mrs. Lucas insisted she give me a ride home. I didn't refuse, and, I NEVER DID THAT AGAIN!

**Once Was Enough**

*Segment II*

I used to go up to Harlee Anderson's farm because there were so many things to see and do. We did a lot of target shooting and hunting.

One day, we climbed to the top of his silo to take some potshots at a couple of mallards that had landed in the pond out in the pasture. Harlee had a scope on his 22-caliber rifle and, with long rifle bullets, we could shoot fairly accurately for long distances. The silo had a tin cone roof on the top of it. We would sit next to the peak since the point of the peak did not feel very good, digging into our rear ends. On sunny days, when the tin got hot, our tennis shoes would not hold us and we would slowly slide down. It was so slow, however, that we had plenty of time to rest our elbows, sight in the rifle and pull off a shot before we cupped our hand over the peak and pulled ourselves back up the top.

One day, we were on top of the silo and Harlee ran out of shells, so he went down to get some more. I had one shell left, so I climbed up to the peak and started sighting in on the mallards. I took careful aim, judging wind and distance, and pulled off a shot. When I reached back for

*Ad courtesy of White Bear Press.*

the peak, I couldn't reach it! I was slowly sliding down to a 45-foot drop. I laid the gun in my lap and thought if I was going over the edge, I would try to jump for the barn roof to help break my fall. I kept sliding, ever so slowly, until I got to the edge of the silo roof where there was about 8 or 10 inches of wood that the tin did not cover. I stopped sliding when I got to the wood but I was on the opposite side of the silo from the ladder. Even though the diameter of the silo was 18 feet, it seemed like a half mile around to the ladder. I kept saying to myself, "Just don't make any quick moves; take it slow." I was on the very of edge of disaster for such a long time, my heart was in my mouth, but I kept saying my prayers and tried to keep cool as I slowly inched myself, one foot at a time, all the way around the silo roof. When I approached the ladder, I told myself, "Don't lunge for it." I didn't, and slowly reached for it, but I swear I left my fingerprints in the iron!

Harlee finally got back and I handed him the gun. I hardly had enough strength to climb down. He looked at me and asked what happened. I just said, "I missed!" I NEVER DID THAT AGAIN!

### *Once Was Enough*

*Segment III*

When I was young, I liked to throw things; rocks, baseballs, footballs, knives, hatchets, etc. One day I was playing catch with my brothers, and the softball we were using rolled into the culvert that went under the road in our lower yard. I decided to crawl in and get it. I got down on my belly and started in. However, as I reached for the ball, I accidentally pushed it in further, so I had to squirm in further after it. When I finally reached it, I was almost in the middle of the culvert and I discovered I could not back out! I could see light at the other end of the culvert, so I decided I would squirm all the way through, but the sand was so built up I did not have enough room to get by. What a claustrophobic predicament! Both my arms were out in front of me so I decided it I could push enough of the sand with my fingers and spread it out, maybe I could get by it. I did not want to make a mistake, because I could not bring my arms back to try again. Besides, I had already made a big mistake! I was finally able to spread enough sand out with my fingertips that I was able to push the ball out ahead of me and squirm through to the other end. I NEVER DID THAT AGAIN!

### *Once Was Enough*

*Segment IV*

When I was twelve, my father bought a new bike for me. It was a Hawthorne from W. T. Grant and Company. It was maroon and white, and had a headlight and horn. It was just about the best bike ever made and I was so proud of it! In late August when the State Fair was in St. Paul, I decided I would take my new bike and ride it to Aunt Signe's house.

*Silo ad, circa 1914, courtesy of White Bear Press.*

She lived near the State Fairgrounds, so I could leave my bike there and go to the Fair. I had asked some of my friends to bike with me, but they didn't want to, so I went by myself. I didn't tell my mother where I was going, because she probably wouldn't have approved. I got to the fairgrounds and met some boys who knew how to get into the grounds without paying. (I didn't have any money.)

They distracted the guard who was on horseback, and I crawled under the fence. Boy, was that exciting! Even though I was by myself, the excitement of the Midway, the smell of the swine barn, the cotton candy and seeing all those people was overwhelming.

After a few hours, I was starting to get hungry. I knew I was a long way from home (18 miles), so I thought I had better start for home before it got dark. I reluctantly left the fair. I walked over to my aunt's house, got on my bike, and headed out Hamline Avenue to Highway 36, and on toward Highway 61. I got as far as Edgerton and Highway 36 when a car slowly came to a stop beside me. It was Dad! He had set out looking for me after my mother had called several friends to find out where I had gone. He was both happy and very upset at me for what I had done. We put my new bike in the car and when we got home, I got a lecture that I would not soon forget. I NEVER DID THAT AGAIN!

### Once Was Enough

*Segment V*

I was in the third grade (about age eight,) during the Depression in the mid-thirties. One day after I had gotten home from school, my mother gave me 20 cents and told me to go down to the Bald Eagle grocery, on Eagle and Park streets, and get a loaf of bread. She told me to be sure to get home before Dad came home from work.

As I walked past Bobby Schickle's house, I asked him if he wanted to come with me. I told him I would give him a jawbreaker if he would. We went down O'Connor's Alley, and when we got to Buffalo Street, we decided to walk the railroad tracks to the store. I was good at walking the rails and I liked to see how far I could go without falling off. As we walked, we found a coil of wire near the railroad's battery cylinder, which powered the signals. Since we used to put pennies on the rail and have the train flatten them out, we decided we would do it with the wire. We unrolled a short piece of wire and laid it over the rail.

The "4:05" was due and we could hear it coming from the north. As the train went by, it suddenly slammed on its brakes. The conductor climbed down from the caboose and called to us. He was a very friendly man. We always waved at him and the engineer as they went by. He asked my name, and I proudly told him, "Allen Lindholm." Bobby and I then continued down to Monte Schur's grocery store, got the bread and jawbreakers and went home without incident.

The next day while I was in Miss Freeman's third grade classroom, there was a knock on the classroom door. Miss Freeman answered, and there was Jerry Fornell, the Ramsey County Sheriff. He asked if she had a boy in her class named Allen Lindholm. She said she did and I was called out of the room. At that moment, I promptly wet my knickers! I had no idea why the Sheriff should be looking for me.

In the hall, the Sheriff asked me if I had been down by the railroad tracks the day before. I answered, and then he asked me if I had put anything on the tracks. I could not remember—I was so scared. He finally helped me remember the wire. He told me the wire had caused the signal arm to turn red which indicates traffic on the crossing Soo Line train tracks. The engineer was forced to make an emergency stop.

I must have been quite a sight to the Sheriff – a little third grade boy with a speech impediment and urine running down his leg. I am sure he was convinced I WOULD NEVER DO THAT AGAIN—AND I DIDN'T!

## Once Was Enough

*Segment VI*

I belonged to the Eagle Patrol in Boy Scout Troop 112, and one summer, we were going on an overnight to the Scout Camp on the St. Croix River across from Stillwater. We were warned about poison ivy, and told to be careful where we walked.

That first night when we were all sitting around the campfire, I showed my friends how to become immune to poison ivy. I made a poison ivy sandwich and I ate it!

One of the boys ran and told the Scout Master, Gil Gehranbeck. what I had done. He just about died! I told him I didn't get poison ivy, and he didn't believe me. They were going to take me to the hospital and have my stomach pumped. He was also worried that some other boys would try the same thing.

I was finally able to convince Mr. Gehranbeck and Paul Manship, the Assistant Scout Master, that I didn't need to have my stomach pumped; however, they told me I should NEVER, NEVER, NEVER DO THAT AGAIN!

# The Outhouse Gang

*As Remembered by*
*C. M. Ingham*

In the history of pre-indoor-plumbing, we date back to prehistoric times when people acted like animals and did their bodily eliminating behind bushes, against trees and rocks, and into natural holes in the ground.

As we became more civilized it became necessary to do our "business" away from public viewing and in private. In the Middle Ages, people started setting aside a place in their yard to relieve themselves. Eventually, Thomas Crapper, an Englishman, developed the enclosed outhouse, which is still in use worldwide in a variety of models. The most common is a shanty style shed with a single door, having a shelf inside with a hole in the shelf to sit over. Below the opening is a pit to receive the emanations. Near the top of the shack walls were frequently cut a half-moon, a star, a square, or drilled holes, to allow circulation of air—which is a necessity.!

## The Outhouse Gang: Part I

My first recollections of the outhouse and its rules and regulations are when I was six years old and living in a prairie town in Montana.

Our outhouse was a deluxe edition, as I compared it with the others I came to know in our town. We had a two-holer, one large for the parents, one smaller for the kids. Our outhouse had real toilet seats also. The kids seat was hinged and was to be flipped up when the boys stood to pee. The parents' hole was never to be used by the youngsters—poor aim.

Our parents' toilet seat was kept in the house behind the kitchen range where it was always warmer. It was carried to the outhouse, slipped into the framed slot, used in comfort, then returned to the kitchen afterward. It was a godsend when the weather was 50 degrees below zero outside and about 49 degrees below in the outhouse. You did not linger there no matter how warm the seat was to start. Using the boys' seat was like sitting on a cake of ice, except I wore my woolen mittens to sit on which helped. Even using the Sears catalog sheets was a cold shock.

When we moved to Minnesota and joined my grandparents in their house I found what a pretty place an outhouse could be. My grandparents had their outhouse on the edge of their property, covered with ivy and morning glories, surrounded by bird feeders. The flowers gave it a visual and nasal improvement and the birds thrived on the bugs and flies and made pretty music.

It was here that I first saw and heard of the Outhouse Gangs. In Montana, no one ever had an outhouse tipped over because there were only 6 or 8 teenage boys in our town who could easily be isolated and dealt with harshly.

In Willernie, Minnesota, it was Anytown, USA and outhouses were fair game to tip over (if not guarded) on the fateful Halloween. Outhouses were always fair game two to three days before or after the holiday. The tippers were roving gangs of senior teenagers. They had to be older because some of those houses were heavy to move.

Many stories survive about their escapades and the heroic attempts to keep the buildings from being violated. Frequent tales told of pushers who were so exuberant that, in their zeal, one or more fell into the pit, which ended their evening's fun.

Another anecdote described an ingenious and energetic homeowner who put his outhouse on skids and moved the house four feet forward of where it had been. This left the pit open to catch the villains coming from the back.

Two of our neighbors had worked for the railroad and sunk eight-foot sections of railroad track in all four corners of their outhouses. Several cases of dislocated shoulders were reported the next day. The following year our gang, in a "get-even" mode, tied chains around one of these rail-enforced houses, and hooked it to their car. The unsuspecting owners tore off at high speed, leaving their back wheels and transmission in the dust, the outhouse intact.

Some of the owners chose to sit in their outhouses armed with shotguns that were loaded with rock salt—which stung, but didn't kill. However, sitting inside was not always wise because the tippers could arrive silently in a rush, push, and trap the owner within.

The object of the game was to anonymously tip over the building but not hurt anyone. Dad used to patrol our back yard with a box of tomatoes and a seven-battery flashlight so he could step forward, flash the light on the guys and say, "Hello, Vern Phillips" or "Brother Youka" or "Harold Lyle." Or if he didn't recognize them, he'd pelt them with tomatoes.

*Ad courtesy of White Bear Press. Circa 1914.*

Another retaliation technique was to send out the younger kids to scout out the tippers' cars and let the air out of their tires.

I don't know if my older brother Bob was on a Tipping Gang, but I was on a Deflation Team and had as much fun as the tippers, with less mess.

### *The Outhouse Gang: Part II*

Memories of my brother Bob include the one of Mr. Clayton, at the end of our block, who let it be known that he would be "on watch" at Halloween inside his outhouse WITH A LOADED SHOTGUN.

Bob and his cronies thought it would be fun to tip his house over on the door, trapping him inside. They sneaked up quietly and tried to dump it, but he had staked it down with 2 x 4 boards so that it only rocked back and forth. Inside, Mr.

Clayton became excited and the gun went off, blowing several holes in the roof. The boys figured that was good enough fun and no one was hurt, so they took off.

Another Halloween, a neighbor who was a constable, deputized several men to help him maintain order. They chased Bob and his cohorts down Weinrich's hill, a long steep decline going down to Lake Washington. The boys hid in the tall swamp grass, but a couple guys were detailed to slow the deputies: they stretched a clothesline across the road as a trip-rope. Bob was on this team, but got caught. He was offered a trip to jail if he didn't tell who the others were. Bob got out of it by saying that he and the other guy thought they were tripping the outhouse tippers, who they thought were "those mean kids from Mahtomedi".

### *Other Sewage Stories:*

A rather rotund gentleman from White Bear Lake pumped septic tanks around the lake into his leaky wagon, which was drawn by two very slow horses. By the time he got home, the tank wagon was often empty. One day, I saw him open the septic tank at a house by the lake and start pumping it into his wagon by hand. When I arrived he was sitting on the edge of the hole with his feet dangling down, eating his lunch. When I asked how he could do that, he said "This is my bread and butter." Thank heavens it wasn't ever mine.

A lot of the people who lived on the lakeshore had cesspools, septic tanks, or drain fields in their front yards, before the sewer system came into the villages.

In the winter, when there was about two feet of snow, residents would run the waste under the snow. Most of them had a small pump hooked up to a hose which they could push down into the sewage holding tanks and pump it up onto their lawns during the night. The noise of pumps running and the smell was a dead giveaway, but hardly anyone got caught because it didn't take long to do. You could be through, back in your house reading the paper before anyone reported it. During the night the sewage would freeze over and there was no odor. In the spring, however, everyone who pumped had healthier, greener grass that those who didn't pump.

We had a friend whose wedding was to be in her mother's lake house yard. The day of the wedding, the bride called us to say she thought the septic tank was leaking. I raced down there and, sure enough, there was seepage on the lawn. No one could be found who would come to pump it out, so I bought 50 gallons of bleach and put signs in the bathroom telling all 150 guests not to "go" in the house. It made for a short reception and much embarrassment for the hostess.

# Prohibition

*As Remembered by*
*C. M. Ingham*

Prohibition became a reality in the United States in 1919. This was three years before I was born in Montana, long enough for bootleggers, smugglers, and other crooks to set up methods of bypassing the law. Even good citizens who were thirsty found ways around the stringent illegal sale of spirits.

One story took place in Willernie, Minnesota, after the end of Prohibition in the 1930s. A neighbor, Wally S., who lived three doors from us stayed very busy making and selling bootleg booze. When asked what kind, he would say, "Any kind you like, Scotch, Gin, Bourbon." It didn't make any difference—it was all made in the same bathtub. The flavoring and color were added later to suit the need. A little tobacco juice gave the scotch its color and taste, some kerosene for the gin, and nutmeg and some other "secret ingredients" for the bourbon.

Wally was the spitting image of movie star Wallace Beery in size, build, voice and manner. He wore a long overcoat that his mother made him, which had about 25 pockets inside, each of which could hold a pint bottle. He scrounged the back doors of liquor joints to find pint bottles, preferably with labels on them. He rinsed these briefly before refilling them with his concoctions and transferring them to his overcoat. His places of business were in the parking lots outside the legitimate booze emporiums in our village. He would ply his trade with people going home, and sold his merchandise at $1.25–$1.50 per bottle, Scotch was $2.50.

On busy weekends he would plan ahead by stashing 20–30 bottles in the culvert under the road so he wouldn't have to go far for more. One winter day he fell down on some ice with his pockets full and put himself out of business. It took him three days to recuperate his losses: one day to make it, one day to bottle and flavor it, and one day to age it. Then to the market it went.

One summer day, Wally was sporting his new $19.95 suit, purple with white chalk stripes, at one of the local watering holes when the fire alarm went off. Being an over-zealous volunteer fire fighter, Wally ran two doors to the fire hall, opened the door of the fire truck, jumped in, and waiting for no one, tore out. He drove about three blocks before he realized he didn't know where the fire was, so spun back to the fire hall. Waiting for him was one of his cohorts in the Fire Department and the number two town drunk, Old Mac. He gave Wally the address and went around to jump on the back of the fire truck, but Wally took off leaving Old Mac sitting in the dust, cussing.

Wally arrived at the fire, three doors from my house, a summer cottage that rented out by the hour. It was only a three-room job with front and back porch, and had a good blaze going on the front porch.

I ran down to watch. I saw Wally pull up, leap off the rig, grab a can of chemical fire retardant and crash right through the screen door. He began pumping the chemical all over the porch floor, walls, screens and himself, then proceeded right through the house and out the back door. He had the fire out in one minute, but came out of the house with his clothes singed and smoking. He dropped the chemical tank, scrambled under the house, and pulled out a crate of his filled, labeled pint bottles. He got up, patted the smoldering suit, now with holes in it, and said, "Boy, that was close. If the fire had gotten to this crate the whole block would have gone up!"

The owner had placed oil-soaked rags in all the corners of the house and touched them off with a match, figuring the insurance company would pay him for the tragedy. He didn't know that Wally had used his crawl space for a liquor warehouse. The company didn't pay and it didn't buy Wally a new suit, either.

*Courtesy of White Bear Press.*
*Circa 1914.*

# PLANTATION TO OPEN TUESDAY

## Engages 70 People; On KSTP Every Night; Dozen National Conventions to Banquet Here

The Plantation, the finest night club in Minnesota, with 70 people, opens the season next Tuesday evening, the 16th, when it is anticipated that the S. R. O. sign will be hung out by the time the program begins.

Phil Lavant and his splendid orchestra who were here last year have been engaged for this season. This orchestra is one of the top-notch musical organizations of Chicago, and is nationally known.

The interior of the Plantation has been gone over, renovated and refreshed, and will present the same inviting and pleasing atmosphere as of last season and Manager Harris says it will be continued this season on the same high scale as before.

Manager Harris stated to The Press yesterday: "We expect to have during the season at least a dozen banquets for national organizations meeting in St. Paul, among them being the Knights Templar, State Sheriffs and Police Association, National Manufacturers of Ready Made Clothing and others. We are today closing a deal for the entertainment of 700 members of B'nai B'rith for July 5, 6 and 7.

"There will be two floor shows each evening by artists of the first class and the programs will be broadcast over KSTP every night by direct wire which should be quite an advertisement for White Bear. Everything in these entertainments will be refined and acceptable to all, there being nothing rough or coarse.

"We are now placing large billboards throughout the state and northwest, advertising 'The Plantation on the shores of White Bear lake.' We cater to none but nice people and never have had any roughness—nor won't have."

# Nude Water Skiing

*As Remembered by*
*C. M. Ingham*

For ten years I served on the Board of Directors of the White Bear Lake Conservation District. Each year, the County Sheriff's Department would submit a resume of the offenses perpetrated on the lake the previous year, along with their budget requests.

One year an item noted two adults arrested for nude water skiing. When questioned, the officer said they had a complaint from two fishing parties about these people bothering them. He also said it took them two hours to catch the perpetrators. When I asked why, he said, "Did you ever try to drive a boat around the lake while looking through binoculars?"

I then asked if the water skiers were wearing PFDs (Personal Flotation Devices, or life jackets), as required by law. His answer: "Gee, I never noticed; I was looking at other things!"

*Ad, circa 1931,*
*courtesy of White Bear Press.*

# The Hula Hut

*As Remembered by*
C. M. Ingham

If you wanted to get to Mahtomedi, Willernie or Wildwood Amusement Park by car, you had to take the Stillwater Road from Highway 61 east or through North St. Paul and over the County Line Road to the Stillwater Road. Now, all these routes are the same but are named differently. The Highway Department did make one huge change in the path to our town by straightening out the road down Wildwood Hill. About one mile east of the Ramsey County line, Stillwater Road took a slow turn to the right, then a serpentine series of curves, arcs, hills and valleys as it wound down Wildwood Hill. In the winter it could be fun or a nightmare with sleet and ice. For a narrow, two-lane road it held the record in the state for the most repairs to its guardrails and adjacent scarred trees and brush. Along near the bottom of the hill lurked a non-descriptive, ugly hovel of a tavern called the Hula Hut.

The Hula Hut was built by Herman Meinke, from North St. Paul. Everyone called him Heime. The building was about the same size as a small house, but was covered on the outside with tarpaper held in place with slats of lathe. This made for easy repairs when cars hit the building or storms lashed at the thin siding. There was no insulation, just the bare studs for inside walls and naked rafters above. Except for the trap door behind the bar, the floor was covered with large slabs of linoleum of various colors and shapes. The trap door opened into a hole dug in the dirt, which was the beer cellar.

It became a busy and well-attended joint by people stopping on their way home from work for a drink or to celebrate the fact that they successfully negotiated the Wildwood Hill Road. It was also a welcome relief station for the employees of Wildwood Amusement Park, about two blocks further down the road, after the Park closed at midnight. They would party 'til the Hula Hut closed at sunup. You knew it was dawn because Heime would start at one end of the bar bumping people with his huge beer belly and shouting in his broken German-English that, "Da sun is op. Go to home and Bet."

The building was so poorly built that when people started dancing, the floor would go up and down two inches at a time. Fred and Millie Bruening were great dancers, but put the building at peril. Fred was about 6 feet 6 inches and weighed close to 300 pounds. Millie was over 6 feet and about 250 pounds. She could run like a deer and was the lady who used to chase us when we tried to "borrow" her baby watermelons. The Bruenings loved to polka, a dance that involves much stomping. People used to tell Heime to put some supports under the floor or it would cave into the cellar. He would answer, "Yah, Yah, dots the reason I only valk around the etches not in the mittle!"

The drinks at the Hula Hut were simple — only spiked beers. Heime would sell near beer made by Schmidt's Brewery in St. Paul. This was made of rice, and came in bottles that were not filled up into the neck. When the waitress brought it to you she pried off the cap and you added the 100% alcohol to the brim. Heime would sell the alcohol to you in pint bottles, supposedly washed and refilled from a local still.

No glasses were furnished for drinking your beer, so the procedure was to hold your thumb over the top of the bottle and upend it a couple of times to mix the beer and alcohol. As you drank it down, you added more alcohol so that it became as potent as you liked or could stand.

After Wildwood Amusement Park closed, Heime's business declined about the same time his legs gave out. He tried adding fried chicken to his menu but there were cleaner, neater, nicer places doing that, so he sold out to some brothers from St. Paul. They were Oscar, the big money man, Joe, the cook, and Al, the bouncer. All tended bar.

They changed the name of the place to the Wildwood Tavern and it became a blind pig—a place to buy illegal booze. It was also the hangout of tough St. Paul hoods, pals of the proprietors.

One time a mild-mannered guy named Bob from Mahtomedi got belligerent after a few drinks and started a fight. The brothers were their own enforcers and did not call the police. Al threw Bob out twice and, in the melee, broke Bob's back. He was in a body cast for a long time. Bob sued and the brother's insurance company settled out of court for a healthy amount. Bob and his dad, who had been a cigarette salesman, started a very successful wholesale cigarette, tobacco and candy business in White Bear. They eventually added a retail liquor store, but Bob stayed away from The Wildwood Tavern ever after.

The Wildwood decided to become a Steak House and they served the largest, not the best, steak, so big it hung over your platter, huge hamburgers, and fries. It was so much meat that there was open speculation whether it was stolen, hijacked beef, or horsemeat. Quite a few horses started disappearing in Washington County, but no one dared ask the brothers.

Strangely, at this time, a World War II veteran rented a storefront shop as a shoe and leather repair place. He had heavy-duty leather sewing machines, but before anyone got to know him much, the brothers called on him one evening and nearly killed him by beating him. He had both legs, one arm, and several ribs broken and heavy contusions everywhere. He spent months in the VA hospital, then disappeared. He had paid his rent for three months ahead but, when he did not return, the owners of the building found all his sewing machines in the basement along with a huge supply of horsehide. No one ever complained or investigated.

When liquor came back and other places purchased liquor licenses, the Tavern didn't buy one. They did not need one since their building was in an unincorporated area and had no one to buy it from, so they continued to sell moonshine rotgut as a Bottle Club. Everyone was supposed to have a locker with his own bottle and his name on it, but they kept them on an open bar because they claimed they were regulars, or had lost the key to the locker.

Eventually, we had a change of Sheriff and the brothers had to change the place into a private club. They issued membership cards for $5.00. The only way you could get in to partake of the dubious meat and booze was to produce your card.

Eventually, the two older brothers sold out to Al and his wife. They ran it for a few years, then sold it two or three times to people who could not make a go of it when they had to buy a liquor license and stop selling cheap moonshine.

One of the moonshiners was an active bathtub chemist named Jim. He was, by real profession, a house painter and wallpaper hanger. He made some money buying summer cottages in Willernie and Mahtomedi. He would slap a coat of paint on the outside and finish the inside with wallboard, which he papered with bright, cheap floral wallpaper. He would invest $1,200 to $2,000 in the house and repairs, then sell quickly, for $5,000 to $6,000, as winter homes. He left town before winter arrived and his client found out the insulation was the glue on the wallpaper.

Bob Ingham hired Jim to paint the ceiling of his grocery store and, thereby, work off his grocery bill. Jim hired George, one of his steady customers, who owed him money, to help.

The ceiling had many cracks and holes in it, but they painted it all in one night while the store was closed. Next morning when Bob opened for business he was pleasantly surprised at how nice it looked, smooth and cracks gone. Later in the day where George came by, Bob asked how they filled and covered the cracks and holes. The answer was they just took a couple of bars of Fels Naptha soap off the shelves and plugged the cracks with that, and painted over it. Of course, when the soap dried out, it fell out, leaving the holes again, but by that time Jim had moved away.

Jim's moonshine business was expanding so he needed more room for a bigger still and more distance between him and his creditors, police, and former painting customers. He told everyone that he was going to move upstate near Morrison to retire and fish. Every week or so he appeared back in town with the back end of his car nearly dragging on the ground. He had made another delivery of freshly "aged lightning." It was "aged in the woods" for at least a day or two while he scrounged up more bottles.

The Hula Hut is still in existence, but the mystique and danger has gone. No more horsemeat or moonshine. It's now legit.

# Willernie and the Paperboy

*As Remembered by*
*C. M. Ingham*

This small village on the southeastern shore of White Bear Lake in Minnesota, twelve miles northeast of St. Paul, was unique in many ways. I don't know the derivation of the name Willernie or what it means, but I am very familiar with its size, inhabitants, reason for being, and am uncertain of its future.

It appeared as a portion of Lincoln township, which was a large expanse of farmland with no town or central headquarters. It probably was an Indian encampment or a streetcar stop on the St. Paul to Mahtomedi to Stillwater run, or where a drunken Englishman found himself one morning, penniless and hung over.

At any rate, the English part is true because the meandering streets have names such as Paddington Road, Chatham Road, Chelsea Place, and Glenmar.

It apparently appeared before 1900 as a summer resort area because it had easy access by streetcar and was near the lake. My grandparents purchased five lots about one mile from the lake in 1913. These lots were each 50 x100 feet, upon which my ancestors built a typical summer cottage. It had two fair size sleeping porches fore and aft with a kitchen, living room, and one bedroom. The bathroom was a wash basin and the "necessary room" an outhouse surrounded by a trellis of morning glories. It was many years before I realized morning glories didn't smell so bad.

My grandmother was a avid gardener. She built a beautiful grape arbor, a strawberry patch, planted currant bushes at the lower lot borders, an ash tree just outside her bedroom, hedges of hawthorn on north and south perimeters, and abundant pots of brilliant flowers throughout the yards, and along walks and stairs. She also made great jams and jellies from her produce and baked my favorite, sugar cookies. Hers were laced with caraway seeds, which I carefully picked out, thinking they were ants.

My grandfather apparently cut the grass with a pusher type mower which must have taken him all week, which, soon enough, my brother and I came to hate. My grandfather's favorite pastimes were watching or listening to the Minneapolis Millers baseball team, and fishing. If he could get tickets to the ballgame at Nicollet Park he'd ride the streetcar all day to and from the Lake to take in the game. One day, he tried to catch a pop foul with his straw bowler: the ball went on through, taking the top of the hat with it. It was a prized trophy.

He offered to show me how to fish, if I would just row the boat. We carried the rods, reels, tackle box, and our lunch one-and-a-half miles to Carlson's boathouse on White Bear Lake, where we rented a boat for the afternoon. We were assigned a fourteen-foot Leviathan that weighed 600 pounds dry and had only two oars. Grandpapa showed his ten-year-old grandson how to fit the six foot oars in the oarlocks and sit facing the rear. He sat on the rear seat facing forward and told me where to go and how to get there. He did show me how to rig the rods, bait the hooks with minnows, drop the line in the lake, and troll while I pulled. Fortunately, one of his favorite spots was in the lily pads in the back bay beyond Wildwood Amusement Park, just across the lake from the boathouse, 3/4 miles away.

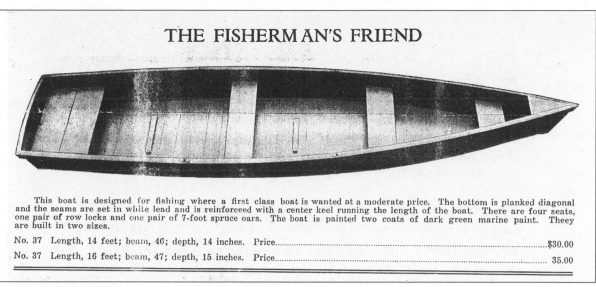

# THE FISHERMAN'S FRIEND

This boat is designed for fishing where a first class boat is wanted at a moderate price. The bottom is planked diagonal and the seams are set in white lead and is reinforced with a center keel running the length of the boat. There are four seats, one pair of row locks and one pair of 7-foot spruce oars. The boat is painted two coats of dark green marine paint. Theey are built in two sizes.

No. 37   Length, 14 feet; beam, 46; depth, 14 inches.   Price.............................................................$30.00
No. 37   Length, 16 feet; beam, 47; depth, 15 inches.   Price................................................... 35.00

*Sales brochure courtesy of Bob Borowski.*

My grandparents lived in the summerhouse from May to October and then in an apartment in Minneapolis or St. Paul the rest of the year.

My family, my parents, a brother four years older than I, and another brother seven years younger, moved into the cottage with the grandparents the summer of 1931 and stayed there all winter. The cottage was barely warm with no insulation, but hardly anyone had insulation then, so what you don't have you don't miss.

Out behind Willernie was a large wooded pasture where a farmer, Fred Bruening, kept his cows. It was here that in later years I learned to play the tuba. Banished from practicing in the house, I walked three blocks to the pasture. Quite often I scared the cows, but as I got better they would gather around and add their moos to mine.

Mrs. Bruening had a large vegetable garden near the house and grew melons. The older boys, my brother and his friends, often talked about how good her melons were that they swiped by moonlight. When I was about thirteen, my friends thought we were old enough to get in on the game, so I asked my brother for advice. He told me where the melons were and how to do it, but to watch out for Mrs. B., who could run like a deer, or Mr. B., who would shoot with rock salt from his shotgun.

Three of us assembled and did the deed and, as we each crept away from the field with a melon, the door to the house opened and out came the tallest blonde I'd ever seen. We three took off for the wooded pasture like streaks of light with the big woman hot on our trail. Somehow, we all leapt the fence with melons intact. They were the best tasting melons I've ever had, at least the excitement and danger made them seem so.

We repeated our escapade a few more times with lots of anticipation each time, and each time was successful, barely. The next year we plied our piracy again with the same results—almost. When we settled into the clearing in the woods and broke open our melons, we found they were terrible. Roy had a matchbook and lit a fire. We found we had stolen three large cucumbers! We lost all heart in the game that night and did not touch the melon patch again.

Thirty years later I met Mrs. B. with her son at a local fair and could not keep from admitting my thievery to her. She laughed and laughed and hugged me greatly. When I asked what she would have done to us if she ever caught us, she said, "Throw you to the ground and kiss you all over your faces. That would have been too embarrassing to take at your age." When I asked if Mr. B. had real rock salt in his shotgun, she said, "No, Fred loaded his own shells and he just put gunpowder in the shells with cotton wadding. They were blanks! We had so much fun planting those melons so you boys would come steal them so we could have some fun, too."

The small town had very few stores, only one grocery, one filling station, one garage, three saloons, and one dairy store where the proprietor's cat slept in the fruit.

My older brother, Bob, and I had a newspaper route delivering the morning, evening, and Sunday papers, seven days per week for 65¢ a month. In the winter we had 100 customers, but in the summer this swelled to 300, due to the rental cottages. There were many cottages, which rented for $25 a week and were full from May to October. I was very young and naive and did not realize that many of the renters were prostitutes and the ladies who owned the cottages were madams. I thought it nice that there were so many pretty younger ladies who had jobs that allowed them to take such long vacations.

We had our paper route for about ten years. I carried from ages 11 to 18 when I left for college. I left the route for Jack, who was 11, but it was too large for him to handle alone for long.

My naivete extended to other experiences on this paper route. One customer I had was a group of young men with big new Buick and LaSalle cars. When I went to collect they gave me a dollar and said, "Keep the change, kid." We received very few tips in those days, so I was really impressed and thought, "Boy, when I grow up I hope I'm successful enough to be able to tip the paperboy."

A few weeks later I opened the paper and there was a picture of my customer and his friends on the front page with the headline "'Babyface' Nelson and his Accomplices are Caught!" No wonder they could afford to tip me; it wasn't their money.

At first, dogs were bothersome at some houses. The one the owners said, "Oh, he won't bite you. He is so gentle," was always the sneaky devil dog that would wait until you walked past, then nip you on the ankle. I wore high boots for years to protect my ankles.

Most of the dogs were all bluff and if you showed no fear and talked to them they would back down. I always extended my left hand toward them to smell, to see that I had no fear, but I kept a tightly rolled paper in my right hand ready to swat him on the ear if he desired to taste. Several did, once.

There were only two dogs I truly feared, and still do. One was a seeing-eye dog that belonged to a blind man on my route. He was excellently under control when he was on the lead with his owner, but off-leash and free, he was a vicious watchdog. One day, when I went to collect, as the mother of the blind man opened the door to pay me, the dog, a Doberman Pinscher, lunged through the door. It grabbed at my knee and caught my brand new $2 blue jeans from Monkey Ward's and ripped the leg open up to the belt. If it hadn't been for Mrs. Eakins grabbing the dog, I'm sure I would have been hurt—or wet my pants—or worse.

The other was a huge German Shepherd that had killed and eaten half a baby in Minneapolis. The guy who owned it couldn't kill the dog, so he gave it to his brother, who lived in Willernie. The dog was so vicious that he was chained inside a garage from both sides all day then let loose to roam at night. I came down the alley by his home one day about 5:30 AM when I heard a growl and, just in time, ducked as he sailed over my head from a high bank on my right. He landed on the slope across the alley, rolled down the bank and crashed into the back of a garage. I was two blocks away when he untangled himself.

The next morning, he jumped me at the end of the alley and I jammed a fully rolled newspaper down his throat, tight. This was a tactic I had used many times on dogs that were too curious about my legs.

I did this stunt a couple times and his owner called and complained about getting his paper. I told him to ask the dog; he had it. He claimed I irritated the dog, but I felt it was vice versa.

Next time the dog attacked, I was ready with a water pistol full of ammonia. Several squirts over several days partially blinded him temporarily. He rallied, but so did I. The water pistol was one of two defense mechanisms we had to protect us from muggers when collecting for the papers. This was during the Depression, and several paperboys were attacked. Our other weapon was an 18-inch cudgel my Dad made. Dad had found this club as a branch of an oak with a knot in one end, in which he drilled a hole and filled it with lead. On the other end, he peeled the bark and drilled a hole for a wrist thong so it wouldn't slip out of my hand.

The time I used the cudgel on my stubborn nemesis, I tapped him only once and sent him home howling with a headache. The next time, I laid him out, temporarily. The third time, I took a two-handed swing and knocked him cold. He apparently lived to stagger home, because when I came to his house after that, he ran into the garage and closed the door.

# A Death on Bald Eagle Lake

*As Remembered by*
*C. Allen Lindholm*

When I was about eight years old, Ruth and Hayden Stright rented the Quincy cottage that was on top of the hill behind our house. They had three children: Paul, Dick and Jeanne. Hayden was a Professor of Religion at Macalester College and had written several books on the subject.

One summer, Ruth's mother, Mrs. Brown, and a live-in nurse stayed with them for the season. On this particular morning, Mother and I were in our backyard when the Strights' nurse came running down the alley and asked if we had seen Mrs. Brown. Mother said we hadn't. However, she asked me to walk along the top of the bank where the path was close to the edge, and see if Mrs. Brown might have fallen. When I got to the top of the bank near Mrs. Johnson's house, I saw what I thought was a huge fish floating in the water by Mrs. Johnson's dock, which was next to the creek. I ran down the bank and when I went out onto the dock, I discovered it was a body!

Mr. Shickle, a neighbor, was out fishing in his boat, so I called to him to come in because there was a body in the water, and to pull it into shore. Mrs. Johnson, who never wanted kids on her property, started yelling at me to get off her dock. But when I told her there was a body down there and to call the police, she went Bananas! She told me to come up and call, but I had never used a telephone before.

I ran home to tell Dad, but found he had heard all the commotion and had already been over to O'Connors to call the police. We could hear the sirens almost immediately, and Dad and I went down to the corner to meet Art Long, the Chief of Police from White Bear, to tell him where to find the body. By this time, quite a crowd had gathered, and my father made me go back to the house so I wouldn't witness the gruesome event.

We later found out from our neighbor, Ralph Tuttle, that he had heard a scream the night before but assumed it was kids having a swimming party down at the lake. That was not uncommon in those days.

According to Ruth Stright, her mother hated the water. Ruth believed she may have walked in her sleep and fainted when she realized where she was. Mrs. Brown was a very kind and pleasant woman, and I liked her very much, but I will never forget this very frightening day.

*One of the first log cabins located in Bald Eagle Lake area. This photo was taken in 1909. Postcard courtesy of Lawrence R. (Bob) and Eileen Whitaker.*

# Hot
# Off the
# Iron

**Editor's Note:**

*In the fall of 1998, as stories and photos were pouring in for this book, we received a mysterious photo of a man in a black cat costume. The photo was submitted by Bob and Eileen Whitaker of White Bear Lake. Attached was a very fragile piece of paper with the names of 39 members of the Black Cat Club, dated April 19, 1912. The photo was slightly damaged after having been removed from an old scrapbook. On the back was the name F. E. Whitaker, father of Bob.*

*Who were the Black Cats and what's with the eerie costume? There was a rumor that the Black Cats may have been a vigilante group, or perhaps they were a theatre troupe. Local newspaper reporters, including Cynthia Boyd from the St. Paul Pioneer Press and Gary Mortenson from the White Bear Press, couldn't resist the mystery, either. They both published stories asking the public to come forward with information on this secret club. The mystery began to unfold.*

*L. D. H.*

*Thus begins the story of…*

# The Black Cats, a Retrospectus

*Story courtesy of the White Bear Breeze, circa 1900*
*Submitted by Sharon Bruckner and retold by Pat Terry*

Owing to a slight deviation from the strict rules and precedents of the order of "Black Cats," we are at last enabled, through the kindness of their worthy Historian, and at great expense to ourselves, to give on this occasion a few details concerning their origin.

One cold, wintry night early in December, in the year of 1896, there assembled at the home of W.H. Whitaker, at the bequest of the host, 12 loyal followers of Hoyle. All had received cordial invitations to be present on the evening in question, for the purpose of trying a hand at "cinch" or whist. None of the company that arrived promptly at 8:30 to enjoy the pastimes and refreshments so plentifully set before them had any thought as to the outcome, or manner in which the evening was to be brought about.

They were there to enjoy themselves, and the shouts arising from each table, attested as much. The "Historian" had just proclaimed his bid of 13 on the ace and deuce. In his mind's eye, the prize glimmering down the line and beyond his reach, was soon to become a fading memory. He was brought to a stern realization of his reckless bid by a tug at the tassel of his score card that dangled from the capacious pocket of the cardigan jacket that did him duty as a coat. Reaching for the indicator of the triumphs and failures, he was much surprised to see, staring him in the face, slowly winking one yellow convex eye, a huge "Black Genii" in the shape of a giant "Black Cat." The cat, belonging to the host, had, in some mysterious manner, gained entrance to the scene of the contest, and deported himself to the head table.

The sudden appearance of this apparition so excited the Historian, that he wildly led the cards around the table, and made all his points. As the bell rang out his victory, he arose, and in a voice subdued only by the metallic click of the punch as it found its way through his score card, proclaimed that thereafter they would be known as the "Black Cats." And, as not one dissenting voice was raised, another social success was launched.

Urged on by the spirit of good fellowship, many subsequent meetings followed suit. The original 13 members all had friends who were welcomed to the order. Consequently, the trend of the affairs of the Black Cat's meetings was moved from assemblage in private homes to larger lodge facilities.

Although made up of many gentlemen from different walks of life, all contrast ceases once the lodge doors close behind them. There are no by-laws, no rules, hence, no disputes. Their only motto, "Be a Gentleman," is strictly adhered to by all. The order stares fate in the face, by holding all their meetings on Friday and as near the 13th of the month as possible. They play 13 games and pay 13 cents for Booby prizes. In the face of this array of Voodoo-ism there has as yet occurred no deaths during the life of the Order, and only one had temerity to become a benedict. It has also unconsciously served a good purpose in cementing the friendly feeling and good fellowship that exists among them all. It claims as its members, persons from all the different fraternal orders in our village, and a few outside. Also, members that belong to no other organization, whatever their lodge rooms, serve as neutral ground, whereon, they can all caterwaul to their heart's content.

We cannot forbear touching upon their repasts, which have been renowned owing to their variety and close association with cabbage in a state of fermentation.

**Editor's Note:**

*The Black Cat's Annual Balls were given in the month of April and were always pronounced "the social success of the season." Following that, they all looked forward anticipating their annual "Cruise" around the lake in August. In early December, many meows could be heard as the High Carnival of Black Cats hosted their seasons-ending galas. The Black Cat events became a mainstay in White Bear Lake in the early part of the 20th century. Their annual hops and picnics were intended to "please and delight" the participating guests. The association grew to include a vivacious and successful bowling and baseball team. Many of the Black Cat officers were elected for life and duly christened. The club disbanded sometime in late 1939, some believe due to the beginning of the war.*

*In celebration of this, the White Bear Center for the Arts decided to revive the legacy of the Black Cats Club. In 1999, they hosted the "High Carnival of the Black Cats Gala" and hope to carry on the tradition of providing the "premiere social event of the year" for this community.*

P.T.

# Just a Little Trivia...

The famed cat of nine lives was domesticated around 2400 BC, although, history tells of their close association with man up to 4000 years before that. Many legends and myths surround this nocturnal creature. The Egyptians worshipped the feline, which is a well known, and documented source of the nine lives theory. The globed cat eyes reputed to be able to see in the dark have been likened to the waxing and waning of the moon. Actions of cats were gleaned to predict the weather or even foretell the next love of your life. Did you know for example, that it is bad luck to kick a cat, but good luck to have a cat at your wedding? Then, of course, we can only begin to dabble at the superstitious aura of beliefs surrounding the Black cat. Norse mythology ingrained the belief that a black cat could turn itself into a witch whose worshippers assembled on Friday. This witch and cat relation was almost fatal to the proliferation of the cat in early history. Well known is the superstition of the black cat crossing your path, but lesser known is the belief that if a black cat comes to your door, there will soon be a lover in your life, and that possessing a black cat assures wealth. To quote an anonymous author: *"Cats are wonderfully independent creatures—they obey no one because they are not obedient. In some circles they have a bad reputation—similar to independent women. But what kind of world would it be without cats—or independent women?"*

P.E.

To stroke a black cat's tail seven times assures you will have good luck in cards . . .

## Black Cats Have a Picnic

Last Sunday will be a day "Jack" Schlee, of Pine Tree Lake, will remember for a long time. Jack has a fondness for cats, but his especial favorites are the Black Cats, of which there are a great many in and around White Bear. It was decided by the White Bear Black Cats that they would take advantage of their friend's fondness for them and congregate around his premises on a given date, the same being Sunday, June 11th. So eager were they for the fray that some of them went the night before "So as to have things ready for the rest." Among the latter were George Farnen, F. E. Lindgren and we believe Art Long. We are informed by the former of this trio that they were successful in gathering in nine chickens, but we were not informed whose flock suffered the loss, which Ben Clewett converted into the best bouillon ever tasted. It must have been an all-night's job for a sort of tired feeling took possession of the advanced delegation of company, and as the morning light was breaking "Rocky" took possession of a boat and announced he was going fishing. He must have lost interest in the finny tribe however, for he alarmed the others by disappearing from sight, and an investigation showed that he had converted the bottom of the boat into a couch and was indulging in peaceful slumber.

As the morning advanced others of the Black Cats began to arrive and continued to arrive until thirty-five were on the grounds. We are told that the only 'Onory Cats present' were W. H. Felkner, of St. Paul, and Ern Bacon, of Stillwater.

Games were enjoyed such as baseball, pitching horseshoe, etc. It is claimed that Sew Smith was there with his two dogs and yet not a single Cat got up on his back nor went up a tree.

We have always taken Harry Getty to be one of those individuals who could never be persuaded under any circumstances to forget true etiquette, but on this occasion he forgot there was such a thing. It happened this way: Our friend Jack of the Pine Tree locality has for a long time been the champion at hitting the stake with the horse shoe. It was proposed that he and Harry each choose a partner for a game and Harry's combination won out. Thinking perhaps his partner was to blame Jack challenged Harry for a game and here was where Harry fell down on etiquette. He forgot that Jack was his host and proceeded to "do" his antagonistic host to a finish.

Mr. and Mrs. Thos. Daniels have moved into their new home at Dellwood.

C. H. Wiegand is attending the I. O. O. F. Grand Lodge at St. Paul this week.

A lively game of ball was on also with our friend Mehlhorn as umpire. Mehl is about as good a judge of good baseball as most cats are of an old boot. His decisions were on a par—and they had to stand. The nearest to a genine thrill came when Doc. Voges made his famous "slide" at the home plate. They called it a slide but were not sure but what it was a "roll" for could anyone who knows Doc imagine he could slide without rolling—in fact how could he? It must have been during this game that one of Jack's hens laid an egg in Bill Spink's pocket, for there was an egg there and surely no cat could lay it there, but we are not here to tell what happened when Bill found it out—ask someone who was there, or ask Billy. It must have been in the excitement of this game also that Jim King lost his hat and didn't know it until after he became "sunstruck," but he survived and all was well.

It surely was a pleasant day for all who participated and especially for Frank Reif who was on the grounds about eight hours and thought he had been there only "a few minutes," and Dr. Francis says he wishes they would have a Black Cat picnic every Sunday.

*Story from the White Bear Press, 1916. Submitted by Lynne Hagen.*

## THE BLACK CATS

### Entertained Their Friends in Their Usual Felicitous Manner.

The Ancient and Extraordinary Order of Black Cats gave their fourth annual hop last night for the pleasure of their large, select and appreciative circle of lady friends. The Twin City Mandolin Club furnished the music; a floor committee consisting of Dr. C. L. Clark, Messrs. F. P. Harbaugh and Geo. H. Wells, assisted by numerous other Cats as aids and lieutenants, looked after the comfort and pleasure of the guests; Mrs. Harbaugh had charge of the refreshments, which were very nice indeed; all arrangements made by the committee, Messrs. F. P. Harbaugh, J. M. King and Wm. H. Felkner, were well planned and smoothly carried out. Under these conditions, a grand success was the only possible outcome. The hall was comfortably filled but not crowded and all present were imbued with the intention to please and be pleased. The result was a delightful evening for every one of the participating guests and a fitting close for the Black Cats' season.

Those who enjoyed the festivities were:

Mr. and Mrs. F. E. Hemstreet, S. C. Smith, J. A. Haussner, George E. Schnabel, T. E. Fellows, W. B. Thomson, E. A. Bacon, Martin Garvin, Dr. and Mrs. Clark.

Mrs. Stocker, of St. Paul, Mrs. W. W. Webber, Jr., Mrs. Harbaugh, Mrs. M. M. Fulton, Mrs. J. D. Ramaley, Mrs. John Long, Mrs. Snell.

Misses Barbara O'Connor, Marguerite O'Gorman, Nannie Conroy and Mamie O'Neill, of St. Paul; Misses Jean Fulton, Sophie A. Hubman, Dora Kinyon, Alice Kinyon, May Kinyon, Marie Heffernan, Ada Palmer, Leona Palmer, Elizabeth Whitaker, Roxana Hardy, Irene Dunn, Emily Extrand, Mabel Extrand, Kathryn Bunghard, Lillian Bunghard, Lula Bunghard, Mabel Thomson, Lucy Clewett, Anna Davis, Ruby Davis, Daphne Murray, and Winnie Gage.

Messrs. G. H. Michaud, C. Avando Levens, of St. Paul, F. P. Harbaugh, J. M. King, Wm. H. Felkner, George H. Wells, T. C. Fulton, J. C. Fulton, George H. Reif, Jas. H. Bacon, F. E. Whitaker, W. H. Whitaker, J. S. Chisholm, John Taylor, Bert King, Frank Lindgren, Henry Extrand, Gene Ramaley, J. J. McGrath, Fred Murray, Frank Murray, George Supple, Joseph Dunn, Alden Blood, Arthur Baldwin, Felix Mainzer, F. J. Reif, R. N. Clewett, Wm. Goesch, Jr. and E. L. Falesi.

## High Carnival of Black Cats.

WHITE BEAR MINN, DEC. 1, 1896.

To White Bear Life

The "Black Cats" held High Carnival at "Park Place" last Monday evening, their Meows being heard until late into Tuesday morning. Roll being called, the official business of the Order was gone through with, including the initiation of Jack Wampler, after which the contests were entered into. Mr. Mainzer ran all the way home with first prize and Mr. Fellows, after a terrific struggle against countless odds, succeeded in perpetuating a lease on the Booby. His record on this kind of a style remains unbroken. Dean Leaman carried off a pocketfull of flour, which has since been returned by his folks. Barring Mr. Leaman's eccentricities the specialty work of comrades Drake and Supple were the features of the evening. Not overlooking in anyway Mr. Thompson and Chisholm's rendition of Tann Hauser. But what of the night? None but Black Cats were put on guard, and yet, with all our alertness our poet "Laurate escaped, and this is the result. We make no apologies for these touching lines, but are duty bound to shield the author:

Thirteen Black Cats went one cold evening to
    play cards;
Fellows and Leaman, two jolly old Pards,
Sat down to the table determined to win,
With never a smile not even a grin.

When McCully and Supple with their winning
    ways,
Very quickly sat on these "Jolly Jays."
They, too were determined to win the Prize.
And all through the evening looked very wise.

And, Alas! for their looks, they were not in it,
To the foot they went that very minute,
For Wampler and Harbaugh in their droll way,
Had come to the head where they meant to stay.

Said the serene Thompson to Gage Mainzer,
    and Drake,
Say, Boys! lets go and jump in the lake,
Oh, No, said Pihlgren we would each spoil our
    face,
Wait for Jack and Felkner and at the table we
    without a place.

*Story taken from the White Breeze.*
*Submitted by Sharon Bruckner.*

# History of the White Bear Center for the Arts

The White Bear Center for the Arts was originally formed in 1968 as the White Bear Arts Council by a group of area residents, organized by Sister Florentine (a nun at St. Jude's School in Mahtomedi) and Janet Schuneman. This group of people shared a passion for the arts and wanted to see them fostered in our community.

The vision of the organization at that time was to provide art classes and start a choral group. Under the direction of Bill Goyer, the Council's first president, the classes began at Birchwood once a week and a choral group began with Paul Hedrickson taking the lead. (The White Bear Choral Association spun off and is still going strong today.)

Over the years, the Arts Council sponsored many events, including The Fair in the Fields, Art Explosion, and the Northern Lights, an annual juried art exhibit held at Century College. The Northern Lights, which started in 1974, continues to be a very prestigious and well attended exhibit. This exhibit draws participants from our five-state region, representing over 100 artists each year.

In May 1996, the White Bear City Council offered the Arts Council use of the fourth floor of the Armory as an arts center. At that time, the organization changed its name to the White Bear Center for the Arts. The Arts Center now offers classes and workshops in a variety of media for children, youth and adults including painting, drawing, ceramics, performance, literary and fiber arts, year round. The emphasis has been on children's programming, with a variety of after-school, non-school and weekend classes.

Other programs and special events the Center offers include: hosting "Artrain," a national touring museum on a train, sponsoring art workshops for Alzheimer's patients at the White Bear Care Center, as well as lectures, exhibits, travel opportunities and art retreats.

"*Krumkake, Tales of Wit, Wisdom and Wanderings,*" our largest project, was an effort to celebrate the art of the written word and the rich history in our community. We hope you have enjoyed it.

*The Center is building for the day in which it will have permanent space and resources to sponsor a regular rotation of gallery exhibitions by local, regional and national artists. The Center is also seeking collaborations with other area organizations toward the development and expansion of our current programs and facility in order to serve the needs of our community better.*

## Lastly

**"The older I get the faster time flies!"**

**How many times have you heard or said that phrase?**
**Or**
**"Remember when we used to....?"**
**Or**
**"I wish I would have asked Grandma…"**

**Life is precious and short.**
**Everybody has a story to be told.**

*No matter how many times you hear the tragic story of the Titanic, you know what happens in the end, the ship sinks. But…what about all the people on the Titanic? They all had a history, each one was affected differently. They all had a past that led up to that date.*

*Just like in our "small town," we may be from the same place but we all have a different experience to draw from. It is our hope that "Krumkake" inspires readers to want to preserve their own memories as a legacy to future generations.*

*In this fast-paced, highly mobile, and technological world we live in, people need to make an effort to preserve the American small town…a place where everybody knows your name, where Mom and Pop's family business can still provide a decent living, and where children can play with their friends safely.*

## What is your legacy?

*Mix a little sugar (those sweet thoughts), flour (the foundation and values) butter (don't let those memories slip away), spice (keep the humor and mischief in perspective) and….*

*L.D.H.*

**Why not Share this recipe of**

# "Krumkake"
## Tales of Wit, Wisdom and Wanderings

**with others**

## BOOK ORDER FORM

Name _____

Address _____

City, State, Zip_____

Phone _( _____ )_____

Name _____

Address _____

City, State, Zip_____

Phone _( _____ )_____


Number of books ordered _____ @ $17.95 = _____

Add shipping & handling: $4.00 each      = _____

                                  Total  = _____


❏ Check        ❏ Visa/MasterCard

Account number _____

Expiration date _____

Signature _____


**Mail completed form to:**
White Bear Center for the Arts
2228 Fourth Street
White Bear Lake, MN 55110
or
**Fax to:** 651-429-1569

Why not Share this recipe of

# "Krumkake"

## Tales of Wit, Wisdom and Wanderings

### with others

## BOOK ORDER FORM

Name _____

Address _____

City, State, Zip_____

Phone (_____)_____

Name _____

Address _____

City, State, Zip_____

Phone (_____)_____


Number of books ordered _____ @ $17.95 = _____

Add shipping & handling: $4.00 each　　　　= _____

　　　　　　　　　　　　　　Total　=　_____


❏ Check　　　❏ Visa/MasterCard

Account number _____

Expiration date _____

Signature _____


**WHITE BEAR CENTER FOR THE ARTS**

**Mail completed form to:**
White Bear Center for the Arts
2228 Fourth Street
White Bear Lake, MN 55110
or
**Fax to:** 651-429-1569